Inside Criminal Law

What Matters and Why

Inside Criminal Law

What Matters and Why

Second Edition

John M. Burkoff
Professor of Law
University of Pittsburgh

Russell L. Weaver
Professor of Law &
Distinguished University Scholar
Louis D. Brandeis School of Law
University of Louisville

Wolters Kluwer
Law & Business

AUSTIN   BOSTON   CHICAGO   NEW YORK   THE NETHERLANDS

Printed in the United States of America.

1 2 3 4 5 6 7 8 9 0

ISBN 978-0-7355-9497-5

Library of Congress Cataloging-in-Publication Data

Burkoff, John M.
    Inside criminal law : what matters and why / John M. Burkoff, Russell L. Weaver.—2nd ed.
        p. cm.
    Includes index.
    ISBN 978-0-7355-9497-5
    1. Criminal law—United States. 2. Criminal law. I. Weaver, Russell L., 1952- II. Title.

    KF9219.B83 2011
    345.73—dc22
                                            2011001584

About Wolters Kluwer Law & Business

Wolters Kluwer Law & Business is a leading provider of research information and workflow solutions in key specialty areas. The strengths of the individual brands of Aspen Publishers, CCH, Kluwer Law International and Loislaw are aligned within Wolters Kluwer Law & Business to provide comprehensive, in-depth solutions and expert-authored content for the legal, professional and education markets.

CCH was founded in 1913 and has served more than four generations of business professionals and their clients. The CCH products in the Wolters Kluwer Law & Business group are highly regarded electronic and print resources for legal, securities, antitrust and trade regulation, government contracting, banking, pension, payroll, employment and labor, and healthcare reimbursement and compliance professionals.

Aspen Publishers is a leading information provider for attorneys, business professionals and law students. Written by preeminent authorities, Aspen products offer analytical and practical information in a range of specialty practice areas from securities law and intellectual property to mergers and acquisitions and pension/benefits. Aspen's trusted legal education resources provide professors and students with high-quality, up-to-date and effective resources for successful instruction and study in all areas of the law.

Kluwer Law International supplies the global business community with comprehensive English-language international legal information. Legal practitioners, corporate counsel and business executives around the world rely on the Kluwer Law International journals, loose-leafs, books and electronic products for authoritative information in many areas of international legal practice.

Loislaw is a premier provider of digitized legal content to small law firm practitioners of various specializations. Loislaw provides attorneys with the ability to quickly and efficiently find the necessary legal information they need, when and where they need it, by facilitating access to primary law as well as state-specific law, records, forms and treatises.

Wolters Kluwer Law & Business, a unit of Wolters Kluwer, is headquartered in New York and Riverwoods, Illinois. Wolters Kluwer is a leading multinational publisher and information services company.

Dedicated, with love, to Nancy, Amy and Sean, David and Emmy, Emma, Molly, and Hannah.
-JMB

To Ben, Kate, and Laurence, with love.
-RLW

Summary of Contents

Contents

Preface and Acknowledgments

Every state in the United States—and the federal government and the District of Columbia—has (literally) tens of thousands of criminal statutes on the books. These bodies of criminal statutes (sometimes collected in a so-called Crimes Code) are different as well as constantly changing—in every single one of these jurisdictions. But there are, nonetheless, important similarities in the history, approach, coverage, and application of *all* the major criminal offenses in *each* of these jurisdictions. It is these similarities, as well as the most significant differences in approach and coverage, that are discussed in appropriate detail in the chapters that follow.

This book—the first and second editions—was written primarily for use by law students who are taking a law school course in criminal law. We have each taught just such a course for longer than we care to admit, and we have tried to include herein all the information necessary for a law student to obtain an informed overview of everything that is typically taught in such a law school course.

This book should prove helpful to non-law students as well. It would serve as a useful overview of criminal law in the United States for undergraduate students enrolled in criminal justice courses. Moreover, this book would serve as a useful tool for criminal justice professionals working in other countries who might want to look to American criminal law as a basis for comparison to their own criminal codes. Indeed, this book would be helpful for many others as well, such as journalists, legislators, and administrators working in the U.S. criminal justice system and interested laypeople who would simply like to gain a better understanding of—and more informed insights into—the nature of substantive criminal law in this country.

It is our hope that the unique features of this book will be particularly useful for readers. The Overview at the beginning of each chapter positions the material that follows in that chapter within the whole field of criminal law. The Frequently Asked Questions feature (FAQs) gives readers clear and cogent answers to issues that commonly pop up in a criminal law course. Sidebars add some color to the coverage of substantive criminal law, offering readers some parenthetical insights. (Use that material to show off in class!) The Summary feature near the end of each chapter offers you a quick and easy guide to the most basic points covered in that chapter. And the Connections feature at the end of each chapter helps you fit the points made in that chapter with the other chapters in the book and the whole body of substantive criminal law.

A number of different types of updated material was added to this second edition. In particular, there was an unusually large number of Supreme Court decisions bearing upon substantive criminal law issues that were decided since the first edition was published. Reference to these various decisions can be found throughout the chapters in this second edition. Particularly noteworthy, however, are the newly included decisions relating to justifications for punishment—e.g., when the death penalty can be imposed—that are referenced in the first chapter.

Finally, we wish to acknowledge with our sincere gratitude the assistance in the production of the first edition of this book of Barbara Roth, the managing editor for this project at Aspen; the editorial assistance of Dana Wilson; the research assistance of Corrie Thearle (Pitt Law, Class of '12) and Sarah Drinkwater (Pitt Law, Class of '09); and the drawings of Dan Schneider (in the conspiracy chapter). We also wish to express our gratitude to our families, not only for their forbearance during the time we took to accomplish this project, but for their crucial role as well in spending all of the (modest) amount of money generated by sales of this book.

John M. Burkoff
Pittsburgh, Pennsylvania

Russell L. Weaver
Louisville, Kentucky

January 2011

Inside Criminal Law

What Matters and Why

Purposes of the Criminal Law

1

O V E R V I E W

Why do we use the criminal law to meet our societal objectives, rather than relying instead on the civil law? Or simple moral force? And even when we have made the decision that a particular act should be criminalized, how do we determine the severity of the punishments that should be imposed? When is a fine sufficient? Imprisonment necessary or desirable? Capital punishment? The answers to these questions are of critical importance to lawyers for many reasons, not the least of which is that the "whys" of the criminal law often determine the "whats"—that is, why we punish often dictates what sentence (if any) a convicted defendant may receive.

A. JUSTIFICATIONS FOR PUNISHMENT

1. Retribution
2. Restraint
3. Specific Deterrence
4. General Deterrence
5. Rehabilitation
6. Expressing Community Values

B. APPLICATION OF THE JUSTIFICATIONS FOR PUNISHMENT

1. Scenario # 1
2. Scenario # 2
3. Scenario # 3

The criminal law is unique in that it provides a mechanism for controlling individual behavior through the medium of punishment. Punishment can take the form of imprisonment, fines, restitution, and, in the most extreme cases, even execution. In this respect the criminal law is distinguishable from other areas of the law.

A. Justifications for Punishment

For moral and ethical reasons, we need sound justifications for imposing criminal penalties. Criminal convictions usually carry a stigma and moral condemnation,[1] which can and usually do affect an individual's reputation, status in society, personal relations, and professional career.[2] In addition, some punishments entail relatively severe personal consequences, such as significant deprivations of individual liberty or even death. Even when criminal punishment involves nothing more than a fine, the loss of money as a result of a criminal conviction is rarely taken lightly.

Civil tort law, by contrast, is designed to provide appropriate *economic* compensation to those injured by the conduct of others. Our criminal law would likely be quite different if it was driven strictly by economic considerations:

From the comic strip "Tom the Dancing Bug," © Ruben Bolling.

---

[1] *See, e.g.,* Henry M. Hart, Jr., *The Aims of the Criminal Law*, 23 Law & Contemporary Problems 401 (1958) ("[A crime] is conduct which, if duly shown to have taken place, will incur a formal and solemn pronouncement of the moral condemnation of the community.").

[2] *See, e.g.,* Louis Michael Seidman, *Soldiers, Martyrs, and Criminals: Utilitarian Theory and the Problem of Crime Control,* 94 Yale L.J. 315 (1984) ("[B]lame not only makes the threat of other punishment credible, but also provides a kind of deterrence that other punishment cannot achieve. . . . [But] moral condemnation is a unique sanction because it inflicts suffering on individuals even when the conduct is otherwise efficient.").

While tort damages also serve as a mechanism for controlling individual behavior in the sense that people may alter their conduct in an effort to avoid liability and civil damages, tort remedies do not include in their repertoire forcible imprisonment or execution. In addition, again unlike criminal offenses, tort damages are usually awarded for compensatory rather than punitive purposes, except in the limited case of civil punitive damages.

Because of the potentially dramatic and life-altering consequences resulting from a criminal conviction, criminal punishment is usually reserved for the more serious departures from societal standards of conduct. Indeed, relatively minor deviations from the prescribed norms are sometimes referred to as only "violations" rather than as "crimes."

The commission of actual criminal offenses is typically punished on the basis of the perceived severity of the offense. Crimes such as murder, manslaughter, robbery, and rape typically carry the most severe punishments. In addition, certain necessary elements of proof are included in virtually all crimes as prerequisites to the imposition of criminal sanctions—for example, a voluntary act, a culpable mens rea, and, in some instances, a specific result and/or an appropriate causal link between the act and the result.[3]

But it is one thing to convict someone of a crime by establishing all of these prescribed elements of a statutory criminal offense, and it is another thing entirely to forcibly punish that person, whether that punishment be a fine, imprisonment, or execution. Unless we are to reflexively legitimize the gratuitous infliction of suffering upon others, society must have reasons—*good* reasons—for imposing such punishment.

Many people contend that it is appropriate to punish a convicted criminal by looking primarily to application of the moral principle of "just deserts." That is to say that criminal punishment is appropriate when scaled to the offender's culpability and the level and scope of the harm that he or she has caused. If an offender is less culpable, then he or she "deserves" less punishment; more culpable, then he or she "deserves" more punishment.

Not everyone agrees, however, that punishment for crimes should be determined strictly by looking to the accused or by applying the principle of just deserts. Some critics point out that even if we all agreed on that rationale, how in the world are we to determine what an offender justly deserves in fact? *What are just deserts?* A prison sentence rather than a fine? If prison, for how many months or years? What is just?

There are a number of reasons why it is important as a practical matter to know why particular activity has been criminalized. When sentencing, judges often consider, for example, the purposes of the criminal law in making discretionary judgments about the length of criminal sentences, at least where such discretionary judgments are permissible because no mandatory sentence is required.

Over the years, a number of different justifications have been discussed both for the imposition of criminal sanctions and for the determination of the severity of those sanctions. Most commonly, these justifications include the following:

- Retribution
- Restraint
- Specific deterrence
- General deterrence

---

[3]See Chapters 2-4.

- Rehabilitation
- Expressing community values[4]

(1) Retribution

The concept of **retribution** is quite elementary, really. It is the notion that society should punish criminals in a fashion similar to the crime actually committed in order either (depending upon point of view) to exact just deserts or simply to exact vengeance for the wrong-doer's own violation of the law. The Biblical "eye for an eye": "Thou shalt give life for life, eye for eye, tooth for tooth, hand for hand, foot for foot, burning for burning, wound for wound, stripe for stripe."[5]

The concept of retribution as justification for punishment is often premised upon the view that we can and should require people to be—and to be held—responsible for their own actions. If a person acts in a morally blameworthy manner appropriately criminalized by the force of law, he or she should be called to account for his or her improper and antisocial actions.[6] Justice demands a sort of moral compensation for the wrongdoing.

Moreover, when ordinary citizens refer to the criminal law, they often do so in just such patently retributive terms. People frequently state, for example, that criminals should be required to "pay their debt to society." And when convicted criminals are released from prison, many people say that they have paid their "debt." In the most extreme examples of retributive sentiment, the families of murder victims sometimes seek to have the perpetrators put to death for their crimes. A "life for a life."

Despite these popular sentiments, many commentators question whether punishment can be justified sensibly based only upon such retributive grounds. Indeed, some commentators have argued that criminal punishment serving *only* to exact retribution is inherently cruel. One well-known commentator argued that the primary justification for punishment should simply be to diminish further instances of such anti-social conduct (see discussion of deterrence, *infra*) and that society should only make such "concessions to retaliatory passions as are practically necessary for the system to survive."[7]

Nonetheless, retribution continues to survive as a common justification, popular and philosophical, for imposing criminal punishment. The public perception, that retaliation or retribution is a valid and important basis for punishment, may simply be too strong to ignore. In addition, some fear that if society does not retaliate against the perpetrators of crimes, the victims will. Some argue further that "'[r]esentment (perhaps even some hatred) is a good thing,' that forgiveness of wrongdoers is overvalued in our culture, and that there is little room for mercy in the sentencing of wrongdoers."[8]

---

[4]*See also, e.g., Kennedy v. Louisiana*, ___ U.S. ___, 128 S. Ct. 2641, 2649, 171 L. Ed. 2d 525 (2009) ("punishment is justified under one or more of three principal rationales: rehabilitation, deterrence, and retribution").

[5]Bible, Exodus 21:23-25, King James Version.

[6]*See, e.g.,* Immanuel Kant, 6 The Metaphysics of Morals 331 (1785) ("Punishment by a court . . . can never be inflicted merely as a means to promote some other good for the criminal himself or for civil society. It must always be inflicted on him only because he has committed a crime . . . . He must previously have been found punishable before any thought can be given to drawing from his punishment something of use for himself or his fellow citizens. The law of punishment is a categorical imperative.").

[7]Herbert Wechsler, *The Challenge of a Model Penal Code*, 65 Harv. L. Rev. 1097 (1952).

[8]Joshua Dressler, *Hating Criminals: How Can Something that Feels So Good Be Wrong?*, 88 U. Mich. L. Rev. 1448 (1990).

The Supreme Court has concluded that a legislature might reasonably conclude that the death penalty serves legitimate retributive (and/or general deterrent) aims.[9] But the Court has also ruled that the death penalty does *not* serve legitimate retributive aims when, for example, it is imposed upon juveniles and mentally retarded persons;[10] someone who had raped but not killed an adult woman;[11] someone who had aided and abetted a robbery during which a murder was committed but did not himself kill, attempt to kill, or intend that a killing would take place;[12] and someone who raped but did not kill a child and did not intend to assist another in killing the child.[13]

As the Court has reasoned in the latter and most recent of these decisions, "The incongruity between the crime of child rape and the harshness of the death penalty poses risks of overpunishment and counsels against a constitutional ruling that the death penalty can be expanded to include this offense. The goal of retribution, which reflects society's and the victim's interests in seeing that the offender is repaid for the hurt he caused, does not justify the harshness of the death penalty here. In measuring retribution, as well as other objectives of criminal law, it is appropriate to distinguish between a particularly depraved murder that merits death as a form of retribution and the crime of child rape. . . . It is not at all evident that the child rape victim's hurt is lessened when the law permits the death of the perpetrator. . . . With respect to deterrence, if the death penalty adds to the risk of non-reporting, that, too, diminishes the penalty's objectives. Underreporting is a common problem with respect to child sexual abuse."[14] The justification of retribution also does not support a sentence of life without possibility of parole for a juvenile.[15]

(2) Restraint

Restraint or incapacitation, the notion that criminal punishment is appropriate because criminals should be isolated or otherwise confined in order to prevent them from doing further harm, is also a widely accepted justification for punishment.

---

[9]*See Gregg v. Georgia*, 428 U.S. 153, 183-184, 186, 186-187 (1976):

Retribution is no longer the dominant objective of the criminal law, . . . but neither is it a forbidden objective nor one inconsistent with our respect for the dignity of men. . . . Indeed, the decision that capital punishment may be the appropriate sanction in extreme cases is an expression of the community's belief that certain crimes are themselves so grievous an affront to humanity that the only adequate response may be the penalty of death. . . . The value of capital punishment as a deterrent of crime is a complex factual issue the resolution of which properly rests with the legislatures, which can evaluate the results of statistical studies in terms of their own local conditions and with a flexibility of approach that is not available to the courts. . . . In sum, we cannot say that the judgment of the Georgia Legislature that capital punishment may be necessary in some cases is clearly wrong. Considerations of federalism, as well as respect for the ability of a legislature to evaluate, in terms of its particular State, the moral consensus concerning the death penalty and its social utility as a sanction, require us to conclude, in the absence of more convincing evidence, that the infliction of death as a punishment for murder is not without justification and thus is not unconstitutionally severe.

See also Graham v. Florida, ___ U.S. ___, 130 S. Ct. 2011, 2028, 176 L. Ed. 2d 825 (2010) ("Retribution is a legitimate reason to punish . . . .").
[10]*Roper v. Simmons*, 543 U.S. 551, 125 S. Ct. 1183, 161 L. Ed. 2d 1 (2005); *Atkins v. Virginia*, 536 U.S. 304, 122 S. Ct. 2242, 153 L. Ed. 2d 335 (2002).
[11]*Eberheart v. Georgia*, 433 U.S. 917, 97 S. Ct. 2994, 53 L. Ed. 2d 1104 (1977); *Coker v. Georgia*, 433 U.S. 584, 97 S. Ct. 2861, 53 L. Ed. 2d 982 (1977).
[12]*Enmund v. Florida*, 458 U.S. 782, 102 S. Ct. 3368, 73 L. Ed. 2d 1140 (1982). *See also Graham v. Florida*, ___ U.S. ___, 130 S. Ct. 2011, 2022, 176 L. Ed. 2d 825 (2010) ("capital punishment is impermissible for non-homicide crimes against individuals").
[13]*Kennedy v. Louisiana*, ___ U.S. ___, 128 S. Ct. 2641, 171 L. Ed. 2d 525 (2009).
[14]*Kennedy v. Louisiana*, ___ U.S. ___, 128 S. Ct. 2641, 2662, 2663, 171 L. Ed. 2d 525 (2009).
[15]*Graham v. Florida*, ___ U.S. ___, 130 S. Ct. 2011, 2022, 176 L. Ed. 2d 825 (2010).

Imprisonment, pure forcible, physical removal of a convicted criminal from society, placing him or her in a correctional institution, is the classic example of restraint. Once a convicted criminal is securely behind bars, he or she cannot (ordinarily) engage in further criminal conduct, at least not in criminal conduct involving non-prisoners. Execution is the most extreme and most effective form of incapacitation. Whereas an imprisoned criminal might eventually be released and returned to society (and thereby given the opportunity to commit further crimes), an executed criminal will never commit another crime. Not in this world, at least.

The efficacy of restraint is, accordingly, virtually unquestionable. But significant normative questions remain. When, for example, has someone committed an offense so heinous that society *should* be empowered, morally and justly, to deprive such an offender of his or her freedom . . . or life? Indeed, to the extent that restraint is arguably most sensible and efficacious when it is used to incapacitate people who are likely to be the most dangerous offenders in the future when and if they are released, the question arises: How do we predict who is likely to be dangerous? Past behavior, including past criminal behavior, may not be a good indicator of a person's future propensity to commit criminal activity.

(3) Specific Deterrence

A third commonly proffered justification for criminal punishment is **specific deterrence**. The hope is that by imposing punishment on a particular ("specific") criminal, he or she will realize the seriousness of society's determination to punish the type of anti-social behavior in which he or she has engaged and will thus be deterred from committing future crimes. Through punishment, in other words, the wrongdoer will presumably learn to recognize the potential consequences of his or her own conduct and, accordingly, will desist from engaging in criminal behavior.

Deterrence justifications for punishment—specific and general—are utilitarian in nature—that is, they weigh the costs of imposing punishment against the social benefits to be obtained in crime prevention.

Some people question, however, whether criminal punishment is truly an effective specific deterrent, and they often point to the high level of recidivism in the United States. Moreover, there are at least two practical problems with the specific deterrence rationale for criminal punishment. First, if prisons do nothing more than warehouse criminals (as sometimes occurs), we run the risk of ignoring the underlying causes of crime and thus losing an opportunity to address those causes. In the case of drug addicts, for example, there is a high risk of recidivism if addicts do not receive treatment. With thieves, there is a similar recidivism risk when convicted thieves do not receive job counseling and job training. Second, when convicted criminals are incarcerated, they sometimes become embittered and hostile and more (not less) likely to commit crimes when they are released.

(4) General Deterrence

General deterrence is the utilitarian notion that by imposing punishment on criminals, society will benefit by deterring *others* from committing crimes in the future. In other words, unlike specific deterrence, which focuses on the particular individual facing punishment, general deterrence posits that the conviction and punishment of a present criminal is appropriate and desirable to serve as an example to other potential criminals about the pitfalls and consequences of criminal conduct.

The hope is that by imposing punishment on a particular criminal, *others* will realize the seriousness of society's determination to punish the type of anti-social behavior in which this particular criminal has engaged and that these others will thus be deterred from committing future crimes.

Principles of general deterrence suggest why prosecutors sometimes attempt to "throw the book" at famous or notorious criminal defendants. Virtually everyone has heard of the most celebrated defendants (e.g., O.J. Simpson, Michael Jackson, Martha Stewart) and the punishments imposed on them are thought more likely to be noticed by others who might be inclined to—and then deterred from—the commission of crimes.

But general deterrence theory is not without its critics. After all, society is punishing one person in an effort to achieve a societal objective with respect to another person. Is this fair? Is it just? We might be able to successfully deter a good deal of petty theft if we cut off the hands of thieves, for example, but is that what we *should* be doing? We think not. The costs to the thieves would be much too great in comparison with the gains in crime prevention that the rest of us might obtain.

F   A   Q

Q: Do retributive justifications for punishment invariably punish wrongdoers more harshly than utilitarian justifications for punishment?

A: No. Utilitarian justifications for punishment—like deterrence—can sometimes be harsher than retributive justifications. If stealing a loaf of bread "deserves" a small fine or a day in jail from a retributive point of view, for example, but deterring bread theft would take much more punishment, then the utilitarian might be harder on the criminal than the retributivist. In this sense, utilitarianism is "forward looking" (what will we gain in the future from punishing this individual now?) while retribution is "backward looking" (what punishment does this individual deserve as a result of what he or she did in the past?).

Some commentators also question the effectiveness of the criminal law as a general deterrent to crime as an empirical matter. They question whether or to what extent criminal punishment in and of itself actually works to deter future criminal misconduct. Is it possible to gauge such general deterrence without also factoring in considerations such as the severity and certainty of punishment resulting from the commission of a crime?

Moreover, in some instances, criminals clearly act for irrational reasons, in a fit of rage, perhaps, that seemingly precludes the reasoning and reflection that general deterrence theorists presume exists (e.g., a woman finds her husband in bed with another woman and, furious, kills them both). In other instances, there is doubt about whether a particular degree of punishment really serves to deter future crimes of a similar nature. For example, wholly aside from the obvious moral considerations, there is significant controversy about whether the imposition of the death penalty actually works to generally deter other people from committing murders.

KILLING MAY NOT DETER KILLING

Is capital punishment "justified" because it "generally deters" future murderers? Consider the following:

Since 1996, more than a dozen studies have been published claiming that each execution can prevent anywhere from three to thirty-two homicides. [All] of the[se] studies . . . suffer from an important and avoidable aggregation error: they examine the relationship between death penalty variables and total non-negligent homicide rates, despite the fact that three-fourths of all such killings do not meet the statutory criteria to be eligible for the death penalty.

[Once] these . . . types of killings have been separated, . . . [none] of the distinctive patterns one might expect from marginal death penalty deterrence can be found in the [past] three decades[.]

In fact, the incidence of death-eligible cases . . . is remarkably stable over time, insensitive to variations in the incidence of executions or to the large swings from one decade to the next in the number or rate of nondeath-eligible killings. Even in Texas, the leading execution state by far in the nation, the proportion of death-eligible killings is no smaller than in other categories of states, and there is no differential decline in death-eligible killings as the execution rate increased in the 1980s and 1990s. . . . *There is simply no visible evidence of the marginal deterrent impact of the death penalty on death-eligible killings.*

Jeffrey Fagan, Franklin E. Zimring & Amanda Geller, *Capital Punishment and Capital Murder: Market Share and the Deterrent Effects of the Death Penalty*, 84 Tex. L. Rev. 1803, 1805-1806, 1859-1860 (2006) (emphasis added).

(5) Rehabilitation

Rehabilitation, the notion that criminals can be "cured" or otherwise changed for the better during incarceration and then returned to society no longer posing a threat to others, provides perhaps the most appealing justification for the operation of the criminal justice system. The hope is that, through appropriate (albeit involuntary) incarceration and/or treatment, criminal offenders will be encouraged or trained to shed their anti-social and criminal tendencies and can be reintegrated into society as productive and functioning members. In other words, the drug addict should receive drug rehabilitation, the thief should receive job training and career counseling, the poorly educated criminal should take classes and improve and educate himself or herself.[16]

In theory, rehabilitation could and perhaps should take many different forms. As the Supreme Court has recently pointed out, "The concept of rehabilitation is imprecise; and its utility and proper implementation are the subject of a substantial, dynamic field of inquiry and dialogue. . . . It is for legislatures to determine what rehabilitative techniques are appropriate and effective."[17] Besides drug rehabilitation or job training or additional education, *true* rehabilitation might even involve more dramatic forms of bodily intervention. "Chemical castration" of convicted sex offenders, for example, can be viewed as rehabilitative in intent, although some might view this as "punishment" instead, more like incapacitation or restraint.

Chemical castration temporarily impedes sexual functioning in individuals due to the administration of certain hormonal drugs. An example like this does, however, beg the question of the government's right, moral and legal, to perform such a dramatic procedure. And, more to the point, since rehabilitation is not the only justification for the imposition of criminal punishment, this now-castrated, "rehabilitated" accused might well still receive a severe criminal sentence, but not (at least logically) for rehabilitative reasons. Perhaps for reasons of general deterrence. Or retribution. Or specific deterrence or restraint.

---

[16]*See* Henry M. Hart, Jr., *The Aims of the Criminal Law*, 23 Law & Contemp. Probs. 401 (1958) (suggesting that a "leading alternative [to criminalization], to judge from contemporary criticism of the penal law, would be to provide that people who behave badly should simply be treated as sick people to be cured, rather than as bad people to be condemned and punished.").

[17]*Graham v. Florida*, ___ U.S. ___, 130 S. Ct. 2011, 2029, 176 L. Ed. 2d 825 (2010).

Most commonly, rehabilitative efforts take the form of education or training. Suppose, for example, that a man commits a theft out of economic necessity. He has been unable to maintain a job, he's hungry and penniless, and he steals to provide food and support for his family. Isn't it logical to suppose that if we provide him with additional education and useful training designed to help him obtain and hold a job, he would be better off . . . and society would be as well? If this training succeeds, he might be able to hold a job and to avoid further criminal activity.

A number of important questions are once again begged by this example. Do we have the right, moral or legal, to paternalistically force someone to improve his lot in life? Should we force a convicted criminal to receive such training or should we simply facilitate its availability? Is a person's life so simple and straightforward that we can say with any assurance that a crime was committed only for one particular reason, in this case, economic necessity? Does training of this sort actually work? And, as noted previously, even if we take the most optimistic view and assume that we can indeed identify and rehabilitate such an individual, what of the other justifications for criminal punishment? If we can rehabilitate a convicted criminal, does that obviate the legitimacy of the imposition of punishment for deterrent purposes? Retributive purposes? These are not easy questions to answer.

To the extent that rehabilitation can and does work, many but by no means all commentators believe that it provides a preferable basis for criminal punishment than the other justifications discussed. As one well-known commentator made the point many years ago, the "grim negativism and the frequent seeming futility of the criminal law when it is considered simply as a means of preventing undesired behavior no doubt help to explain why sensitive people, working at close hand with criminals, tend so often to embrace the more hopeful and positive tenets of a curative-rehabilitative philosophy."[18]

There is, however, an additional, somewhat more practical and political problem that stands in the way of the creation and implementation of a truly rehabilitative

Sidebar

REHABILITATION: A PRISONER'S VIEW

"The concept of rehabilitation versus punishment has raged within the American Penal community since its inception. The last decade has seen the concept of punishment and retribution all but extinguish the concept of rehabilitation from prisons in the United States. [Ironically,] it is not the Department of Corrections that supported the complete removal of rehabilitation programs from the prisons. [The] push for punishment over rehabilitation was pushed by politicians catering to a public that was frustrated with rising crime rates and expressed crime as their number one concern. [All] across the country state legislatures passed harsh sentencing laws that increased the punishments for committing certain crimes.

"[The] consequences of these harsh sentencing guidelines and laws was more people being imprisoned in . . . already overcrowded prisons, teeming with prisoners from the War on Drugs in the 80's, [which] became even more overcrowded in the 90's . . . . Prisons are so overcrowded only bare bones educational and vocational programs are available. Due to the prevailing public and political climate, emphasizing punishment over rehabilitation, it is no longer a question of does rehabilitation work; it is a question of does rehabilitation have a prominent role in American prisons. [Rehabilitation] works, it is just expensive and time-consuming, two factors which work against it in a society dominated by politicians who want immediate results to gloat over and a public that is accustomed to 15 minute solutions . . . ."

Robert X. Holbrook #BL-5140
SCI Greene, Waynesburg, PA 15370

Does Rehabilitation Work? Does it Exist?, the defenestrator, http://www.defenestrator .org/?q=node/122 (December 11, 2004).

---

[18]*See* Henry M. Hart, Jr., *The Aims of the Criminal Law*, 23 Law & Contemp. Probs. 401 (1958).

correctional regime. True rehabilitative efforts tend to be very costly, requiring a significant investment in new facilities, new equipment, and the employment of new personnel. Our political leaders have generally chosen to spend our limited governmental resources on other social needs. In any event, the political reality is that we have not yet implemented a functioning and effective rehabilitative system on any large scale and, for many of the reasons discussed above, perhaps we cannot and should not even hope to do so.

(6) Expressing Community Values

Many modern commentators add a sixth justification for criminal punishment that has been called the "expressive function" of the criminal law. What this means is that we sanction certain behaviors under the criminal law in order to express the community's strong feelings about the moral wrongfulness of that behavior. The point is not simply to deter the behavior, because punishment is not viewed as justified solely in terms of preventing future harms. Nor is this expressive function simply retribution, because the point of punishment is not to avenge or to ensure just deserts. Rather the point seen as most important is to educate and edify the members of the community about what is morally wrong.

In addition, this expressive function is viewed as an effort to use the criminal law to help shape the outer boundaries of permissible human behavior and to foster a sense of community solidarity by enforcing strongly shared moral norms.

B. Application of the Justifications for Punishment

The common justifications for punishment discussed above are not necessarily or even usually consistent with one other. A sentence that a judge might impose in order to incapacitate a particular convicted criminal, for example, might or might not be consistent with a specific and/or general deterrent aim or a retributive goal or an effort to rehabilitate or the expression of community values. And, in any given case, a judge might decide that one or more of these justifications is a more appropriate basis for a particular sentence. Likewise, a particular sentencing judge might tend to always favor one or more of these goals over others.

In an effort to structure the exercise of sentencing discretion, some criminal codes have attempted to provide guidance to judges in this process. But rarely do these codes dictate that one justification for punishment presumptively trumps another. The American Law Institute's Model Penal Code simply (and not very helpfully) provides, for example, that the "general purposes of the provisions governing the sentencing and treatment of offenders are: (a) to prevent the commission of offenses; (b) to promote the correction and rehabilitation of offenders . . . ."[19] Notably, the MPC omits any reference to retribution as a "general purpose" of sentencing. Is that an appropriate omission, do you think?

---

[19]Model Penal Code §1.02(2).

F   A   Q

Q: Who decides what justifications for punishment are appropriate?

A: While sentencing judges often consider the justifications for punishment in making discretionary judgments about the length and nature of criminal sentences, in the first instance it is legislators who make the judgment about what conduct should be subject to criminal penalties and how severely that conduct should be punished. It is only in the rarest and most unusual of circumstances that a reviewing court should or could find a criminal statute based upon those justifications to be so unreasonable or illegitimate as to render the statute unconstitutional. But *see, e.g., U.S. v. Stevens*, ___ U.S. ___, 130 S. Ct. 1577, 176 L. Ed. 2d 435 (2010) (federal statute criminalizing the commercial creation, sale, or possession of depictions of animal cruelty held substantially overbroad and thus facially invalid under the First Amendment protection of speech).

When the U.S. Sentencing Commission was first created, it was charged, in part, with proposing objective sentencing guidelines in order to reduce the individual variation in criminal sentences that resulted from judges exercising their sentencing discretion, utilizing different and often conflicting justifications for the punishments imposed. But the Commission chose to perform this task empirically, basing its proposals on traditional sentencing ranges for particular crimes, rather than favoring one justification for punishment over another. As the Commission explained:

> A philosophical problem arose when the Commission attempted to reconcile the differing perceptions of the purposes of criminal punishment. Most observers of the criminal law agree that the ultimate aim of the law itself, and of punishment in particular, is the control of crime. Beyond this point, however, the consensus seems to break down. Some argue that appropriate punishment should be defined primarily on the basis of the moral principle of "just deserts." Under this principle, punishment should be scaled to the offender's culpability and the resulting harms. Thus, if a defendant is less culpable, the defendant deserves less punishment. Others argue that punishment should be imposed primarily on the basis of practical "crime control" considerations. Defendants sentenced under this scheme should receive the punishment that most effectively lessens the likelihood of future crime, either by deterring others or incapacitating the defendant.

Sidebar

ALI MODEL PENAL CODE

Founded in 1923, the American Law Institute (ALI) is a private organization made up of prominent judges, lawyers, and law professors from all over the United States. The ALI drafts and publishes Restatements of the Law, model codes, and legal studies intended to promote clarification and simplification of the law.

The ALI's Model Penal Code (M.P.C. or MPC) was adopted in 1962, after more than a decade of debate and discussion, and was intended to be a model for legislatures to use to modernize and standardize their criminal laws. It had a major impact. The MPC played an important role in the widespread revision and codification of substantive criminal law in the U.S. in the 1960s and 1970s. Although some MPC recommendations were almost universally rejected, many jurisdictions made other MPC provisions and/or approaches part of their crimes codes, helping to give some predictability to American criminal law across jurisdictions. Moreover, many courts look to MPC provisions and commentary to help in the interpretation of criminal statutes. However, the criminal law is not static. It keeps changing through new legislation and judicial rulings. Many of the original MPC provisions—enacted by states many years ago now—have been subsequently and significantly amended.

Adherents of these points of view have urged the Commission to choose between them, to accord one primacy over the other. . . . The Commission's empirical approach has . . . helped resolve its philosophical dilemma. Those who adhere to a just deserts philosophy may concede that the lack of moral consensus might make it difficult to say exactly what punishment is deserved for a particular crime, specified in minute detail. Likewise, those who subscribe to a philosophy of crime control may acknowledge that the lack of sufficient, readily available data might make it difficult to say exactly what punishment will best prevent that crime. Both groups might therefore recognize the wisdom of looking to those distinctions that judges and legislators have, in fact, made over the course of time. These established distinctions are ones that the community believes, or has found over time, to be important from either a moral or crime-control perspective.[20]

Although there is no consensus on exactly which justifications for punishment should invariably prevail, as the Sentencing Commission recognized, it is nonetheless valuable to think about how the most common justifications might and should be applied in specific cases.

Suppose, for example, that two men intentionally kill a teenage boy. What punishment should they receive? There is no clear or precise answer. We need to know more about the killers, the victim, and the circumstances of the crime. Consider the following scenarios:

(1) Scenario # 1

Suppose we know that both men were hardened criminals who had murdered before, and that there were no extenuating circumstances. The men killed the boy "just for kicks," and they did so in a horrific and brutal manner. Under such circumstances, absent mitigating circumstances, a number of justifications can be offered for punishing them. Clearly, they need to be restrained so that they do not kill or hurt others. In addition, for those who accept retribution as a justifiable basis for punishment, who more than these men deserves societal vengeance? Indeed, those who believe in an "eye for an eye" type of punitive response might well argue that they should be executed. Specific deterrence might or might not be justified in a case like this. It's not clear at all that these men will "learn" from their punishment and use that learning to avoid future criminal behavior. However, a general deterrence rationale might be served by punishing them and punishing them severely. Arguably, others may be deterred from committing similar crimes in the future because of the severity of the punishment imposed. Rehabilitation? Under these circumstances, it is far from clear that these men could be sufficiently rehabilitated to the point that we would be comfortable releasing them into society in the belief that they would no longer commit criminal acts.

Would a different result be reached under the Model Penal Code? Probably not. Although the MPC tends to focus more on the prevention of future offenses and rehabilitation, the analysis is essentially similar. It is clear that these individuals need to be restrained, and there are clear indications that rehabilitation would be futile.

---

[20]U.S. Sentencing Guidelines Manual §1(A)(3) (November 1, 1987).

(2) Scenario # 2

Now, let's suppose that we alter the facts, and do so by reference to the famous decision in *Regina v. Dudley & Stephens.*[21] In that case, four English sailors were cast adrift in an open boat on the high seas after their yacht was wrecked. They were nearly 1,000 miles from land with no water and only a little food. They survived until the twentieth day on a few canned turnips and a turtle that they managed to catch on the fourth day. During this time, they had no fresh water except for rain water. By the twelfth day, they were out of food. After 20 days, still far from land, with no hope of rescue in sight, they discussed among themselves what was to be done. Fearing they would die unless they took drastic action, two of the men decided that one of them should be sacrificed to save the rest. The two chose as their victim the teenaged boy, Parker, who was already near death, lying in the bottom of the boat. They killed Parker, and they and the third passenger (who had not agreed to the killing) consumed his remains until they were rescued. At that point, Dudley and Stephens were charged with murder.

Arguably, a scenario such as *Dudley & Stephens* presents quite different punishment questions than a situation where two men brutally murder a teenager "just for kicks." Since Dudley and Stephens killed under such extreme circumstances, there is no reason to believe that they need to be restrained. If they were returned to the streets of London, there is no reason to believe that they would attack or kill others. They killed for food to survive, not for the simple pleasure of killing. In addition, there is little reason to believe that they would need to be "rehabilitated" to transform them into "decent, law-abiding citizens." They killed under the most extreme of circumstances, and one could well argue that the only rehabilitation they need is to deal with the psychological consequences of what they have been through and what they have done.

Would a deterrence rationale be well served by punishing these men? From the standpoint of either general or specific deterrence, it could certainly be reasonably contended that punishing Dudley and Stephens is unlikely to prevent them or anyone else from killing when faced with similar circumstances. Faced with the likelihood of death by starvation, very few people would be deterred from killing simply by the threat of some possible punishment down the road. In fact, the worst punishment that could have been imposed on them was death, the same danger that they confronted in the boat. But the British court thought differently, concluding that others might learn that "[t]o preserve one's life is generally speaking a duty, but it may be the plainest and the highest duty to sacrifice it. . . . It is not correct, therefore, to say that there is any absolute or unqualified necessity to preserve one's life."

The most tenable justification for punishing Dudley and Stephens may well have been simple, unvarnished retribution. However, even the case for retribution was less than crystal clear. British public opinion was decidedly to the contrary. The British public recognized that sailors who were cast adrift usually died and typically had little chance of rescue. Indeed, the judges themselves—reflecting British community values?—urged commutation of the death sentences they themselves

S i d e b a r

MAYBE THEY SHOULD HAVE DIED IN THE LIFEBOAT

Stephens remained in England and died in poverty. Dudley emigrated to Australia where he died of the plague.

---

[21][1884] 14 Q.B.D. 273.

imposed, albeit implicitly. Queen Victoria, bowing to this sentiment and to the tide of public opinion, obliged. She commuted Dudley's and Stephens's sentences to only six months in prison. It is certainly possible, in fact, that the judges would have balked at sentencing the pair to death if they had thought the death sentence would really have been carried out without the Queen's intercession.

Would a different result have been reached if the British judges had been transported ahead in time and instructed to follow the dictates of the Model Penal Code? As discussed above, Dudley and Stephens apparently were not good candidates for rehabilitation, and they did not pose any significant risk of committing like offenses in the future. Moreover, it is arguable, at best, whether by punishing them the State could or would truly deter other lifeboat survivors in the future from committing similar crimes. As a result, if retribution is eliminated as a justification for punishment, as it is under the MPC, there is scant basis for imposing criminal punishment in this case.

(3) Scenario # 3

Change the facts one more time. Suppose that a teen-age boy is dying a slow and painful death due to disease. Incapacitated and unable to take his own life, he begs his father to relieve him of his misery. Aware that killing is criminal, but overcome with grief by the plight of his son, the father prays for spiritual guidance about what to do. After weeks of anguish, the father agrees to help his son take his own life. Wanting to kill his son quickly and painlessly, the father enlists the aid of his brother. The two administer a lethal poison that painlessly kills the boy.

Although the facts in Scenario # 3 are significantly different from those in Scenario # 2, the analysis is similar. There is little need to restrain the father or the uncle, is there? Both are extremely unlikely to ever be presented with such extraordinary circumstances again, and both appear highly unlikely to kill absent such circumstances. As for rehabilitation, it is not clear that either of them needs or requires rehabilitation, except for counseling to help them deal with the boy's death and their contribution to its occurrence. Indeed, rehabilitation presumes that there is something to rehabilitate. Did they really do the wrong thing?

The deterrence rationale is also similar to the Dudley and Stephens situation, but perhaps not quite as compelling. From a specific deterrence standpoint, there is little indication that either the father or the uncle need to be deterred because they are not likely to face such horrific circumstances again. However, in the unlikely event that they did, it is true that punishment in this case might well deter them from committing a subsequent murder. As for general deterrence, it is not clear that other people in the father's situation would be deterred by the threat of criminal punishment from engaging in what they see as a loving act of kindness and compassion. However, some people might be deterred. And it is perhaps more likely that someone in the uncle's position might be deterred from helping. Who really knows?

From a retributive standpoint, this situation is arguably comparable to Dudley and Stephens as well. The father anguished over his son's request and only acted to accommodate him because he thought it was morally right. Certainly, individual moral or religious convictions do not trump the law. In addition, some people might argue that the father acted immorally (whatever he thought) and that he deserves retributive punishment as a result. But others would disagree. What are the appropriate community values to vindicate here? What do you think? If a person commits an act that he or she honestly believes is morally correct, but it is in fact a criminal act, should we punish that person for strictly retributive reasons?

Under the Model Penal Code, as in the Dudley and Stephens situation, it is doubtful that either the father or the uncle needs rehabilitation, and neither is any real risk for committing future offenses. Thus, under the MPC, with retribution eliminated as a justification for punishment, the most likely basis for punishing either or both of them is the belief that punishment might deter others from committing similar acts under similar circumstances in the future.

SUMMARY

- The most common justifications for criminal punishment include retribution, restraint, deterrence (both general and specific), rehabilitation, and the expression of community values.

- Retribution as justification for punishment is often premised on the view that people are responsible for their own actions and that justice demands moral compensation when they commit criminal acts.

- Restraint is the notion that criminal punishment is appropriate because criminals should be isolated in order to prevent them from doing any further harm.

- Utilitarian justifications for punishment are those that weigh the costs of imposing punishment against the social benefits to be obtained in crime prevention.

- Specific deterrence is the utilitarian idea that by imposing punishment on a particular ("specific") person, he or she will learn the consequences of his or her behavior and stop doing it.

- General deterrence is the utilitarian notion that by imposing punishment on criminals, society will benefit by deterring *others* from committing crimes in the future.

- It is still debatable whether capital punishment is "justified" because it is debatable whether it generally deters future homicides.

- Rehabilitation is the notion that criminals can be "cured" during incarceration and then returned to society no longer posing a threat to others, but we have not yet implemented a functioning and effective rehabilitative system on any large scale and may not be able to do so.

- The expressive function of the criminal law means that we criminalize certain behaviors to express the community's strong feelings about the moral wrongfulness of that behavior and to educate the community about what is morally wrong.

- Legislators make the initial judgment about what conduct should be criminalized and how severely violations should be punished, and judges often consider those justifications for punishment in sentencing.

- There is no consensus on exactly which justifications for punishment should invariably prevail in any given situation.

CONNECTIONS

Relationship to Excuses

The commission of some criminal acts is deemed to be excused (see Chapter 13) because even though an actor's conduct may have harmed society, it is not deemed to be blameworthy given the purposes of the criminal law discussed in this chapter.

Relationship to Justification Defenses

The commission of some criminal acts is deemed to be justified (see Chapter 12) because the conduct at issue is deemed beneficial to society or because the conduct is in some other way judged to be socially useful or desirable.

Relationship to Sentencing

Sentencing judges often consider the purposes of the criminal law in making discretionary judgments about the length of criminal sentences, where such discretionary judgments are permissible, because no mandatory sentence is required.

Relationship to Sexual Offenses

Much of the history of the evolving definition of sexual offenses (see Chapter 10) reflects legislative enactments and judicial decisions that arguably resulted less from the legitimate purposes of the criminal law, at least as viewed by modern eyes, than from gender stereotyping and outdated notions of women as property and as witnesses lacking in credibility.

Relationship to Substantive Offenses

The purposes of the criminal law help to inform the legislative process. These rationales for criminalization and punishment aid legislators in defining precisely what conduct should be subject to criminal penalties and what the harshness of those penalties should be. Outside of the legislative process, lawyers may also raise questions about why or whether a particular criminal statute accords with appropriate purposes of the criminal law when a statute is ambiguous or when arguing about how a statute should be applied to a particular set of facts. Moreover, albeit very infrequently, a reviewing court may find the legislative justifications supporting enactment of a criminal statute to be so unreasonable or illegitimate as to render the statute unconstitutional (e.g., criminalization of pre-viability abortions).

Actus Reus Requirement

When is a person's "bad" conduct actually worse than that? When is it so bad that it is *criminal* conduct? Establishing the existence of a crime **OVERVIEW** generally requires proof of a criminal act—the *actus reus*— undertaken by an accused with the criminal intent required by law—the *mens rea*—where one is specified. The traditional view has long been that for punishment to be fair and just, a criminal defendant must be found first to have committed a voluntary criminal act. Or that defendant must have failed to act in a situation where he or she was legally required to act. Accordingly, mere "thoughts," as opposed to actual concrete actions, are not punishable as crimes, even if they are viewed as bad or evil or otherwise thought to indicate a risk of future criminal behavior. A person can act, however, simply by being aware of his or her possession and control of something that that person is not permitted to possess.

A. THE VOLUNTARY ACT REQUIREMENT

1. Defining "Voluntariness"
2. Recklessness/Negligence Crimes
3. Strict Liability Offenses
4. Possession Offenses
5. "Status Based" Crimes

B. OMISSIONS

1. Exceptions to the General Rule
2. Duties to Act
3. Predicates to Duty
4. Constitutional Issues

One of the key elements of every criminal offense is the existence of an **actus reus**, a criminal act. We don't punish thought crimes in the United States; there must be an actual criminal act. That act must also be undertaken voluntarily, or, put another way, it is a complete defense that an accused person's actions were involuntary. This defense of involuntariness is completely different from a defense attempting to demonstrate that the requisite mental state (mens rea, see Chapter 3) did not exist. The involuntariness defense can be successful, for example, even when no mental state is required at all because the criminal offense is one of strict liability.

Moreover, an actor is not responsible under the criminal law for a mere failure to act, an **omission**, unless that actor has failed to perform a required legal duty.

A. The Voluntary Act Requirement

Before an act can be regarded as criminal, it must be voluntary. The requirement of **voluntariness** is a fundamental principle of the criminal law, denoting an act that is both a product of the willed response of the actor and that is manifested by a corresponding external body movement. If an act is **involuntary**—i.e., it is *not* a product of the willed response of the actor and corresponding external body movement—there is no just basis for punishing that person.

For example, suppose that a woman attends a baseball game as a spectator. During the game, totally unexpectedly, she has an epileptic seizure and during that seizure, one of her arms happens to strike the man sitting next to her. Under such circumstances, she has not committed an assaultive crime. Not only did she lack the required mens rea for such a criminal offense, but, more important for present purposes, her flailing arms did not involve a volitional—willed—act on her part. (The voluntariness inquiry is part of the actus reus requirement, not the mens rea requirement. See Chapter 3.)

As a result, one cannot argue (fairly, at least) that she deserves retribution for her unwilled act or that punishment is needed in order to deter her or others similarly situated from engaging in similar behavior in the future. Indeed, others who suffer similar, involuntary seizures in the future are just as likely to flail their limbs and perhaps accidentally hit someone else, whether or not this particular woman is punished for her conduct. In addition, there is no indication that the woman needs to be restrained. While she might need "rehabilitation," in the medical sense of the word—diagnosis of the cause of her seizure and treatment to attempt to control it—this is best accomplished outside the criminal justice system.

Q: Can an act still be involuntary if the defendant intended that the result that actually occurred would happen?

A: Yes. A defendant's intention relates only to mens rea. Involuntariness relates only to actus reus. Even if a defendant intended a particular result, she is still not criminally responsible for it, if it happened entirely as a result of her involuntary act.

The Model Penal Code reflects the fundamental requirement found in every American jurisdiction that an act must be "voluntary" in order to permit conviction.[1] As the explanatory note to the MPC provides, the "law cannot hope to deter involuntary movement or to stimulate action that cannot physically be performed," and one's "sense of personal security would be undermined in a society where such movement or inactivity could lead to formal social condemnation of the sort that a conviction necessarily entails."[2] As a result, the Model Penal Code provides that "[a] person is not guilty of an offense unless his liability is based on conduct that includes a voluntary act or the omission to perform an act of which he is physically capable."[3]

Most jurisdictions today treat voluntariness as either an explicit or an implicit part of the actus reus element of every criminal offense. A minority of jurisdictions, however, provide instead that involuntariness is not an element of the crime but rather is an affirmative defense that must be proved by the accused in order to be successful.[4]

(1) Defining "Voluntariness"

In requiring a voluntary act, the criminal law assumes that such an act is a manifestation of the individual's will. As a result, the flailing limbs of the epileptic woman was not regarded as voluntary because it was not a product of her own free will, but rather it was the result of a seizure over which she had no physical control.

Q: Is a voluntary act in criminal law the same as a voluntary act in criminal procedure?

A: No. Voluntariness in the criminal law setting refers to the willed response of an actor. In criminal procedure, in contrast, a voluntary action, such as a volunteered, incriminating statement or a consent to a police officer's request to search, is one that has not been coerced in violation of the Fourteenth Amendment Due Process Clause of the Constitution.

---

[1] See the discussion of the Model Penal Code itself in the Sidebar in Chapter 1.
[2] Model Penal Code §2.01.
[3] Model Penal Code §2.01(1).
[4] *See, e.g., State v. Caddell,* 287 N.C. 266, 215 S.E.2d 348 (1975); *Fulcher v. State,* 633 P.2d 142 (Wyo. 1981).

What other types of movements might not be regarded by criminal law as a manifestation of an individual's will? The MPC sets forth a variety of acts that should not be regarded as voluntary, including: "(a) a reflex or convulsion; (b) a bodily movement during unconsciousness or sleep; (c) conduct during hypnosis or resulting from hypnotic suggestion; (d) a bodily movement that otherwise is not a product of the effort or determination of the actor, either conscious or habitual."[5]

(a) Hypnosis

As previously indicated, the Model Penal Code provides that an act performed as a result of hypnotic suggestion may not be voluntary.[6] But, even where a defendant can prove that he acted while in a hypnotic trance, he still may not prevail on a claim of this sort.

The analysis of the Ninth Circuit Court of Appeals in *United States v. McCollum* is illustrative.[7] In *McCollum*, defendant entered a bank, approached a bank employee, and handed him an envelope. The employee asked defendant about the envelope, and he replied simply, "Open it. I was told to bring it here. I don't know what is in it." The employee opened the note and found that it contained a demand for $100,000, and stated that the person who had delivered it was under a hypnotic spell. When the employee asked defendant to sit down, he complied, and remained seated while the bank was evacuated and police officers entered to apprehend him. Defendant failed to respond to the officers' initial questions and commands, but accompanied them to a police car. Later, in the car, defendant shook violently for 10 to 15 seconds and then asked one of the officers, "What are you doing? Why am I here?" At trial, defendant claimed he had been hypnotized and that his actions were involuntary. Although the court agreed that a hypnotic action *could* be involuntary in the appropriate circumstances, it rejected defendant's involuntariness claim in *this* case, noting archly that he had robbed banks before, presumably in an unhypnotized state.

(b) Forced Movements

Another instance in which a defendant's actions might be regarded as involuntary is when his criminal act was caused by the actions of another person rather than by the effort or determination of the defendant himself. For example, in *People v. Shaughnessy*,[8] defendant was charged with violating an ordinance prohibiting entry upon private property. He claimed that he had not acted voluntarily because he was merely a passenger in a trespassing car. The court agreed, finding that he indeed had not voluntarily entered the property, and therefore had not committed a voluntary trespass.[9]

A similar result was reached in the oft-cited case of *Martin v. State*.[10] In *Martin*, defendant was convicted of appearing in a public place while drunk and manifesting his drunkenness by "boisterous or indecent conduct, or loud and profane discourse." The evidence revealed that the police arrested Martin at his home, where he was already drunk. Then they carried him out of his house and set him down on a public highway. There, the State argued, Martin manifested his drunkenness in violation

---

[5]Model Penal Code §2.01(2).
[6]Model Penal Code §2.01(2).
[7]732 F.2d 1419 (9th Cir. 1984).
[8]66 Misc. 2d 19, 319 N.Y.S.2d 626 (1971).
[9]*See also State v. Boleyn*, 328 So. 2d 95 (La. 1976).
[10]17 So. 2d 427 (Ala. App. 1944).

of the statute by conduct that included "using loud and profane language." The Alabama Court of Appeals held that Martin could not be convicted of this crime because a "voluntary appearance" on the public highway was presupposed by the statute: "[A]n accusation of drunkenness in a designated public place cannot be established by proof that the accused, while in an intoxicated condition, was involuntarily and forcibly carried to that place by the arresting officer."

(c) Automatism

A number of cases deal with the question of whether a defendant who has acted "automatistically" has committed a voluntary act.[11] **Automatism** is an unconscious state in which an actor who otherwise might be capable of voluntary action, is in fact unaware of what he or she is doing. Subsequently, the defendant may not be able to recall part or all of the alleged act.

Automatism might or might not be associated with mental disease or defect. (See Chapter 13, discussing the significance of mental illness in the criminal justice system.) In some instances, an individual might possess an otherwise healthy mind but suffer from a temporary condition—for example, a severe blow to the head that produces an automatistic response. If a defendant commits a criminal act under such circumstances, he may not have committed a voluntary act and, wholly aside from any possible mental illness, he may be able to raise a complete defense to a charged crime based upon that act.

One illustration of the significance of automatism in criminal proceedings is the holding of the California Court of Appeal in *People v. Cox*.[12] In *Cox*, defendant was charged with homicide, but claimed that he had been hit over the head with a bottle and was suffering from traumatic amnesia, resulting in unconsciousness at the time of the killing. The court held that it was error not to give an instruction on unconsciousness where "there is evidence of the existence of that state of the mind wherein the individual's conscious mind has ceased to operate and his actions are controlled

Sidebar

NEUROSCIENCE AND THE VOLUNTARY/INVOLUNTARY DISTINCTION

Professor Deborah Denno has argued that convicting those deemed to have acted voluntarily but excusing those deemed to have acted involuntarily no longer makes sense:

> Recent neuroscientific research indicates that the relationship between conscious and unconscious processes is far more dynamic than these legal dichotomies (voluntary/involuntary, conscious/unconscious) would imply. Such fluidity suggests that human behavior need not be conscious or voluntary in the either/or fashion presumed by the voluntary act requirement. Instead, consciousness is manifested in degrees that suggest multiple levels of awareness.

> Given that the voluntary act requirement is, in theory, the initial filter for individuals brought before the criminal justice system, the concept of a continuum of consciousness is significant. The justice system must evaluate actors with the widest possible range of mental states, behaviors, and potential defenses to determine if they should remain in the system or be acquitted. In the context of such heterogeneity, a forced voluntary/involuntary dichotomy may produce artificial alternatives that risk extreme variations in the punishments for similar acts, depending on how they are ultimately categorized (e.g., involuntary, insane, voluntary and dangerous).

Deborah W. Denno, *Criminal Law in a Post-Freudian World*, 2005 U. Ill. L. Rev. 601, 621 (2005). *See also* Deborah W. Denno, *Crime and Consciousness: Science and Involuntary Acts*, 87 Minn. L. Rev. 269, 388 (2002) (proposing "that the voluntary act requirement should be substantially simplified and constitute three parts: (1) voluntary acts, (2) involuntary acts, and (3) semi-voluntary acts. The third category of semi-voluntary acts takes cases from the first two categories under the presumption that current criminal law paradigms are both too harsh and too lenient, depending on the type of person being adjudicated.").

---

[11] *West v. Addison*, 127 Fed. Appx. 419 (10th Cir. 2005) (denial of jury instruction on automatism held correct because defendant voluntarily consumed drugs that morning); *McClain v. State*, 678 N.E.2d 104 (Ind. 1997) (defendant allowed to use automatism defense as it had bearing on voluntariness).
[12] *People v. Cox*, 67 Cal. App. 2d 166, 153 P.2d 362 (1944).

by the subconscious or subjective mind, it would be error to refuse instructions as to the legal effect of such unconsciousness. . . ."[13]

Likewise, in the widely publicized case of *People v. Newton*,[14] defendant Huey Newton, a well-known political activist, was shot by a police officer and subsequently shot and killed the officer with his return fire. Newton claimed that he was unconscious during the time that he killed the officer. He supported his claim with evidence that, when a gunshot wound penetrates a body cavity, the abdominal or thoracic cavity is likely to produce a profound reflex shock reaction, and it is not uncommon for such a person to lose consciousness for up to half an hour. The California Court of Appeal concluded that Newton was entitled to an instruction on unconsciousness.

(2) Recklessness/Negligence Crimes

Even though a defendant must commit a voluntary act in order to be responsible under the criminal law, as strange as it may sound at first blush, he or she nonetheless does not necessarily need to be conscious at the time the crime is committed. For example, in *State v. Olsen*,[15] the defendant, a shuttle operator, was dispatched to pick up passengers at the airport. On the way, he became sleepy, but kept on driving, opening the window to try and revive himself. At some point, however, he fell asleep, ran off the road, and killed a pedestrian. In sustaining his conviction for involuntary manslaughter, the Utah Supreme Court concluded that the defendant committed a voluntary act by driving under these circumstances: "[He] knew that he had been going without sleep, that he had been drinking that which would disturb his faculties, and that he was not in a fit condition to drive a car. An ordinarily prudent man would have known it." The court found that he "was negligent in trying to drive a car when a man of ordinary prudence would have known it was not safe for him to do so."

Similar principles apply to an actor who drives *knowing* that he is subject to seizures, unlike the hypothetical discussed earlier in which an epileptic baseball fan has a seizure without any prior knowledge of the likelihood of its occurrence. For example, in the well-known case of *People v. Decina*,[16] defendant Decina, aware that he was subject to epileptic seizures, killed a pedestrian when he had a seizure while driving his car. Even though Decina was unconscious at the time of the actual killing, he was deemed to have committed a voluntary act when he chose to drive a vehicle knowing that he was subject to seizures. In the court's view, Decina "took a chance by making a conscious choice of a course of action, in disregard of the consequences which he knew might follow from his conscious act, and which in this case did ensue." The court added that Decina's "awareness of a condition which he knows may produce such consequences as here, and his disregard of the consequences, renders him liable for culpable negligence, as the courts below have properly held."

As previously noted, however, if an actor had no prior awareness of his susceptibility to epileptic seizures and a factual scenario took place otherwise similar to that presented in *Decina*, the fact finder might well find that the actor did not perform a voluntary act. As the *Decina* court made clear, "To have a sudden sleeping spell, an unexpected heart or other disabling attack, without any prior knowledge or warning thereof, is an altogether different situation, and there is simply no basis for comparing such cases with the flagrant disregard manifested here. . . ."

[13]*See also State v. Mercer*, 275 N.C. 108, 165 S.E.2d 328 (1969).
[14]8 Cal. App. 3d 359, 87 Cal. Rptr. 394 (1970).
[15]108 Utah 377, 160 P.2d 427 (1945).
[16]2 N.Y.2d 133, 138 N.E.2d 799, 157 N.Y.S.2d 558 (1956).

(3) Strict Liability Offenses

Where a criminal defendant can make the case successfully that the act with which he is charged was involuntary, it does not matter at all whether the offense was a strict liability crime, as involuntariness is, as previously discussed, an actus reus defense, not a mens rea defense.

(4) Possession Offenses

The act requirement also applies to cases where the government alleges that a defendant illegally possessed contraband, often narcotics, in violation of a criminal statute. However, in order to prove a sufficient act for purposes of establishing possession, the prosecution must ordinarily show that the defendant was aware of her possession sufficiently to be able to exercise control over the item possessed and that she acted knowingly and voluntarily in possessing the contraband.

The Model Penal Code has taken this view, providing that "[p]ossession is an act . . . if the possessor knowingly procured or received the thing possessed or was aware of his control thereof for a sufficient period to have been able to terminate his possession."[17] In this sense, it is also possible to view possession as a failure to act—an omission, see discussion, *infra*—rather than an act because the actor failed to terminate his control over the item possessed.

Whether treated as an act or an omission, it is nonetheless important to recognize that courts often infer voluntary and knowing possession constructively, based on circumstantial evidence. For example, suppose that the police stop defendant's car and an ensuing search of the vehicle reveals a baggie of marijuana in the pocket of defendant's coat found lying on the seat. Under the circumstances, even if defendant denies having any knowledge of the drugs, a fact finder might well infer possession constructively based upon the location of the drugs.

Actual Possession:	Contraband found on the defendant's person.
Constructive Possession:	Contraband found in a place where the defendant is aware of its existence and exercises control.
Joint Possession:	Contraband found on a person or in a place where more than one defendant is aware of its existence and exercises control.

Likewise, more than one person can be and quite often are found to be in possession of the very same contraband items. If a search of an apartment, for example, turns up narcotics in a common area of a kitchen, it is quite possible that the two co-tenants of the apartment will be found circumstantially to have been aware of the existence of the narcotics and to have had control over them sufficient to establish joint and constructive possession and to subject both of them to prosecution under an applicable possession-of-narcotics crimes code provision.

---

[17]Model Penal Code §2.01(4).

(5) "Status Based" Crimes

The act requirement has also been the focus of two important Supreme Court decisions. The Court's decision in *Robinson v. California*[18] involved a California statute that made it a criminal offense to "be addicted to the use of narcotics." The evidence showed that Robinson was a narcotics addict. Not only did he admit his addiction, the police observed "scar tissue and discoloration" on the inside of his right arm, as well as "numerous needle marks and a scab" on his left arm. The jury found that defendant was addicted to narcotics and convicted him.

In striking down the statute, the Supreme Court concluded that it did not require proof that defendant had used narcotics or had possessed narcotics or engaged in anti-social or disorderly conduct in the state. On the contrary, someone could be convicted based solely upon his status or the chronic condition of being "addicted to the use of narcotics." The Court concluded that Robinson could not constitutionally be convicted for this status in the same way that a state cannot make it a crime for a person to "be mentally ill, or a leper, or to be afflicted with a venereal disease." While the Court observed that a state might legitimately conclude that addicts should be forced into treatment or quarantine, criminalizing an individual's mere status was held to be cruel and unusual punishment. As the Court added, addiction can be contracted innocently or involuntarily, as in the case of a baby born to an addicted mother.

Following *Robinson*, questions arose about how far this decision might extend. Subsequently, in *Powell v. Texas*,[19] a defendant contended that he was "afflicted with the disease of chronic alcoholism," that "his appearance in public [while drunk was] not of his own volition," and therefore "that to punish him criminally for that conduct would be cruel and unusual." The Supreme Court disagreed, a plurality of the Court distinguishing *Robinson* on the ground that Powell was not convicted based upon his status as an alcoholic, but rather for "being in public while drunk on a particular occasion." The *Powell* plurality also rejected the notion that "chronic alcoholics in general, and [Powell] in particular, suffer from such an irresistible compulsion to drink and to get drunk in public that they are utterly unable to control their performance of either or both of these acts and thus cannot be deterred at all from public intoxication."

B. Omissions

Even though criminal culpability must be based upon a voluntary act, the term "act" is defined broadly enough to include a *failure to act*—an omission—but only when and if the defendant has a preexisting legal obligation to act. Consistent with this approach, the Model Penal Code provides that criminal culpability can be based on an "omission to perform an act of which he is physically capable."[20]

In general, the criminal law does not require individuals to protect or care for others. For example, even if an individual has the resources to help someone who is starving, his or her failure to help that person does not give rise to criminal responsibility.

On the contrary, and once again, before criminal culpability can attach for a mere failure to act, it must be shown that the accused had a legal duty to provide

[18]370 U.S. 660 (1962).
[19]392 U.S. 514 (1968).
[20]Model Penal Code §2.01.

such assistance. As the Michigan Supreme Court concluded more than a century ago in the partly (but not completely) outdated case of *People v. Beardsley*,[21] "[t]he law recognizes that under some circumstances the omission of a duty owed by one individual to another, where such omission results in the death of the one to whom the duty is owing, will make the other chargeable with manslaughter. [This] rule of law is always based upon the proposition that the duty neglected must be a legal duty, and not a mere moral obligation. It must be a duty imposed by law or by contract, and the omission to perform the duty must be the immediate and direct cause of death."

(1) Exceptions to the General Rule

Should the law impose a broader duty to help those in need? One can certainly make a reasonable argument for such a change in the law. In many places in this country, a significant number of people suffer from starvation, as well as from homelessness and poverty and the effects of severe weather. Should the government impose a *criminal obligation* on its better-off citizens (most of the rest of us) to help those in need, and should it impose punishment upon those who fail to meet this obligation?

Although you can certainly argue reasonably that we *should* all be required to assist those in need, it is a large jump from that ethical proposition to argue further that criminal responsibility as opposed to moral responsibility should follow from a refusal to help others. No American jurisdiction has taken such a leap by—currently, at least—imposing such a far-reaching, general duty to help others in need. As a result, the well-heeled citizen can blithely ignore the plight of the homeless and the starving—at least he or she can do so without any criminal consequence.

Perhaps the most notorious example of the application of the present law in this regard is the Kitty Genovese case, which took place in Queens, New York.[22] Genovese was sexually assaulted and brutally murdered while 38 people heard her screams from inside their apartments and did nothing. Indeed, the evidence revealed that she screamed repeatedly for help while her attacker stabbed her, then moved his car, and then came after Genovese again, attacking her again, and ultimately killing her. None of the nearby residents who heard her screams did anything—nothing at all—to help her, except that a couple of people yelled out of their windows for the attacker to stop. But none of these people were prosecuted. How could they be? Remember, they failed to act. They didn't act, and an omission to act is not punishable under the criminal law—*ordinarily*—in the absence of a legal duty.

We say *ordinarily* because there are some few exceptions to this rule. Some states and municipalities do impose some duties upon their citizens in specific sorts of emergency situations. For example, a Wisconsin law requires citizens to come to the aid of crime victims provided that they can do so without danger to themselves.[23] Likewise, a Rhode Island law requires one present at the scene of an emergency to

[21]150 Mich. 206, 113 N.W. 1128, 1129 (1907).
[22]Reported as *Moseley v. Scully*, 908 F. Supp. 1120 (E.D.N.Y. 1995).
[23]*See* W.S.A. 940.34(2)(a) ("Any person who knows that a crime is being committed and that a victim is exposed to bodily harm shall summon law enforcement officers or other assistance or shall provide assistance to the victim."); W.S.A. 940.34(2)(d) ("A person need not comply with this subsection if any of the following apply: 1. Compliance would place him or her in danger[;] 2. Compliance would interfere with duties the person owes to others[;] 3. In the circumstances described under par. (a), assistance is being summoned or provided by others[; or] 4. . . . the crime or alleged crime has been reported to an appropriate law enforcement agency by others.").

render assistance to those exposed to "grave physical harm" if he or she can do so "without danger or peril to himself or herself or to others. . . ."[24]

One of the most controversial cases involving omissions, the failure to assist, involves the car crash in a Paris tunnel that led to the death of Princess Diana of England. After the crash, many of the photographers, following in their own cars, stopped to take photos, but did not offer assistance to the crash victims. Under traditional American law, in the majority of states that do not have failure-to-assist statutes, that failure to come to Princess Di's aid would not raise issues of criminal culpability. France does have such a statute. Nonetheless in 2002 France's highest court dropped manslaughter charges against nine photographers who pursued the car before it crashed or who took photos at the site.

(2) Duties to Act

Taken from the common law, there are at least five situations in which the law ordinarily imposes a duty to act, failure to comply with which may result in criminal culpability based upon an omission. First, a duty to act exists when a statute expressly imposes such a duty. Second, a duty exists when an actor stands in a recognized "status relationship" (e.g., parent or spouse) to or with another person. Third, a legal duty exists when one has assumed a contractual duty to perform certain specified tasks. Fourth, a legal duty exists where a person has voluntarily assumed the care of another person. And fifth, a duty exists where a person is responsible for actually creating the victim's dire situation.

DUTIES TO ACT:

(a) Statutory Obligations
(b) Status Relationships
(c) Contractual Duty
(d) Voluntary Assumption of Duty
(e) Creation of Peril

Each of these situations is discussed below.[25]

(a) Statutory Obligations

A few statutes impose duties of care upon individuals in carefully specified circumstances. For example, public school officials may have a general statutory duty of care toward children entrusted to their care. Or they may have a more specific

---

[24]R.I. Gen. Law §11–56–1 ("Any person at the scene of an emergency who knows that another person is exposed to, or has suffered, grave physical harm shall, to the extent that he or she can do so without danger or peril to himself or herself or to others, give reasonable assistance to the exposed person. Any person violating the provisions of this section shall be guilty of a petty misdemeanor and shall be subject to imprisonment for a term not exceeding six (6) months, or by a fine of not more than five hundred dollars ($500), or both.").

[25]The Model Penal Code essentially incorporates these common law rules by use of the following language: "Liability for the commission of an offense may not be based on an omission unaccompanied by action unless: (a) the omission is expressly made sufficient by the law defining the offense; or (b) a duty to perform the omitted act is otherwise imposed by law." Model Penal Code §2.01(3).

statutory duty—to look for and to report instances of apparent child abuse, for example. Likewise, in many jurisdictions, a driver who is involved in an automobile accident may have a legal obligation imposed by statute to stop and render assistance to those injured in the accident. Doctors and other health care workers may have a statutory duty to report the admission to a hospital of patients with gunshot wounds.

There are any number of other specific circumstances in which specific statutory duties of care might be imposed. California, for example, imposes a statutory obligation of care on those charged with the care of elderly or dependent adults.[26]

(b) Status Relationships

One of the most common status relationships that gives rise to a duty to provide aid is the relationship between a parent and his or her child. For example, in *State v. Williquette*,[27] a mother was charged with child abuse for failing to protect her children while her husband repeatedly beat and sexually abused them. Despite the severity of the beatings—their father sometimes beat the children so hard with a metal stick that they had bruises all over their bodies—the children's mother did nothing other than to tell her kids "not to worry about it." The Wisconsin Supreme Court sustained the mother's conviction, ruling that she had a duty to protect her children because of her special—parental—relationship to them: "It is the right and duty of parents under the law of nature as well as the common law and the statutes of many states to protect their children, to care for them in sickness and in health, and to do whatever may be necessary for their care, maintenance, and preservation, including medical attendance, if necessary. An omission to do this is a public wrong which the state, under its police powers, may prevent."

A number of other parental omission cases have involved a failure to obtain medical care for a sick child. For example, in the well-known case of *State v. Williams*,[28] defendant father,[29] a laborer with only a sixth-grade education, had a 14-month-old son who was suffering from an abscessed tooth that developed into a gangrenous infection of the mouth. Even though both defendant and his wife loved the child, neither took him to the doctor even though they had the means to do so. Both parents admitted that they realized that their baby was very sick for about two weeks before the baby died. Not realizing that death was a possibility, they attempted to treat him only with aspirin. The evidence showed that neither parent realized the dire significance or seriousness of the baby's symptoms. Nevertheless, both were found to have possessed a legal duty toward their son, and both were deemed to have failed to perform that duty. That failure to care, given their status as parents, led the court to one conclusion: "We therefore hold that the violation of

---

[26]Cal. Penal Code §368(b)(1) ("Any person who knows or reasonably should know that a person is an elder or dependent adult and who, under circumstances or conditions likely to produce great bodily harm or death, willfully causes or permits any elder or dependent adult to suffer, or inflicts thereon unjustifiable physical pain or mental suffering, or having the care or custody of any elder or dependent adult, willfully causes or permits the person or health of the elder or dependent adult to be injured, or willfully causes or permits the elder or dependent adult to be placed in a situation in which his or her person or health is endangered, is punishable by imprisonment in a county jail not exceeding one year, or by a fine not to exceed six thousand dollars ($6,000), or by both that fine and imprisonment, or by imprisonment in the state prison for two, three, or four years.").

[27]129 Wis. 2d 239, 385 N.W.2d 145 (1986).

[28]4 Wash. App. 908, 484 P.2d 1167 (1971).

[29]The father in *Williams* was not actually the boy's natural father. The court concluded nonetheless that his assumption of that parental role (and consequent duty) provided a sufficient basis for the imposition of criminal responsibility: "[His] assumption of responsibility, characterized in the information as that required of a 'guardian and custodian,' is sufficient to impose upon him the duty to furnish necessary medical care."

the parental duty to furnish medical care to a minor dependent child, the other elements of manslaughter being present, is a sufficient basis on which to rest a conviction of the crime of manslaughter."

In other cases, parents have argued that they should not be held criminally responsible for their child's death because they relied on their religious beliefs in failing to seek medical care and therefore that they were protected under the First Amendment's free exercise clause. For example, in *Walker v. Superior Court*,[30] defendant's daughter died of meningitis, which had been present in her body for at least two weeks at the time of death. The defendant mother knew that her daughter was very ill, but chose nonetheless to treat her daughter by spiritual healing rather than by the use of medical specialists or practitioners. The court upheld the trial court's conviction for manslaughter, holding that the "point at which parents may incur liability for substituting prayer treatment for medical care for their child is clear— when the lack of medical attention places the child in a situation endangering its person or health."

Q: What other status relationships are commonly recognized as creating a duty to act?

A: Other status relationships—beyond that of parent-child—can also create duties of care. Commonly, for example, there is a spousal duty of care toward one other. Landlords have a duty of care toward their tenants, employers have a duty of care toward their employees, common carriers have such a duty toward their passengers.

However, the fact that such a relationship exists does not necessarily mean that a failure to act will always result in criminal culpability. For example, take the case of *Commonwealth v. Konz*.[31] In *Konz*, a woman failed to seek medical care for her diabetic husband, who subsequently died as an apparent result. The husband, following a visit with an evangelist, had decided to discontinue all insulin treatment in the belief that "God would heal [his] diabetic condition." The court rejected the argument that the wife had a duty to request medical assistance for her husband, distinguishing between a parent's obligation to a child and a wife's obligation to her husband: "The inherent dependency of a child upon his parent to obtain medical aid, i.e., the incapacity of a child to evaluate his condition and summon aid by himself, supports imposition of such a duty upon the parent. . . . Spouses, however, do not generally suffer the same incapacity as do children with respect to the ability to comprehend their states of health and obtain medical assistance."

The defendant wife was simply honoring her husband's desire to avoid the use of insulin; he had in fact refused several offers of insulin. As a result, the court concluded that "[t]he marital relationship gives rise to an expectation of reliance between spouses, and to a belief that one's spouse should be trusted to respect, rather than ignore, one's expressed preferences. That expectation would be frustrated by imposition of a broad duty to seek aid, since one's spouse would then be

---

[30]222 Cal. Rptr. 87 (Cal. App. 1986).
[31]498 Pa. 639, 450 A.2d 638 (1982).

forced to ignore the expectation that the preference to forego assistance will be honored."

It is important to add, however, that many other jurisdictions have imposed a duty on a spouse to seek medical assistance for a husband or wife in need of care, at least in the appropriate circumstances.[32]

(c) Contractual Obligations

In some instances, individuals will have contractual obligations that impose on them legal duties toward others. Such obligations are not only enforceable in private civil actions, but create duties under the criminal law.

These obligations and concomitant duties can arise in a variety of situations. For example, someone hired as a lifeguard at a swimming pool likely has a contractual obligation to assist swimmers in distress. If a lifeguard fails to fulfill that duty in a situation where she can reasonably do so, she may be held responsible for the swimmer's death under the criminal law.

Likewise, when a school or day care center agrees to provide care for the children in its charge, it has a resulting legal obligation to provide food and other necessities—for example, medical care, if needed—during the period of that care. A failure to meet that obligation leading to a child's death, can, accordingly, be punished under the criminal law.

An old, classic example of this legal principle can be found in the decision in *State v. Irvine*,[33] where a locomotive foreman's job responsibilities included the obligation to ensure that trains were on the proper tracks. When an engineer decided to travel inward on the outgoing side of the track, and caused a head-on collision with an outbound train, the foreman was held criminally responsible: "[D]efendant is guilty even if he did not know that the engine was on this wrong track; because, where one is charged with a special duty the nonperformance of which involves danger to the safety of others, the failure to perform the duty even through inattention is gross and culpable, or, in other words, criminal, negligence. . . . 'Where death is the direct and immediate result of the omission of a party to perform a plain duty imposed upon him by law or contract, he is guilty of a felonious homicide.'"[34]

Similarly, in *State v. Harrison*,[35] another older but still controlling case, defendant was employed by a railroad company as a gateman. Since his job was to close the gate when a train approached, he was held to have a contractual obligation that gave rise to criminal responsibility when he failed to close the gate, thereby causing the death of a driver: "Instead of lowering the gates, as his duty to the railroad company and to the public required him to do, he failed and neglected to lower them, although he saw Goble, the decedent, approaching the crossing in his automobile when Goble was about 125 feet away. The result was that Goble was hit by the train and killed. Certainly such failure of duty justified a finding of gross negligence."

[32]*See, e.g., Westrup v. Commonwealth*, 123 Ky. 95, 93 S.W. 646 (1906) ("Where the husband neglects to provide necessaries for his wife, or medical attention in case of her illness, he will be guilty of involuntary manslaughter, provided it appears that she was in a *helpless state and unable to appeal elsewhere for aid*, and that the death, though not intended nor anticipated by him, was the natural and reasonable consequence of his negligence."); *State v. Mally*, 139 Mont. 599, 366 P.2d 868 (1961) ("We are aware that the large majority of homicide cases involving a failure to provide medical aid involve a parent-child relationship. This is undoubtedly due to the fact that a person of mature years is not generally in a helpless condition. However, fact situations do arise, such as the instant case, wherein it is apparent *that an adult is as helpless as the newborn*. The record is replete with evidence that [decedent] could not have *consciously or rationally denied medical aid*.").
[33]126 La. 434, 52 So. 567 (1910).
[34]126 La. 434, 438, 52 So. 567, 569 (1910) quoting 61 L.R.A. 277.
[35]107 N.J.L. 213, 152 A. 867 (1931).

(d) Assumption of Duty

In general, as previously discussed, absent a special relationship or some other obligation established by law, a person has no duty enforceable by the criminal law to provide care for someone else in need. However, there is another common exception to that general rule. If an actor actually assumed the responsibility to help another person or created that person's perilous situation, a duty to assist the victim enforceable at criminal law may well arise.

For example, traditionally, a child was held to have no legal duty to provide or care for an aging or ailing parent,[36] and could not therefore be charged with homicide even if his or her parent died from hunger or neglect. However, if an adult child assumes responsibility for a parent by taking that parent into the child's home, for example, thus assuming a duty of care (and simultaneously making it difficult for other persons to offer assistance or even to know of the parent's need for assistance), the child may well have criminal responsibility if the parent dies as a result of neglect. A legal duty will have been assumed and the failure to live up to that duty can be punished as the actus reus of a crime.[37]

There does not need to be a formal status relationship, however, such as child-parent, between individuals in order for someone to assume a duty and risk criminal responsibility of this sort. Any individual who invites another person into his or her home and agrees to provide for that person and thereby effectively secludes him from the public, can be held criminally responsible when that person suffers from neglect.

In *Commonwealth v. Pestinikas*,[38] for example, a man was released from the hospital after a serious illness and a couple invited him to live with them. Although they were aware that he had special medical needs and that he required special medicines in addition to his ordinary need for food and shelter, the couple never filled his prescriptions. Just as bad, they placed him in a dilapidated house that had cracks in the walls and that lacked insulation, refrigeration, a bathroom, a sink, or a telephone. When the man's family tried to find out where he was, the couple provided them with misleading information, telling them they didn't know where he'd gone. The couple also withdrew more than $30,000 from his bank accounts. After the man died, the coroner found him to be emaciated, with his ribs and sternum protruding from his body. The cause of death was starvation and dehydration. Because the couple had assumed responsibility for the man and then secluded him, the Pennsylvania Superior Court held that they were criminally responsible for his death.[39]

(e) Creation of Peril

Finally, although it does not occur very often, on occasion a legal duty to assist may arise because an actor was responsible for actually "creating the victim's peril."

---

[36]In some few jurisdictions, however, in more recent cases, an obligation to provide care has been created pursuant to the status relationship of child-parent.
[37]*See, e.g., Davis v. Commonwealth*, 230 Va. 201, 335 S.E.2d 375 (1985) ("Davis accepted sole responsibility for the total care of Carter. . . . In return, Carter allowed Davis to live in her home expense free and shared with Davis her income from social security. Additionally, Carter authorized Davis to act as her food stamp representative, and for this Davis received food stamp benefits in her own right. From [this] evidence, the trial court reasonably could find the existence of an implied contract. . . . Davis was more than a mere volunteer; she had a legal duty, not merely a moral one, to care for her mother."); *People v. Sealy*, 136 Mich. App. 168, 356 N.W.2d 614 (1984).
[38]421 Pa. Super. 371, 617 A.2d 1339 (1992).
[39]*See also People v. Montecino*, 66 Cal. App. 2d 85, 152 P.2d 5 (1944).

For example, in *Jones v. State*,[40] a man brutally attacked and raped a young girl and left her in great emotional and physical distress. In that state, she fell into a stream and was unable to get herself to shore. But her attacker refused to help her even though he could have easily done so.

In concluding that that he was criminally culpable not just for the rape but for her death as well, the Indiana Supreme Court reasoned: "Can it be doubted than one who by his own overpowering criminal act has put another in danger of drowning has the duty to preserve her life? . . . The recital in the indictment of [defendant's] failure to rescue her is not the allegation of a separate public offense but the statement of one link in a chain of causation, beginning with [his] wrongful acts, and leading directly to the death of [the victim]."

(3) Predicates to Duty

Even if an individual has a legal duty to provide assistance to another person, that duty may not result in a criminal conviction unless and until the individual is actually aware of the need to act or is reckless or negligent, as applicable criminal statutes might require. Suppose, for example, that a parent drops his child off at school in the morning with the intention of picking the child up that afternoon. During the day, the child suffers a severe injury requiring immediate medical assistance. Under such circumstances, the parent's duty of assistance might not attach unless and until the parent has actually been notified by the school of the child's need for assistance.

In addition to being aware of the need to act, an individual must also have the physical ability to perform the required duty. For example, if a mother and her children are involved in an automobile accident, and all of them require medical care, the mother's failure to obtain medical care for her children would certainly be excused where her own immediate medical condition rendered her physically unable to help her children.

F A Q

Q: Can someone who watches a swimmer drown be held criminally responsible for the death?

A: It depends entirely upon who the "someone" is and what his or her abilities are. Ordinarily, failures to act are *not* punished unless they are failures to satisfy a preexisting legal obligation. In this hypothetical, if the person who failed to act was a parent (status relationship) or a lifeguard (contractual duty), for example, he or she would have a duty, and a failure to meet that duty could result in a homicide conviction, assuming that the other elements of homicide are satisfied. See Chapter 8. In addition, however, if a bystander watching the swimmer drown couldn't swim (that is, he or she was "physically unable to act"), even if a legal duty to act existed—for example, the bystander was the swimmer's father—there would be no criminal responsibility.

---

[40]220 Ind. 384, 43 N.E.2d 1017 (1942).

Similarly, if a father and his children are lost in a remote wilderness area and are starving, but have no means of obtaining food under the circumstances, the father cannot be held criminally responsible for failing to provide food for his children. He would be, in short, physically unable to act. However, each case of this sort must and will be evaluated on its own facts. In the latter example, if the father and his children were homeless and starving in an urban area, rather than in a remote wilderness area, the parent's obligation to act on his duty of care to his children would likely be viewed quite differently. Even if he lacked the means to buy food for them, he might none-theless still possess a legal obligation to seek help from others to care for the children, including calling upon the resources of public welfare agencies.

(4) Constitutional Issues

Also relevant to the issue of omissions is the Supreme Court's oft-cited but con-troversial decision in *Lambert v. California*.[41] That case involved a Los Angeles ordinance that required "any convicted person" to register with the police within five days of arriving in the city. Defendant Lambert failed to register, an omission, and she was subsequently prosecuted and convicted for her failure. In overturning her conviction, the Court emphasized that her action was "passive" in that it involved a mere failure to register. While the Court acknowledged the continuing vitality of the general rule that "ignorance of the law will not excuse," it nonetheless concluded that due process places "some limits on its exercise," more specifically, that Lambert and others in her situation needed to be given fair notice of their need to register. The Court applied these principles to the Los Angeles ordinance, con-cluding that

> notice is required in a myriad of situations where a penalty or forfeiture might be suffered for mere failure to act. [The] principle is equally appropriate where a person, wholly passive and unaware of any wrongdoing, is brought to the bar of justice for condemnation in a criminal case.
>
> [At] most the ordinance is but a law enforcement technique designed for the convenience of law enforcement agencies through which a list of the names and addresses of felons then residing in a given community is compiled. [Lambert] on first becoming aware of her duty to register was given no opportunity to comply with the law and avoid its penalty, even though her default was entirely innocent. She could but suffer the conse-quences of the ordinance, namely, conviction with the imposition of heavy criminal pen-alties thereunder. We believe that actual knowledge of the duty to register or proof of the probability of such knowledge and subsequent failure to comply are necessary before a conviction under the ordinance can stand.

The *Lambert* decision does not mean that criminal laws cannot be enforced against a person who doesn't know that the law exists. To the contrary. The maxim that "ignorance of the law is no defense" still retains vitality. *Lambert* is a very limited decision. First, it's important to note that *Lambert* involved an individual who *failed* to act (so-called *passive* conduct, an omission), rather than someone who was acting. Second and perhaps more important, *Lambert* does not apply to situa-tions where a person reasonably should have been on notice that there might be criminal or regulatory statutes in existence.

---

[41]355 U.S. 225 (1957).

SUMMARY

■ An involuntary act does not satisfy the actus reus element of a criminal offense.

■ Involuntariness is an actus reus defense, not a mens rea defense, hence it still applies even if the criminal offense in question is strict liability.

■ To establish the act of possession of contraband, the defendant must have been aware of his possession sufficiently to be able to exercise control and have acted knowingly and voluntarily.

■ Voluntary and knowing possession is often inferred constructively, based upon circumstantial evidence.

■ An omission can only satisfy the actus reus requirement where the accused had a legal obligation to act.

■ A legal duty to act exists when a statute imposes such a duty, there is a status relationship, such as parent or spouse, with another person, a contractual duty exists, or where a person has voluntarily assumed the care of another.

■ An omission cannot be criminalized constitutionally unless the accused is or should be aware that criminal or regulatory rules might exist governing such conduct.

CONNECTIONS

Relationship to Attempt

Attempts (see Chapter 6) have their own actus reus, different from the actus reus of the criminal offense that the actor tried but failed to commit. Defined differently in different jurisdictions, that actus reus might focus on the actor's proximity to completion of the intended criminal act or simply upon the question whether or not the actor took a substantial step toward his or her criminal goal.

Relationship to Causation

Where an act element requires the accused's completion of a specified result— for example, the death of a human being for homicide offenses (see Chapter 8)— the criminal offense ordinarily will also require that the State establish that the accused person "caused" that result (see Chapter 4).

Relationship to Excuse and Justification Defenses

The actus reus and mens rea (see Chapter 3) of a crime are elements of the criminal offense. The classic defense to a criminal charge is to establish the prosecution's failure of proof of one of those or any other element of the crime. In contrast, excuse and justification defenses (see Chapters 13 and 12) are usually affirmative defenses that need to be proven by the accused without regard to proof of the elements of the offense.

Relationship to Mens Rea

Ordinarily, the prosecution needs to establish the concurrence of a criminal act (actus reus) and criminal intent (mens rea) elements (see Chapter 3) in order to establish the basic minima of a criminal conviction.

Relationship to Mental Illness Defenses

An involuntary act might or might not be associated with the actor's mental disease or defect. See Chapter 13 (discussing the significance of mental illness in the criminal justice system). In some instances, for example, an individual might possess an otherwise healthy mind, but suffer from a temporary condition, such as a severe blow to the head that produces an automatistic response. If a defendant commits a criminal act under such circumstances, he may not have committed a voluntary act and, wholly aside from any possible mental illness defense he may have (e.g., insanity), he may be able to raise a complete defense to a charged crime based upon involuntariness.

Relationship to Sexual Offenses

Significantly, unlike the common law, modern rape statutes in most jurisdictions (see Chapter 10) do *not* require proof of *both* the actus reus elements of the use of force *and* the absence of consent. Instead, they typically require proof of one of those elements or the other, not both.

Relationship to Theft Offenses

The prosecution of theft crimes (see Chapter 11) traditionally relied heavily on the clear proof of specified actus reus elements. If a prosecutor at trial actually established the actus reus element of a theft offense that had not been charged, the prosecution failed. Today, with the consolidation of many theft offenses in most jurisdictions, this is far less of a problem.

Mens Rea

3

OVERVIEW

We do not generally want to punish someone who did not intend to commit a punishable act. Accordingly, one of the key elements of most criminal offenses is proof beyond a reasonable doubt of the **mens rea**, the specific criminal intent expressly deemed requisite for that particular criminal offense. As noted in Chapter 2, establishing the existence of a crime generally requires proof both of a criminal act—the *actus reus*—and of this *mens rea*, where one is specified by law. But legislatures also can and do sometimes enact **strict liability** criminal statutes, eliminating the necessity for the prosecution to prove a mens rea. Nonetheless, *most* criminal statutes do require expressly that the prosecution prove that the accused acted with a specifically enumerated, culpable state of mind.

A. MENS REA FORMULATIONS

1. Concurrence of Act and Intent
2. Common Law
3. Changes in the Common Law
4. Purpose
5. Knowledge
6. Recklessness and Negligence
7. Construction of Criminal Statutes

B. STRICT LIABILITY OFFENSES

1. Traditional Aversion to Strict Liability
2. Public Welfare Offenses
3. Impact of Strict Liability

C. INTOXICATION AND DRUGGED CONDITION

D. MISTAKE OF FACT

E. MISTAKE OF LAW

Except where a criminal statute imposes culpability based on strict liability, criminal responsibility almost always requires proof of, *inter alia*, a specified mens rea or mental state. In other words, most criminal statutes require the State to prove beyond a reasonable doubt that the accused engaged in a prohibited act or caused a prohibited result while acting with a specific state of mind.

The mens rea requirement plays an important role in the criminal justice system as it is commonly used to distinguish between criminally culpable (blameworthy) and nonculpable individuals. For example, if a defendant's automobile veered off the road and killed a pedestrian, the defendant's mental state would normally be viewed as highly relevant to—if not dispositive of—the question whether his or her actions violated applicable criminal law. If the defendant acted, for instance, with the express intent or purpose of killing the pedestrian, the State might well impose—and be viewed as morally justified in imposing—the severest forms of punishment, such as incarceration for many years, life imprisonment, or, in some jurisdictions, capital punishment. By contrast, if the reason the pedestrian was killed was that the defendant swerved entirely by accident—for example, a tire blew out—the driver, who was not acting intentionally, might well have no criminal responsibility whatsoever due to lack of appropriate mens rea.

Even as between various culpable individuals, the mens rea requirement helps distinguish between defendants, serving to impose more severe punishment on those defendants who possessed mental states deemed by the legislature to be more culpable than other mental states. In the prior example, involving the motorist who swerved off the road and killed a pedestrian, the most severe punishment would usually be reserved for a driver who acted with the express intention of killing the pedestrian, thus supporting a murder conviction, probably murder in the first degree. By contrast, if the defendant was found to have killed a pedestrian recklessly or negligently, because, for instance, he was traveling on bald tires and knew or should have known as much, the facts might be viewed by a fact finder as supporting conviction only of a lesser homicide offense—involuntary manslaughter perhaps.[1]

A. Mens Rea Formulations

"Even a dog distinguishes between being stumbled over and being kicked."

—Oliver Wendell Holmes

---

[1]See Chapter 8 (Homicide).

The earliest concept of mens rea reflected little more than satisfaction of a "general notion of blameworthiness," a "guilty mind," a "vicious will," or even proof of an accused person's "evil mind." Over time, however, this general, amorphous concept of evil criminal intent shifted from a vague notion of wickedness to a more definite requirement of a *specific* state of mind to do that which is prohibited expressly in specific criminal statutes. Thus, no longer does simple proof of "wickedness" suffice to establish criminal culpability. Put another way, the mere fact that a defendant may have possessed a wicked or felonious disposition, unrelated to the mens rea required for the specific crime for which he or she is charged, is not enough to sustain a criminal conviction.

For example, in the old, classic case of *Regina v. Faulkner*,[2] a seaman was charged with "feloniously, unlawfully, and maliciously" burning a ship. The evidence revealed that the sailor, Faulkner, went into the hold of the ship intending to steal rum. In the process, he accidentally set a cask of rum on fire with a lighted match, and the resulting blaze destroyed the whole ship. He was convicted of the crime of maliciously burning a ship. The conviction was reversed, however, because the court rejected the notion that "the defendant, being engaged in the commission of, or in an attempt to commit a felony, was criminally responsible for every result that was occasioned thereby, even though it was not a probable consequence of his act or such as he could have reasonably foreseen or intended."

In short, just because Faulkner intended to do something bad (steal rum) did not necessarily mean that he was guilty of the particular criminal act that resulted (burned ship). Where a criminal statute specifies a particular mens rea as an element of the criminal offense, that particular mens rea—not simple wickedness or evil intent—must be established in order to satisfy the statute.

F   A   Q

Q: Why wasn't Faulkner guilty of a crime when he clearly started the fire that burned the ship?

A: He may well have been guilty of a crime, just not the crime with which he was charged (burning the ship) on the basis of the instructions that were given to the jury. He certainly would have been found guilty of stealing the rum if that offense had been charged. And he may well have been convicted of burning the ship if the jury had been properly charged on the mens rea of recklessness. Certainly, a strong argument could have been made by the prosecution that—by holding a lighted match next to the rum—he consciously disregarded a substantial risk that the rum might catch fire and burn the ship.

(1) Concurrence of Act and Intent

There must also be a "concurrence" between the accused's mens rea and the accused's culpable act. Suppose, for example, that a person intends to kill his victim, and concocts

---

[2]13 Cox Crim. Cas. 550 (1877).

a plan to shoot him the following week. To that end, the would-be killer purchases a gun, reconnoiters the place where he plans to shoot from, and plans his getaway. However, on the way to work the next morning, his tire unexpectedly blows out, causing his car to swerve off the road. He tries to avoid hitting any pedestrians, but unavoidably, he does hit and kill one. When he gets out of his car, he realizes, to his astonishment, that the deceased pedestrian is none other than the very victim he planned to kill the next week, and he is overjoyed. He is not criminally responsible for the death because there was no concurrence between his intent to kill his victim and the actual killing act.

In the real world outside of criminal law hypotheticals in books, however, this particular defendant may have a *very* difficult time convincing a judge or jury that he didn't intend the particular automobile "accident." More bluntly, the driver's lack of blameworthiness depends entirely on the prosecutor or the fact finder believing the entire implausible account of the facts spelled out above.

(2) Common Law

Historically, the mens rea requirement has been formulated in various ways. At common law, a variety of mental states existed, including "maliciously," "feloniously," "unlawfully," "fraudulently," "corruptly," "willfully," and the "intent to steal." Additionally, at common law, a distinction was made between a **specific intent crime** and a **general intent crime**. The precise dividing line between the two types of intent has not always been clear. However, broadly speaking, a crime is a general intent crime when the required mens rea entails only an intent to perform the act that causes the harm (for example, assault); a crime is often treated as a "specific intent crime" when the required mens rea entails an intent to cause a further harm (for example, assault with intent to rape).

The common law offense of burglary, as another example, was a specific intent crime because it entailed the breaking and entering of the dwelling of another at night *with the intent to commit a felony*—that is, an action undertaken with the intent to cause a further act aside from the triggering criminal act. Burglary was a specific intent crime, in other words, because in addition to the general intent to break and enter, to be convicted, an accused burglar had to be shown to have possessed the specific intent—the *further* intent—to commit a felony inside the dwelling.

Given the confusing nature of this distinction between general and specific intent crimes, you will no doubt be pleased to learn that this distinction is no longer significant today in most American jurisdictions, except as it relates to the defense of intoxication or drugged condition in some states, as is discussed later in this chapter.

(3) Changes in the Common Law

Because the common law array of mens rea requirements was—at best—confusing and—at worst—inconsistent, the drafters of the Model Penal Code sought to simplify the notion of mens rea by creating a standardized system.[3] Although many jurisdictions do not or do not any longer follow this MPC approach, and because even in those jurisdictions that still do, interpretations of the various mens rea terms vary widely and are usually non-exclusive, the Model Penal Code mens rea approach and terminology nonetheless is still quite useful to examine in order to understand just how mens rea elements are commonly utilized and defined in this country.

---

[3]*See* discussion of the Model Penal Code itself in the Sidebar in Chapter 1.

F   A   Q

Q: What do we mean when we say that the MPC mens rea terms are usually used in a "non-exclusive" manner?

A: The drafters of the MPC intended that the four mens rea terms that they created and so carefully defined would be the *only* mens rea terms to be used in jurisdictions adopting a version of the MPC as that jurisdiction's Crimes Code. That simply has not happened. Since legislators have the authority to enact and define criminal offenses just as they wish (and perhaps because so many legislators are not lawyers, too), most jurisdictions that have adopted the MPC mens rea elements also possess dozens—sometimes hundreds—of criminal statutes that use other non-defined mens rea terms of art.

Except when criminal culpability is based upon strict liability, the MPC provides that proof of commission of a particular crime should be based on a showing that the accused acted with one of four defined mental states to be included in the statutory description of the offense: purpose, knowledge, recklessness, and negligence.[4]

(4) Purpose

Because they are mental states that are deemed to suggest a high degree of culpability given the actor's express criminal object, both the Model Penal Code's purpose and knowledge mens rea tests are more difficult to satisfy than the tests of recklessness and negligence, each of which can be established without a showing of express antisocial intention.

For the mens rea of "purpose," the Model Penal Code requires a showing that "(i) if the element involves the nature of his conduct or a result thereof, it is his conscious object to engage in conduct of that nature or to cause such a result; and (ii) if the element involves the attendant circumstances, he is aware of the existence of such circumstances or he believes or hopes that they exist."[5]

In some instances, it will not be difficult at all to show that an actor acted purposely. Suppose, for example, that a defendant is charged with murder under a statute that requires that he purposely killed another human being. The prosecutor would be able to prove purposeful murder if the defendant flatly admits that his intention was to kill his victim. But where such a clear inculpatory admission does not exist, purposefulness is commonly established on the basis of circumstantial evidence.

That circumstantial evidence often includes the defendant's own actions. If, for example, the defendant had pulled out a gun and carefully aimed it at his victim and then pulled the trigger, *well*, it doesn't take any enormous stretch of the imagination to suppose that a jury might infer from those facts that he intended to kill his victim and that he engaged in *purposeful* conduct. Moreover, evidence of appropriate

[4]*See* Model Penal Code §2.02(1) ("Except as provided in Section 2.05, a person is not guilty of an offense unless he acted purposely, knowingly, recklessly or negligently, as the law may require, with respect to each material element of the offense.").
[5]Model Penal Code §2.02(1)(a).

planning behavior and/or other circumstantial evidence can assist the fact finder in establishing an actor's purposefulness.

(5) Knowledge

The Model Penal Code makes a distinction between an actor who is acting purposefully and one who is merely acting "knowingly." Unlike acting purposefully, knowingly acting or causing a result (depending on the particular statutory requirement) does not require proof that the act or result in question was actually the actor's conscious object. Rather, the Model Penal Code requires only a showing that "(i) if the element involves the nature of his conduct or the attendant circumstances, he is aware that his conduct is of that nature or that such circumstances exist; and (ii) if the element involves a result of his conduct, he is aware that it is practically certain that his conduct will cause such a result."[6]

In many settings, it is relatively easy to distinguish knowledge from purpose. Suppose, for example, that a person places a bomb on a plane intending to kill her arch enemy. In the process, she kills not only her enemy, but the other 200 passengers on the plane. Under such circumstances, one might readily be able to conclude that the defendant's purpose was to kill her enemy because it was her conscious object to achieve that result. However, assuming that she was indifferent regarding the death of the other passengers, it cannot be said that she had the conscious object of killing all of them, and therefore it was not her purpose to kill them. Nevertheless, since she must have been practically certain that her conduct— putting a bomb on a plane—would cause the death of the other passengers as well as her target, she knowingly caused their death. Accordingly, with respect to the other passengers, she would assumedly be guilty of 200 counts of whatever homicide offense exists in that jurisdiction that uses *knowingly* as the mens rea. But she would not be guilty—at least as to the *other* passengers—of homicide charges based upon a statute that required a *purposeful* act.

F   A   Q

Q: Would a terrorist who blows up an airplane and kills all its passengers *not* be guilty of first-degree murder of those passengers?

A: No. Remember that hypotheticals in law school depend strictly upon the factual assumptions to which they are applied. In a jurisdiction requiring purposefulness to establish first-degree murder, if a jury were to find that a person's conscious intention was to kill *only* one targeted person on an airplane with a bomb, then that person would *not* be guilty of first-degree murder of the other passengers. But, a jury—for good reason—might well not believe such a story. Terrorists often have the aim of killing *everyone* with their bombs. If a jury found that to be the case, a terrorist who planted a bomb on an airplane *would* be guilty of as many counts of first-degree murder as the number of passengers he or she killed with a bomb.

---

[6]Model Penal Code §2.02(1)(b).

(6) Recklessness and Negligence

Although the concepts of recklessness and negligence are similar in some respects, there are important differences as well. Recklessness contains a subjective element because a defendant must *consciously* disregard a substantial and unjustifiable risk in order to act recklessly. Negligence, by contrast, is strictly objective—that is, the focus is on the question whether the defendant *should have* been aware of a substantial and unjustifiable risk, rather than actually being aware in order to consciously disregard the risk.

> Recklessness: conscious disregard of risk
> = subjective test
> Negligence: should be aware of risk
> = objective test

The MPC defines "recklessness" in the following way: "A person acts recklessly with respect to a material element of an offense when he consciously disregards a substantial and unjustifiable risk that the material element exists or will result from his conduct. The risk must be of such a nature and degree that, considering the nature and purpose of the actor's conduct and the circumstances known to him, its disregard involves a gross deviation from the standard of conduct that a law-abiding person would observe in the actor's situation."[7]

The MPC defines acting "negligently" in the following way: "A person acts negligently with respect to a material element of an offense when he should be aware of a substantial and unjustifiable risk that the material element exists or will result from his conduct. The risk must be of such a nature and degree that the actor's failure to perceive it, considering the nature and purpose of his conduct and the circumstances known to him, involves a gross deviation from the standard of care that a reasonable person would observe in the actor's situation."[8]

F   A   Q

Q: What's the difference between recklessness and negligence in torts and in criminal law?

A: The Model Penal Code's definitions of recklessness and negligence are similar to the parallel tort definitions, but require a more aggravated disregard of reasonable behavior than tort law. In criminal law, the risk the actor disregards must be of such a nature and degree that the actor's failure to perceive it "involves a *gross* deviation from the standard of care that a reasonable person would observe in the actor's situation."[9] That "gross" requirement distinguishes criminal law from tort law.

---

[7]Model Penal Code §2.02(1)(c).
[8]Model Penal Code §2.02(1)(d).
[9]Emphasis added.

As discussed, because of the subjective requirement of "conscious disregard," there is a significant difference between recklessness and negligence. Suppose, for example, that a person is traveling in a car at a high rate of speed on a city street when he loses control of his vehicle, causing it to veer off the road and kill a pedestrian. Before he can be convicted of any sort of *reckless* homicide offense, it must be established that he consciously disregarded the risk that his driving might cause death. Not just that he *should* have known better (that is negligence). That he *did* in fact know better . . . and then that he disregarded that risk anyway (that is recklessness).

In this instance, whether or not this actor consciously appreciated and disregarded the risk of harm to others, it would appear clear that by traveling at a high rate of speed on a city street, assumedly with a much lower speed limit, he acted, at the very minimum, negligently. He should have been aware that his excessive speed created a substantial and unjustifiable risk of death. Accordingly, he would be guilty of any homicide offense that is premised only upon negligent behavior resulting in death.

Recklessness and negligence can also be readily distinguished from purpose and knowledge. Assume that a defendant is driving a car when she suffers a blown-out tire that causes her to veer off the road, killing a pedestrian. Suppose further that the evidence reveals that she was driving on bald tires and that she was also traveling 20 mph over the speed limit. Even though it might be possible to show that she acted recklessly or negligently with regard to the pedestrian's death, as previously discussed, it will be far more difficult to prove that she either purposely or knowingly caused the death. In all likelihood, it was not the driver's purpose to kill the pedestrian because it was not her conscious object to cause that death. Similarly, in all likelihood, the driver did not knowingly cause the victim's death because that result was not practically certain to ensue from the driver's pre-blowout conduct.

Nevertheless, as previously mentioned, a fact finder might well find that the actor in this hypothetical acted negligently . . . or perhaps even recklessly. Whether or not she actually consciously disregarded the risk that her driving presented a substantial and unjustifiable risk of death (recklessness), a jury might find that she should have been aware of the risk that she disregarded (negligence). In cases of alleged recklessness, it can be difficult for the prosecution to prove that defendant possessed the necessary subjective mental state. Occasionally, a defendant may actually admit that she was aware of the risk and that she consciously disregarded it. But that is not the typical case. Far from it. In most instances, the jury must infer the mental state from circumstantial evidence if it is to conclude that the defendant acted recklessly.

Even though recklessness and negligence differ with regard to the conscious disregard requirement—recklessness requires it; negligence does not—they otherwise utilize precisely the same test for risk assessment. Both mental states focus on whether a "substantial and unjustifiable" risk existed. In the case of homicide offenses based on either of these two mental states, the question is whether the defendant disregarded a substantial and unjustifiable risk of the victim's death. For recklessness, the "risk must be of such a nature and degree that, considering the nature and purpose of the actor's conduct and the circumstances known to him, its disregard involves a gross deviation from the standard of conduct that a law-abiding person would observe in the actor's situation." The negligence standard asks whether defendant should have been aware of the risk and, instead of focusing on whether there was a gross deviation from the standard of care that a "law-abiding person" would observe, the focus is on whether there is a similar deviation from the standard of care that a "reasonable person" would have observed in the actor's situation.

Both mens rea requirements, recklessness and negligence, involve a subtle balancing analysis. If, for example, two teenagers decide to play Russian roulette, the two are certainly negligent (they should have known better), and they are likely reckless as well (they consciously disregarded the risk). The social utility of engaging in this activity for amusement purposes is quite low, unlike driving, for example, where the social utility is high. Moreover, the risk of death in a game of Russian roulette is sufficiently high that it cannot be counterbalanced by the social utility of the activity. It is, in short, a "gross deviation from the standard of conduct that a law-abiding person would observe in the actor's situation," creating a substantial and unjustifiable risk of death.

As a result, even if the teenagers placed only a single bullet at random in one of the revolver's six chambers, so that the risk of death was only one in six on a single pull of the trigger, the risk is too great to justify the activity. Since these actors *should* have known better—that is, since they *should* have been aware that this act was a "a gross deviation from the standard of care that a reasonable person would observe in the actor's situation"—they are negligent. Furthermore, since it is also possible to conclude that they "*consciously* disregard[ed] a substantial and unjustifiable risk" that a death might result from their actions, it is quite likely that a fact finder would conclude that they acted recklessly as well.

A similar analysis would apply to an individual who knows that he is subject to periodic epileptic seizures, but who nonetheless decides to drive a vehicle to and from work. There is social utility in the defendant's desire to use his car to get to work. However, given the risk of an epileptic seizure, and the possible

horrific consequences that could result if he suffers a seizure while driving, the risk of driving under these circumstances is clearly substantial and unjustifiable. This analysis might well be different if the individual had been taking medicine to control his seizures and had not actually suffered a seizure for some time. Under those circumstances, the likelihood of a seizure might not be viewed as substantial enough to render his decision to drive unjustifiable. That determination would be up to the fact finder, and, in the first instance, up to the prosecutor who has to decide initially whether or not to bring criminal charges at all.

However, the mere fact that a defendant's conduct creates a significant risk of death does not necessarily result in a finding of criminal culpability. If the social utility of the actor's conduct is high enough, he or she might well be viewed as not having acted recklessly or negligently, even where death results. Suppose, for example, that a medical equipment manufacturer develops and implants a new artificial heart in patients. Although the heart has been approved for experimental use, it nonetheless comes with a very high risk of death. However, the company hopes that its new heart will constitute a major medical advance that will significantly increase the survival chances of individuals with failed hearts.

Under circumstances like these, it might not constitute either recklessness or negligence to implant the heart experimentally in individuals who are fully apprised and accepting of the risks.

However, much depends on how the experiment is structured. It is one thing to implant the heart in individuals who suffer from serious heart disease and are near death. Under these circumstances, the artificial heart, despite its risks, offers some possibility of extending the life of the person in whom it is implanted and may produce a medical breakthrough that will significantly enhance the life expectancy of others. As a result, even if the risk of death from the heart can be regarded as substantial (or worse), it is probably not unjustifiable under the circumstances. At the very least, there is no gross deviation from the standard of care that a law-abiding person would observe in these circumstances.

On the other hand, this analysis would likely be different if the experiment involved young, healthy patients rather than people who are mortally ill. Despite the potential benefit of the experiment to future heart patients, it is unlikely in the extreme that the high risk of death from such an experiment could be justified if the experimental pool is otherwise young and healthy.

IMPORTANT NOTE

A change in a single fact or circumstance can make all the difference in the world in analyzing recklessness or negligence!

This sort of risk assessment will vary dramatically from one criminal case to another, depending on the vagaries of the facts under scrutiny. Suppose that a woman routinely drives 35 mph in a residential neighborhood where the speed limit is 20 mph and hits and kills a child who darts out into the street. Under the circumstances, the woman is probably guilty of at least criminal negligence if her speed was, as is likely, a causative factor in the child's death. There is some social utility to driving fast in a neighborhood. It allows people to get to and from their homes more quickly. But the social utility of such conduct is more than outweighed by the potential risk to young children and others who may happen into the street oblivious of the possible consequences. At the very least, the driver should be found guilty of negligent homicide. Indeed, in some situations—when the weather is particularly bad, for example—a defendant might even be deemed negligent for driving the posted speed limit in a residential neighborhood. Moreover, if a jury finds that the driver consciously disregarded the risk of hitting someone, it might also find her guilty of reckless homicide.

(7) Construction of Criminal Statutes

As previously discussed, even though the Model Penal Code's drafters tried to standardize the available set of mens rea tests, state and federal criminal statutes continue to remain widely variable with respect to mental states. Only a small handful of jurisdictions try to follow the MPC mens rea formulations conscientiously. Some jurisdictions adopted these tests and then amended them, some jurisdictions adopted them and then ignored them (at least as to their exclusivity with respect to mental states), and some jurisdictions never adopted them at all. In addition, quite commonly, criminal statutes are enacted, and they do not appear to include a required mental state or, at least, it is confusing and arguable whether or not they do.

The absence of a mens rea term in a criminal statute does not mean necessarily that the statute is intended to be a strict liability offense. This is an important point. Because we often presume that legislatures mean to include a mens rea provision unless they indicate clearly that they do not, many jurisdictions have enacted default mens rea provisions. The MPC provides, for example, that: "When the culpability sufficient to establish a material element of an offense is not prescribed by law, such element is established if a person acts purposely, knowingly or recklessly with respect thereto."[10]

Some jurisdictions have enacted statutes exactly like the MPC, making recklessness the default minimum mens rea; other jurisdictions have provided, in contrast, that the default mental state is knowing behavior; still other jurisdictions have provided that the default mental state is criminal negligence. These default provisions operate in the absence of evidence of legislative intent that the offense be strict liability, as was mentioned above and is discussed below.

Suppose, for example, that a jurisdiction enacted a breaking-and-entering crimes code provision that provided simply: "It shall be a third-degree felony for anyone to break and enter a building, occupied or unoccupied." In that situation, under the Model Penal Code, for example, the presumption would be that the offense would be made out if the actor committed the specified act and, in so doing, acted, at minimum, in a reckless fashion.

In addition, sometimes a criminal statute clearly contains a mens rea element, but it is unclear whether or not that mens rea term applies to each and every act element included in the definition of the criminal offense. In that situation, a court must decide whether to apply the mens rea to only to a single element of the crime or whether to apply it to some or all of the other elements.

For example, suppose that a statute makes it a crime to "knowingly convert to his use or the use of another any property of the United States or any department or agency thereof." Under that statute, it is not entirely clear whether the stated mens rea ("knowingly") applies only to the word "convert," or whether it also applies to the attendant circumstances ("any property of the United States or any department or agency thereof"). While it is possible to construe the mens rea as applying to *all* of the elements—*both* the act of conversion *and* the attendant circumstances—it is also possible to view the statute as providing only that criminal culpability attaches when the conversion is knowing, using a different (or no) mens rea applicable to the attendant circumstances.

The Model Penal Code attempted to address this sort of confusion by including a rule of statutory construction providing that "[w]hen the law defining an offense prescribes the kind of culpability that is sufficient for the commission of an offense, without distinguishing among the material elements thereof, such provision shall apply to all the material elements of the offense, unless a contrary purpose plainly appears."[11] Applying this MPC provision to the example set out above, the mens rea of knowingly would be applied to *both* the act of conversion *and* to the attendant circumstances ("all the material elements of the offense") since a contrary purpose

---

[10]Model Penal Code §2.02(3).
[11]Model Penal Code §2.02(4).

does not plainly appear on the face of the statute. Many jurisdictions use similar rules of construction.

As one recent example, the Supreme Court interpreted a federal criminal aggravated identity theft statute in 1909 that provides that it is a crime when a person "knowingly transfers, possesses, or uses, without lawful authority, a means of identification of another person."[12] The question before the Court was "whether the statute requires the Government to show that the defendant knew that the 'means of identification' he or she unlawfully transferred, possessed, or used, in fact, belonged to 'another person.'"[13] Observing that "courts ordinarily read a phrase in a criminal statute that introduces the elements of a crime with the word 'knowingly' as applying that word to each element," a majority of the Court "conclude[d] that [the statute] requires the Government to show that the defendant knew that the means of identification at issue belonged to another person."[14]

Similarly, suppose that a criminal statute defined the offense of receiving stolen property, *inter alia*, as "knowingly receiving stolen goods." It is unclear on the face of this statute whether the mens rea applies only to the act of receiving, or whether it also applies to the attendant circumstances—that is, knowing that the goods were stolen. But if the Model Penal Code or a similar provision or rule was applicable, it would resolve the issue by applying the mens rea to *both* the act *and* the attendant circumstances. A contrary purpose does not appear to be present in the statute. If a court reviewed the statute subsequently and found such a contrary purpose, as sometimes occurs, then the mens rea of knowingly would only apply to the act of receiving.

There are situations when a contrary purpose plainly appears in a criminal statute. For example, suppose that a state's crimes code included a provision reflecting the common law offense of burglary, defined as "the breaking and entering of the dwelling of another at night with the intent to commit a felony." The issue arises whether the word "intent" applies only to the phrase "to commit a felony," or whether instead it also applies to the act of "breaking and entering" *and* to all three of the attendant circumstances: (1) "of another"; (2) "at night"; (3) "to commit a felony." Based on the placement of the mens rea term *after* the principal act and two of the attendant circumstances, and before the phrase "to commit a felony," one can argue that the legislative purpose was for the mens rea to apply only to the latter. That is, in fact, just how courts commonly construe statutes of this sort.

The MPC also contains several other statutory construction provisions that are commonly found mirrored in the crimes codes of the various states. For example, there is a provision that states that when a statute provides that negligence will suffice for the mens rea of a crime, that element is satisfied if the defendant acted knowingly as well as if he or she acted purposely, knowingly, or recklessly.[15] In other words, the broader, more inclusive mens rea terms include proof of the narrower, more specific terms.

---

[12]18 U.S.C. §1028A(a)(1).
[13]*Flores-Figueroa v. U.S.*, ___ U.S. ___, 129 S. Ct. 1886, 1891, 173 L. Ed. 2d 853 (2009).
[14]*Flores-Figueroa v. U.S.*, ___ U.S. ___, 129 S. Ct. 1886, 1891, 1894, 173 L. Ed. 2d 853 (2009).
[15]Model Penal Code §2.02(5):

> Substitutes for Negligence, Recklessness and Knowledge. When the law provides that negligence suffices to establish an element of an offense, such element also is established if a person acts purposely, knowingly or recklessly. When recklessness suffices to establish an element, such element also is established if a person acts purposely or knowingly. When acting knowingly suffices to establish an element, such element also is established if a person acts purposely.

In addition, there is an MPC provision that states that when a requirement of knowledge of a particular fact is required for conviction of a crime, that element is satisfied if the person is aware of a high probability that the fact exists.[16]

Moreover, under the MPC, if a statute uses the mens rea of willfully, that mens rea is deemed satisfied by proof that the defendant acted knowingly.[17] However, again under the MPC, when an offense can be committed with any one of the four mens rea terms—purposely, knowingly, recklessly, or negligently—the grading of the offense for purposes of punishment shall be based on the mens rea that was actually established. In other words, if defendant was shown to have acted only negligently, as opposed to purposely, knowingly, or recklessly, the grade and degree of the crime would be based only on negligence.[18]

B. Strict Liability Offenses

Legislatures have the power to enact criminal statutes that do not include any mens rea requirement at all, but instead impose strict liability. By strict liability, what is meant is the imposition of criminal penalties without the necessity of the prosecution having to charge or prove any type of culpable criminal intent. Although the majority of criminal offenses are *not* strict liability offenses, some are, including some quite serious offenses, such as, in many jurisdictions, the crime of forcible rape.

(1) Traditional Aversion to Strict Liability

The concept of strict liability is antithetical to some of the traditional assumptions of how and why the criminal law should operate. Courts and commentators have long said, in a shorthand fashion, that criminal culpability should be premised upon a criminal act (actus reus) committed by an actor who is acting with a culpable mens rea.

For example, if an actor was driving the speed limit in a car that was in perfectly good condition and she was otherwise being careful and obeying the traffic laws, but had an unexpected blow-out that caused her car to swerve and to run over and kill someone, this general rule of thumb tells us that this hypothetical is *not* an appropriate one for the imposition of criminal culpability, as the actor lacked any sort of culpable mens rea at the time of the offending act. In contrast, if the driver acted negligently or recklessly or knowingly or purposefully, culpability might well be appropriate, as previously discussed.

---

[16]Model Penal Code §2.02(7):

> Requirement of Knowledge Satisfied by Knowledge of High Probability. When knowledge of the existence of a particular fact is an element of an offense, such knowledge is established if a person is aware of a high probability of its existence, unless he actually believes that it does not exist.

[17]Model Penal Code §2.02(8):

> Requirement of Wilfulness Satisfied by Acting Knowingly. A requirement that an offense be committed wilfully is satisfied if a person acts knowingly with respect to the material elements of the offense, unless a purpose to impose further requirements appears.

[18]Model Penal Code §2.02(10):

> Culpability as Determinant of Grade of Offense. When the grade or degree of an offense depends on whether the offense is committed purposely, knowingly, recklessly or negligently, its grade or degree shall be the lowest for which the determinative kind of culpability is established with respect to any material element of the offense.

Because the notion of strict liability runs counter to this traditional rule of thumb and because, more importantly, it seems just plain unfair to punish someone criminally who had no actual intention of committing a criminal act, courts have been reluctant to impose criminal consequences without making absolutely sure that the legislative intent in enacting a particular statute lacking an apparent mens rea element was actually to create a strict liability offense.

One of the most important court decisions in this area of the law is the decision of the Supreme Court in *Morissette v. United States*.[19] In *Morissette*, defendant Morissette made an unauthorized entry onto a tract of uninhabited land in a wooded and sparsely populated part of Michigan. The government had used this land as a practice bombing range and the Air Force had dropped simulated bombs there. These bombs consisted of metal cylinders filled with sand and enough black powder to cause a smoke puff. The land was posted with signs that warned people to keep out. Despite the signs, Morissette went hunting on the range and when he failed to bag a deer, he decided to meet his expenses by salvaging some of the casings. Subsequently, he was indicted under a federal statute that provided:

> Whoever embezzles, steals, purloins, or knowingly converts to his use or the use of another, or without authority, sells, conveys or disposes of any . . . thing of value of the United States . . . ; Shall be fined not more than $10,000 or imprisoned not more than ten years, or both; but if the value of such property does not exceed the sum of $100, he shall be fined not more than $1,000 or imprisoned not more than one year, or both.[20]

Morissette argued that, based on the rusty appearance of the casings, he believed they were abandoned. In other words, he claimed that he took the casings without any wrongful or criminal intent. The government argued, however, that the statute should not be construed as requiring a mens rea.

The Supreme Court held that since the criminal offense at issue was taken from the common law ("[s]tealing, larceny, and its variants and equivalents, were among the earliest offenses known to the law that existed before legislation"), the crime retained its traditional common law mens rea element in the absence of any contrary indication of congressional intent. Many lower courts similarly share the Supreme Court's reluctance to assume that a statute, even a statute *without* common law origins, was intended by a legislature to create a strict liability criminal offense, at least in the absence of a clear indication to that effect.

Indeed, the Model Penal Code reflects the general aversion to strict liability by distinguishing between "crimes," defined broadly to include offenses that fall into the categories of felonies and misdemeanors, and "violations."[21] The latter category, violations, consists of more minor offenses, such as the vehicular offenses of speeding, failure to stop for a stop sign, and making an illegal left turn. The MPC provides that strict liability can be imposed for such minor violations. In taking this stance, the MPC essentially reflects the common law idea that petty offenses, like violations, can be treated differently than traditional crimes.

---

[19]342 U.S. 246 (1952).
[20]18 U.S.C. §641.
[21]*See* Model Penal Code §2.05(1)(a).

Q: How can you tell whether a criminal statute without an apparent mens rea term is a strict liability offense?

A: When the offense in question has common law origins and traditionally contained a mens rea element, the presumption usually is that strict liability was *not* intended. In that case, if the jurisdiction has a default mens rea statute, the jurisdiction's default mens rea (negligence? recklessness? knowledge?) will apply. Where the offense in question was not of common law origin, it will ordinarily be interpreted as a strict liability offense where there is a clear indication that this was the legislative intention.

The MPC also permits the imposition of strict liability for "offenses defined by statutes other than the Code, insofar as a legislative purpose to impose absolute liability for such offenses or with respect to any material element thereof plainly appears."[22] However, the requirement that the legislature's intention to impose strict liability must plainly appear is consistent with the general aversion to imposition of strict liability.

(2) Public Welfare Offenses

Legislatures have often enacted strict liability criminal offenses in areas said to involve the so-called public welfare. A good example is the statute at issue in the leading case of *United States v. Dotterweich*.[23] In that case, the Supreme Court was dealing with the vicarious application of a statute criminalizing the shipment of adulterated or misbranded drugs that did not require the actor's knowledge that the items in question were in fact misbranded or adulterated. The *Dotterweich* Court explained that such statutes were "public welfare offenses," namely "a now familiar type of legislation whereby penalties serve as effective means of regulation. Such legislation dispenses with the conventional requirement for criminal conduct— awareness of some wrongdoing."

As the Court explained further in *Dotterweich*, "public welfare offenses have been created by Congress, and recognized by this Court, in 'limited circumstances' involving regulation of potentially harmful or injurious items." As a result, "as long as a defendant knows that he is dealing with a dangerous device of a character that places him 'in responsible relation to a public danger,' he should be alerted to the probability of strict regulation."

A similar conclusion was reached by the Supreme Court in *United States v. Balint*.[24] The *Balint* case involved a federal statute that provided that persons selling opium or coca leaves had to register with the Internal Revenue Service and pay a tax.[25] The defendant, Balint, admitted that he sold an opium-based substance, but he denied that he actually knew that it was criminal to do so. The Court held that even if

---

[22]*See* Model Penal Code §2.05(1)(b).
[23]320 U.S. 277, 281 (1943). *See also* discussion of *Dotterweich* in Chapter 5.
[24]258 U.S. 250 (1922).
[25]38 Stat. 785, 786 (Comp. St. §§6287g-6287q).

that assertion were true, knowledge that the substance was actually cocaine was not required under the statute—that is, there was no mens rea. The imposition of strict liability was perfectly appropriate in this instance, the Court explained, because persons dealing with drugs are on notice of the pervasive regulation of such items. Accordingly, the Court concluded that the statute in question required proof by the government *only* of the fact that the defendant knew that he was selling drugs, *not* that he knew that the specific items he had sold were "narcotics" within the ambit of the statute.[26]

However, where an individual would *not* reasonably be on notice that items that are the subject of a criminal statute are likely to be so regulated, courts will not presume a legislative intention to impose strict liability. A relatively recent decision of the Supreme Court, *Staples v. United States*,[27] illustrates this point quite well. In *Staples*, the Court considered the question whether a criminal statute that imposed strict registration requirements on statutorily defined firearms was a strict liability statute.[28] The statute included machine guns, defined as "any weapon which shoots, [or] can be readily restored to shoot, automatically more than one shot, without manual reloading, by a single function of the trigger." Any fully automatic weapon was deemed to be a firearm that must be registered, and it was a crime, punishable by up to ten years in prison, for any person to possess an unregistered firearm.

Defendant Staples was charged when law enforcement officers discovered an AR-15 rifle during a search of his home. Although an unmodified AR-15 is a *semi-automatic* weapon, Staples's rifle had been modified in such a way as to allow it to function as an automatic weapon. Staples claimed that he was unaware that the rifle had been so altered so he had no mens rea. Before the Supreme Court, the question was whether the prosecution was required to prove that defendant knew of the characteristics of his weapon that made it a firearm thereby triggering his obligation to register. Finding that the legislative intention as to strict liability was unclear, the Court concluded that it had to construe the statute in light of the background principles of the common law in which "the requirement of some mens rea for a crime is firmly embedded." The Court added, significantly, that "offenses that require no mens rea generally are disfavored," meaning that "some indication of congressional intent, express or implied, is required to dispense with mens rea as an element of a crime."

A majority of the Court then rejected the notion that this statute fit within the definition of a public welfare offense. The government had argued that, as in *Balint*, with narcotics, firearms are "dangerous devices that put gun owners on notice that they must determine at their hazard whether their weapons come within the scope of the Act." The majority rejected this argument, noting that the mere fact that an item is dangerous is not dispositive, as it can be "so commonplace and generally available that we would not consider them to alert individuals to the likelihood of strict regulation." More to the point, the majority added that "guns generally can be owned in perfect innocence."

The government also sought to rely on *United States v. Freed*,[29] a case in which the Court held previously that a statute criminalizing the possession of unregistered hand

---

[26]*See also, e.g., Dean v. U.S.,* ___ U.S. ___, 129 S. Ct. 1849, 173 L. Ed. 2d 785 (2009) (statutory sentencing enhancement for defendant's discharge of firearm required no separate proof of defendant's intent to discharge weapon where weapon discharged in the course of what the defendant already knew was unlawful conduct).
[27]511 U.S. 600 (1994).
[28]26 U.S.C. §§5801-5872.
[29]401 U.S. 601 (1971).

grenades was properly deemed to be a strict liability offense. But the majority in *Staples* distinguished *Freed* on the ground that ordinary Americans are on notice that hand grenades are highly regulated, but not on notice that firearms are highly regulated given this country's long history of private ownership of guns. Indeed, the *Staples* majority ruled there was no indication that Congress had intended to "impose criminal sanctions on a class of persons whose mental state—ignorance of the characteristics of weapons in their possession—makes their actions entirely innocent."

In holding that this statute was not one of strict liability, the Court also relied on the serious nature of the penalty imposed: up to ten years' imprisonment. The majority noted that the cases that first defined the concept of the public welfare offense almost uniformly involved statutes that provided for only light penalties such as fines or short jail sentences, not imprisonment. Smaller penalties, the Court added, are more consistent with the absence of a mens rea requirement.

(3) Impact of Strict Liability

At first glance, one might suspect that the existence of strict liability criminal offenses would encourage potential lawbreakers to be especially careful and to steer clear of any possible criminal behavior. However, in the real world, that is not necessarily what occurs. How potential defendants behave depends on a host of complex behavioral and market factors, including whether these actors even know about the possibility of criminal sanctions (even if they reasonably should know about them). Even if they do know such offenses exist, the certainty of their apprehension and prosecution and the severity of the likely criminal penalties if they are prosecuted and convicted are all factors that may well play a role in determining their conduct.

Certainly in some instances, the existence of strict liability criminal offenses should and arguably does encourage individuals to steer clear of particular types of conduct. Suppose, for example, that a statute imposes strict liability on actors who distribute adulterated drugs, as in *Dotterweich*. But, unlike *Dotterweich*, the same statute also contains very severe penalties for violations, including long prison sentences, as in *Staples*. In such a situation, if lawbreakers are really sent to prison for violations, individuals might be expected to be reluctant in the extreme to engage in the business of distributing adulterated drugs. Unless there is an enormous amount of money to be made from that activity, individuals might well not be willing to risk the possibility of imprisonment.

But, in some instances, the existence of strict liability criminal offenses might actually work to discourage regulated entities from taking steps to avoid culpability. For example, suppose that an air pollution statute imposes strict liability for violations of air pollution standards. The evidence reveals that air pollution equipment is expensive and that regardless of whether a regulated entity spends the money for it, the entity is likely to exceed prohibited air pollution levels from time to time and be fined under the criminal statutes. In such a situation, if the penalties for violation of the pollution laws are not sufficiently high, a regulated entity may have a moral—but no economic—incentive to install the latest equipment. If it does, it knows that it will still violate the law from time to time in any event and be forced to pay fines. If it does not install the equipment, it can use the money that it would have spent for pollution control to pay the fines. And, if the penalties for violation are *really* high, such as long prison sentences, then the regulated entity might be discouraged from engaging in the activity at all. Depending upon what the activity is, this result may be as or more socially and economically harmful as the pollution itself.

Now, suppose that the air pollution statute in question in the hypothetical above exists, but requires a mens rea of reckless behavior and provides more substantial penalties for violations. In that situation, if a company spends millions installing the latest air pollution technology, it is unlikely to engage in violations of the statute because its efforts are likely to defeat any claim of recklessness (conscious disregard of risk, etc.). In this situation, the company is again likely to engage in cost-benefit analysis in deciding whether to install the technology. However, if the installation of the latest technology will essentially relieve defendant of the possibility of criminal culpability, and the fines for violations are high enough, the economic incentives may shift in favor of installing the latest technology.

C. Intoxication and Drugged Condition

Criminal offenders are commonly under the influence of drugs or alcohol at the moment they commit their criminal offenses. One federal study found that "[h]alf (50%) of convicted jail inmates were under the influence of drugs or alcohol at the time of the offense . . . [and t]hree out of every four convicted jail inmates were alcohol or drugs-involved at the time of their current offense."[30] This unfortunate fact of modern life raises the significant question when, if ever, a defendant should be able to negate a requisite mens rea element in a criminal offense by establishing that she was so intoxicated or drugged that she did not possess the mens rea required for the particular crime.

Suppose, for example, that an actor is driving a car while intoxicated. Suppose further that this person is so intoxicated that he does not even realize that he is driving a vehicle, let alone appreciate the risk he is posing to others. Under these circumstances, if the actor runs over and kills a pedestrian, can it really be said that he acted purposefully? Knowingly? Recklessly—that is, with a *conscious* disregard for the risk he was running?

For crimes involving criminal negligence, as previously discussed, a defendant may be convicted even if he did not actually foresee or intend the consequences of his actions, assuming that, *inter alia*, considering the circumstances known to him, he should have been aware of and nonetheless ignored a substantial and unjustifiable risk that his actions might lead to death. But the question arises: Should prosecutors be limited to bringing charges involving negligent homicide against an actor like this, excusing him from more serious homicide charges because he was drunk and/or drugged?

The point is that where a criminal offense is not strict liability, it is easy to imagine situations where a defendant does not and, sometimes, virtually *cannot* (due to intoxication or drugged condition) possess the specific mens rea—purposefully, knowingly, recklessly, whatever it is—that is a required element of the criminal offense in question. Nonetheless, legislatures have been extremely reluctant to permit voluntary intoxication or drugged condition to be used as a valid defense across the board in such situations, and courts have likewise been extremely reluctant to acquit on this basis.

---

[30]U.S. Dept. of Justice, Office of Justice Programs, Bureau of Justice Statistics, Profile of Jail Inmates, 2002, http://www.ojp.usdoj.gov/bjs/crimoff.htm#publications. *See also* U.S. Dept. of Justice, Office of Justice Programs, Bureau of Justice Statistics, Alcohol and Crime: Data from 2002 to 2008, http://bjs.ojp.usdoj.gov/content/acf/29_prisoners_and_alcoholuse.cfm ("An estimated 37% of state prisoners serving time for a violent offense in 2004 said they were under the influence of alcohol at the time of the offense").

Many jurisdictions have compromised between excusing virtually all intoxicated conduct (which seems unfair) and excusing none of it (which also seems unfair). These jurisdictions have taken the position that intoxication or drugged condition negates the mens rea for a specific intent crime when it is proven that the impairment was so pronounced as to eliminate the intent entirely. But intoxication or drugged condition cannot negate the mens rea of a general intent crime. Just what general and specific intent mean in this setting has, however, been the subject of considerable controversy and, notably, different jurisdictions take significantly different positions on this subject.

Consider as one example of how this works the California Supreme Court's decision in *People v. Atkins*.[31] In *Atkins*, the court held that the crime of arson was a general intent crime in California and, accordingly, that evidence of voluntary intoxication could not be used as a defense. Arson is a general intent crime, the court reasoned, because "[a] crime is characterized as a 'general intent' crime when the required mental state entails only an intent to do the act that causes the harm; a crime is characterized as a 'specific intent' crime when the required mental state entails an intent to cause the resulting harm. Th[is] statute does not require an additional specific intent to burn a 'structure, forest land, or property,' but rather requires only an intent to do the act that causes the harm. . . . Thus, the intent requirement for arson fits within the . . . definition of general intent, i.e., the description of the proscribed act fails to refer to an intent to do a further act or achieve a future consequence."

Note that if the arson offense discussed in *Atkins* had been defined differently by the California legislature (for example, if it had included the additional element of the intent to burn a structure, forest land, or property, or something of that sort), the court intimated that the result would very likely have been different—the arson would have been deemed to be a specific intent crime and the defense of intoxication would have been permissible.

The *Atkins* court was undoubtedly influenced, as other courts are as well, by the specter of what it would mean to conclude that arson was a specific intent crime and, hence, amenable to the defense of intoxication or drugged condition. As the court acknowledged, the crime of arson "often is an angry impulsive act, requiring no tools other than a match or lighter, and possibly a container of gasoline" and is often committed by intoxicated individuals. Given the prevalence of impulsive, drunken arsonists, the court concluded that the legislature must have intended for intoxication not to be a defense in such circumstances, as it would "be anomalous to allow evidence of intoxication to relieve a man of responsibility for the crime[ ] of [arson], which [is] so frequently committed in just such a manner."

Not every jurisdiction uses the general intent/specific intent approach to determining whether or not an intoxication defense is available. Some jurisdictions eliminate or virtually eliminate the defense altogether. For example, a Pennsylvania statute provides that "[n]either voluntary intoxication nor voluntary drugged condition is a defense to a criminal charge, nor may evidence of such conditions be introduced to negative the element of intent of the offense, except that evidence of such intoxication or drugged condition of the defendant may be offered by the defendant whenever it is relevant to reduce murder from a higher degree to a lower degree of murder."[32] This statute serves to prohibit consideration of *any*

[31] 25 Cal. 4th 76, 18 P.3d 660, 104 Cal. Rptr. 2d 738 (2001).
[32] 18 Pa. C.S.A. §308.

evidence of intoxication or drugged condition to negate the mens rea for any criminal offense, except to mitigate a first-degree murder charge to a lower degree of murder. This means that some defendants who truly did not *actually* possess the mens rea specified for the offense with which they are charged will be convicted in any event.

The Model Penal Code contains a number of different provisions relating to intoxication (which includes drugged condition). It establishes the general proposition that "intoxication of the actor is not a defense unless it negatives an element of the offense."[33] In other words, intoxication cannot serve under the MPC as an affirmative defense excusing criminal conduct that has otherwise been established as affirmative defenses such as self-defense, defense of others, and defense of property operate. However, the MPC does permit intoxication and drugged condition to serve as the functional equivalent of a defense—in the sense that they can relieve a defendant of criminal responsibility—when they are established sufficiently that they negate the specified mens rea of the offense charged.

For example, suppose that a person picks up another customer's pink umbrella when he leaves a bar. He is so drunk that he does not realize that he has taken another person's umbrella instead of his own black umbrella. Suppose that he is charged with theft of movable property, which applicable state law defines as "unlawfully tak[ing], or exercis[ing] unlawful control over movable property of another with purpose to deprive him thereof." If this defendant really was so drunk that he did not realize that he was taking another person's umbrella, then he could not be convicted under the MPC unless the statute was strict liability or premised upon negligence. Since he thought that he was taking his own umbrella, he did not intend to take the property of another.

Under the California approach discussed earlier, however, assuming again that this was not a strict liability offense, whether or not the defendant's actions could be excused by the absence of a mental state caused by intoxication or drugged condition turns on the question whether or not the statute is a general intent (no intoxication defense) or specific intent (intoxication defense) statute. Very likely, given the "with purpose to deprive him thereof" clause in the statute, it would be treated as a specific intent statute and an intoxication defense would be permitted. In Pennsylvania, in contrast, no intoxication defense would be permitted, as Pennsylvania has abolished the defense, as previously discussed, except where a defendant is charged with first-degree murder.

Remember, however, that where an intoxication or drugged condition defense is available, a defendant must do more than simply show that he drank a lot of alcohol or ingested narcotics. Rather, the defendant must prove that he was so severely intoxicated and/or drugged that he did not in fact possess the necessary mens rea for the offenses with which he is charged.

F   A   Q

Q: How can you tell when intoxication or drugged condition will be a defense?

A: First, determine whether the jurisdiction in question permits an intoxication or drugged condition defense in any circumstances at all. Second, if it does, determine if it uses the traditional general/specific intent test to determine whether the

---

[33]Model Penal Code §2.08(1).

criminal offense in question is a specific intent crime. Third, if it is, determine whether the defendant was sufficiently intoxicated and/or drugged not to be able to possess the intent required by the statute.

Parenthetically, *involuntary* intoxication or drugged condition, unlike *voluntary* intoxication or drugged condition, *is* a viable and complete defense to criminal charges. This defense is treated as an involuntary act (see Chapter 2), rather than as bearing on the defendant's mental state. For example, the Model Penal Code provides that intoxication can be a defense if it is not self-induced.[34] The MPC further provides that intoxication is self-induced when it is "caused by substances that the actor knowingly introduces into his body, the tendency of which to cause intoxication he knows or ought to know, unless he introduces them pursuant to medical advice or under such circumstances as would afford a defense to a charge of crime."[35]

Involuntary intoxication might occur, for example, where a person goes to a party, does not drink any alcohol, and does not have any reason to believe that others are putting alcohol into her soft drinks, but, unbeknownst to her, her drink is being laced with alcohol or a narcotic. In an intoxicated or drugged condition, she might drive herself home and cause an accident, killing another person. Under such circumstances, assuming that this actor can establish the truth of all of these factual circumstances, the fact that her intoxication was not self-induced might allow her to raise involuntary intoxication as an actus reus defense successfully.

The Model Penal Code also includes an unusual and not commonly adopted defense for so-called pathological intoxication.[36] The MPC defines "pathological intoxication" as occurring when defendant suffers a reaction that is "grossly excessive in degree, given the amount of the intoxicant, to which the actor does not know he is susceptible."[37] The New Jersey Superior Court has ruled, in any event, that as to the defense of pathological intoxication, "where a defendant . . . voluntarily ingests large amounts of illegal intoxicants and intentionally overdoses on legal drugs, he cannot assert that he unexpectedly reacted violently to those drugs due to an unknown, underlying pathological condition which afflicted him."[38]

D. Mistake of Fact

Sometimes, a person commits a criminal act, believing that she is not acting criminally, due to a mistake about the applicable factual circumstances. Whether such a mistaken belief relieves the person of criminal culpability depends on a number of things, including the law on mistake in that jurisdiction and the specific elements of the crime with which she is charged. Nonetheless, in many instances, a defendant's reasonable mistake may serve to negate the mens rea of a crime and, hence, serve as a complete defense.

For example, suppose that the crime of theft is defined in a jurisdiction in such a way as to criminalize the act of stealing another person's personal property with the

---

[34]Model Penal Code §2.08(4)(a).
[35]Model Penal Code §2.08(5)(b).
[36]Model Penal Code §2.08(4)(b).
[37]Model Penal Code §2.08(5)(c).
[38]*State v. Sette*, 259 N.J. Super. 156, 611 A.2d 1129, 1138 (A.D. 1992).

intent to permanently deprive the victim of the property. Suppose further that an actor went to a restaurant carrying her black umbrella, which she left at the front door in an umbrella rack. On leaving the restaurant, she mistakenly picked up another customer's black umbrella, honestly believing that it was her own. In other words, she neither intended to steal the umbrella nor to permanently deprive the victim of the victim's black umbrella, but she simply intended to reclaim what she thought was rightfully hers. Under these circumstances, this actor's mistake would likely negate the mens rea of the crime (the intent to permanently deprive the victim of the property) and would, accordingly, preclude conviction.

But that would not necessarily be the result if the umbrella mistakenly picked up by the actor was pink and frilly (not black and plain) or in some other way clearly and demonstrably different from her own umbrella. In that event, the actor's mistaken belief might well be viewed as an *unreasonable* one. In most jurisdictions, to make a tenable defense of **mistake of fact**, a defendant must establish not simply that her mistaken belief negated the required mens rea element, but she *also* must establish the objective reasonableness of that mistaken belief.

Sometimes, the mens rea element in a criminal offense *already* expressly contains an objective element—for example, recklessness or negligence—which looks to the standard of conduct that a *reasonable* (objective) person might follow.

For example, in *New Jersey v. Sexton*,[39] a 15-year-old defendant, Sexton, pointed a gun that he thought was unloaded at another boy and it "just went off," killing the boy. The question was whether a mistake of fact defense would apply in a prosecution for reckless manslaughter. Since a mistake needs to be reasonable in order to negate a mens rea element, and since, further, a defendant cannot be convicted of reckless manslaughter in New Jersey without the prosecution proving that he has acted unreasonably, the New Jersey Supreme Court reasoned that "there is no difference between a positive and negative statement on the issue—what is required for liability versus what will provide a defense to liability. What is required in order to establish liability for manslaughter is recklessness (as defined by the [Crimes] Code) about whether death will result from the conduct.

STATUTORY RAPE LAWS TODAY

"Statutory rape laws assume that all sexual activities involving individuals below a certain age are coercive. This is true even if both parties believe their participation is voluntary. [To] complicate matters, few states use the term 'statutory rape' in their criminal codes. More often, a state's code will address legality of different sexual activities involving minors (e.g., sexual contact versus penetration). [A] common misconception about statutory rape is that there is a single age at which an individual can legally consent to sexual activity. . . .

"*Minimum age of victim.* Some state codes define the age below which an individual cannot legally engage in sexual activities, regardless of the age of the other party. For example, in [one state], the age of consent is 16, but under certain circumstances—that is, the defendant is no more than four years older and under age 19—individuals who are at least 13 years of age can legally engage in sexual activities. It is illegal to engage in sexual activities with someone under 13 years of age under all circumstances.

"*Minimum age of defendant.* Some states define the age below which an individual cannot be prosecuted for having sex with a minor. In [one state], sexual activity with someone below the age of consent is only illegal if the defendant is at least 18 years of age. Thus, in order to understand a specific state's laws, one must look to see which of these elements is included."

The Lewin Group, *Statutory Rape: A Guide to State Laws and Reporting Requirements*, Overview, Executive Summary, pp. ES-1 to ES-2, http://www.lewin.com/NR/rdonlyres/6F92A2EI-526A-4FD6-9D22-7374CCA5E16A/0/3068.pdf. See further discussion of statutory rape in Chapter 10.

---

[39] 160 N.J. 93, 733 A.2d 1125 (1999).

A faultless or merely careless mistake may negate that reckless state of mind and provide a defense."

Moreover, a mistake of fact defense is wholly inapplicable to strict liability offenses since, where no mens rea is required, the actor's intention is always totally irrelevant. For example, in *Iowa v. Freeman*,[40] defendant Freeman agreed to sell a controlled substance to someone else, but he actually delivered only acetaminophen, which is not a controlled substance. Freeman was charged with the offense of delivering a simulated controlled substance, but he argued that he had a good mistake of fact defense to that charge as he actually had thought that he was delivering cocaine, an *actual* controlled substance, not a simulated controlled substance. The Iowa Supreme Court held, however, that Freeman's mistaken belief was no defense—in fact, it was irrelevant—because the simulated controlled substance statute in Iowa required proof that Freeman knowingly represented the substance to be cocaine, but "clearly does not require knowing misrepresentation of the nature of the substance delivered."

Similarly, mistake of fact is often *not* allowed as a defense to a charge of statutory rape, as that offense is a strict liability offense in most jurisdictions. For example, in *Rhode Island v. Yanez*,[41] 18-year-old defendant, Yanez, engaged in sexual intercourse with a 13-year-old girl. He claimed she told him that she was 16 years old; she denied telling him that. The trial court did not permit the introduction of any evidence regarding the alleged mistaken nature of Yanez's beliefs, and the jury convicted him of statutory rape. The Rhode Island Supreme Court affirmed, construing the statute in question as imposing strict liability with respect to the attendant circumstance of the victim's age. Since the legislature was fully entitled to create such strict liability offenses, Yanez's conviction was affirmed since he had no right to attempt to introduce irrelevant evidence of his mistaken intention, reasonable or not.

Nonetheless, despite the general rule that there is no mistake of fact defense to statutory rape, some legislatures and some courts—a minority—have permitted such a defense where the accused's mistaken belief about the victim's age was a reasonable one.

E. Mistake of Law

Sometimes, a person commits a criminal act while believing—due to a mistake about the applicable law—that he or she is not in fact acting criminally or doing anything that is otherwise prohibited by law. Ordinarily, however, **mistake of law** is not a defense. Just as at the common law, simply put: *Ignorance of the law is no excuse.*

This longstanding rule of law was adopted at common law as a matter of perceived social necessity. A defense of this sort would both reward a person's ignorance and create a disincentive for him or her to learn what the criminal law actually permits and prohibits. The societal costs of permitting an actor's rape or murder or robbery or assault or theft or kidnapping—or even less violent, but no less criminal offenses—to be excused due to his or her ignorance (even reasonable ignorance) of the fact that such offenses are prohibited by law have simply been deemed too great to allow such a defense to exist.

---

[40]450 N.W.2d 826 (Iowa 1990).
[41]716 A.2d 759 (R.I. 1998).

There are some limited exceptions to this general rule, however. The law in a number of jurisdictions allows a defendant to defend against criminal charges on the ground that he mistakenly relied on the advice of a public official.[42] However, even where such a defense is possible, some statutes limit it to mistaken reliance only on the word of an official actually charged with the responsibility for the interpretation, administration, or enforcement of the law defining the offense in question.

For example, in *Hawaii v. DeCastro*,[43] defendant DeCastro was convicted of the offense of resisting an order to stop a motor vehicle. After a police car nearly caused an accident while pursuing a suspect, DeCastro pulled up behind the car and took down the officer's license plate number. The officer approached DeCastro and, at that point, he claimed that the officer became belligerent and ordered him to produce his license and registration and get out of the car. When the officer walked away, DeCastro dialed 911 and told the operator that he was being harassed by a policeman. The 911 operator, apparently not understanding what she was being told, indicated that he should drive on to his warehouse, and that another officer would be sent there. When DeCastro left the scene, however, the original officer gave chase and apprehended him. On these facts, the Hawaii Court of Appeals concluded that the limited mistake of law defense in that jurisdiction[44] did *not* apply because a 911 operator is not "the public officer or body charged by law with responsibility for the interpretation, administration, or enforcement of the law defining the offense" of resisting an order to stop a motor vehicle.

Additionally, sometimes, albeit infrequently, legislatures include as one of the elements of a regulatory crime the requirement that the actor actually know that what he is doing is a crime. In that case, a defendant may defend successfully if he or she can negate that express knowledge of the law element. In *Liparota v. United States*,[45] for example, the Supreme Court analyzed a statute providing criminal penalties for anyone who "knowingly transfers, acquires, alters, or possesses [food stamp] coupons or authorization cards in any manner not authorized by [statute] or regulations."[46] The Court found that Congress intended that the word "knowingly" in that statute to modify the final phrase of the statute, thus making knowledge of the statutes and regulations an actual element of the offense. It held, in other words, that the statute required that a defendant know that his activity—the transfer or possession of food stamps in proscribed settings—was not actually authorized by law. Significantly, however, the Supreme Court rejected the idea that it was somehow creating a generic mistake of law defense. The *Liparota* decision merely held that, as to that one statute, Congress intended to make knowledge of an attendant legal rule (authorized possession of stamps) an element of the offense.

---

[42]The Due Process Clause of the Fourteenth Amendment requires states to recognize some version of this defense where an actor acts in reliance on the advice or command of an appropriate public official. *See, e.g., Cox v. State of La.*, 379 U.S. 559, 571 (1965) ("The Due Process Clause does not permit convictions to be obtained under such circumstances").
[43]81 Haw. 147, 913 P.2d 558 (Ct. App. 1996).
[44]Haw. Rev. Stat. §702-220 (1985) ("Ignorance or mistake of law; belief that conduct not legally prohibited. In any prosecution, it shall be an affirmative defense that the defendant engaged in the conduct or caused the result alleged under the belief that the conduct or result was not legally prohibited when he acts in reasonable reliance upon an official statement of the law, afterward determined to be invalid or erroneous, contained in: . . . (3) An . . . administrative grant of permission; or (4) An official interpretation of the public officer or body charged by law with responsibility for the interpretation, administration, or enforcement of the law defining the offense.").
[45]471 U.S. 419 (1985).
[46]7 U.S.C. §2024(b)(1).

Moreover, in another handful of cases, courts have recognized a mistake of law defense premised largely on a "reasonable reliance" or "estoppel" type of fairness argument. For example, in *Kipp v. Delaware*,[47] defendant Kipp was charged with possession of a deadly weapon by an individual prohibited from carrying a weapon. Kipp did, in fact, have possession of a deadly weapon, and he was a person prohibited within the meaning of the law due to a prior conviction. But Kipp argued that he was told at the time of that conviction that he would not be prohibited from possessing weapons as a result of his guilty plea. Indeed, the evidence showed that the guilty plea form relating to the conviction contained a space in which it could be indicated whether a guilty plea would result in loss of the right to possess deadly weapons and that portion of the form was marked "N/A." Ultimately, when faced with this evidence, the prosecution "confessed error" and conceded that Kipp should be able to make a mistake of law defense.

The Delaware Supreme Court agreed, holding that "the mistake of law defense is based upon principles of fundamental fairness. A review of the record and the applicable law supports the State's confession of error. The State's confession of error 'is in accordance with the highest tradition of the Delaware Bar and the prosecutor's unique role and duty to seek justice within an adversary system.'"

You should bear in mind, however, that such exceptions to the no mistake of law rule rarely apply. The overwhelming majority of the time, once again, the basic common law rule still applies: *Ignorance of the law is no defense.*

SUMMARY

- Except for strict liability statutes, criminal responsibility requires proof of a specified mens rea or mental state. Demonstrating general wickedness or felonious intent is not enough to establish mens rea.

- Except for strict liability offenses, the MPC provides that proof of a crime should require a showing that the accused acted with one of four defined mental states: purpose, knowledge, recklessness, or negligence.

- Under the MPC, to establish purposeful conduct, it must be shown that the defendant's conscious object was to engage in conduct of the specified nature or to cause a specified result.

- Under the MPC, knowing conduct is established where the defendant was aware that his conduct was of a specified nature or that it was practically certain that his conduct would cause a specified result.

- Under the MPC, a defendant must have consciously disregarded a substantial and unjustifiable risk in order to have acted recklessly.

- Under the MPC, to establish negligence, the defendant should have been aware of a substantial and unjustifiable risk that the criminal result in question would occur.

- Legislatures may enact strict liability criminal statutes, but the absence of a mens rea term does not mean necessarily that the statute is one of strict liability. Courts

---

[47]704 A.2d 839 (Del. 1998).

often presume that legislatures meant to include a mens rea element unless they indicated clearly that they did not.

■ Many jurisdictions have intoxication defenses that apply to specific intent crimes, but not to general intent crimes.

■ To establish intoxication, an accused must prove that she was so severely intoxicated that she did not possess the mens rea for the offense with which she is charged.

■ Involuntary intoxication is a complete defense to criminal charges, treated as an involuntary act.

■ To make a good mistake of fact defense, a defendant must ordinarily establish that her mistaken belief both negated the required mens rea element and was reasonably held.

■ Ordinarily, mistake of law is not a defense.

CONNECTIONS

Relationship to Actus Reus
Ordinarily, the prosecution needs to establish the concurrence of a criminal act (actus reus—see Chapter 2) and criminal intent (mens rea) in order to establish the basic minima of a criminal conviction.

Relationship to Causation
The situation where an actor intends to kill one person but instead kills another person by mistake is often treated as a causation question (see Chapter 4) but perhaps should be treated instead as an issue of mens rea and an appropriate application of transferred intent.

Relationship to Complicity
Many public welfare offenses are not only strict liability offenses, but vicarious liability statutes as well (see Chapter 5).

Relationship to Excuse and Justification Defenses
The actus reus (see Chapter 2) and mens rea of a crime are elements of the criminal offense. The classic defense to a criminal charge is to establish the prosecution's failure of proof of one of those or any other elements of the crime. In contrast, excuse and justification defenses (see Chapters 13 and 12) are usually affirmative defenses that need to be proven by the accused without regard to proof of the elements of the offense.

Relationship to Homicide Offenses

In most jurisdictions, each of the basic mens rea concepts adopted by the Model Penal Code—purposefully, knowingly, recklessly, and negligently—can be found as a component of a different homicide offense, see Chapter 8.

Relationship to Rape and Sexual Offenses

Sexual offenses, see Chapter 10, are unusual in that many of the most serious offenses—forcible rape, for instance—often are deemed to be strict liability offenses. As discussed in this chapter, most strict liability offenses are less serious offenses, often involving so-called public welfare, regulatory offenses.

Causation

4

Did the accused actually "cause" the crime with which he or she is being charged? Most criminal codes draw a distinction between "conduct" and

OVERVIEW

"result" crimes. The former require proof that the actor committed the *actus reus* of the crime, and that he or she did so with the necessary *mens rea*, if there is one. The latter, however, require additionally that the prosecution prove that the defendant *caused* some particular result to occur. The crime of homicide, for example, is the quintessential result crime, where a defendant must have caused the death of another human being. Establishing the causation element in a criminal proceeding requires proof *both* that the accused was the actual cause of the result in question and that the relationship between the act and the result was legally sufficient.

A. COMMON LAW APPROACHES

1. Actual Causation
2. Legal Causation

B. SPECIFIC APPLICATIONS

1. Transferred Intent
2. "Eggshell" Victims
3. Unexpected Acts of the Victim
4. Negligent Medical Care
5. Crimes Involving Recklessness or Negligence

The decision whether or not a criminal offense will be based on conduct, circumstances, and/or a particular result is entirely up to the legislature that enacts the statute in the first instance. While there are common statutory patterns—homicide offenses typically include a result element—legislatures have the authority to define criminal offenses however they see fit. Nonetheless, when causing a specified result is made an element of a crime—a so-called *result* crime—the prosecution must establish beyond a reasonable doubt *both* that the defendant was the actual "but for" cause of the result in question *and* that his or her acts were connected sufficiently to that result to justify a finding of criminal responsibility. Jurisdictions use a variety of different tests to assess the existence of this latter legal sufficiency prong of the criminal causation test.

Why does the criminal law distinguish between conduct crimes and result crimes? Most jurisdictions reason that—in general—more severe punishments should be imposed on convicted defendants who have actually caused particularly heinous results, such as the death of another person, as opposed to those actors who have merely engaged in certain anti-social behaviors without causing particularly heinous results. For example, one who tries to kill another but does not succeed is generally, but not invariably, thought to have caused less societal damage than one who tries to kill another person and succeeds. The attempted murderer might still be convicted of attempt and subjected to the usually lesser punishment attendant to that crime, but more severe punishments are reserved commonly for crimes causing more serious criminal results.

A. Common Law Approaches

Today, most American jurisdictions assess causation in the criminal setting by using a two-pronged test that requires a showing of *both* "actual causation" and "legal causation." The former (actual causation) inquiry focuses on the question whether there is sufficient evidence to conclude that the defendant was *a* cause of the victim's death. The latter (legal causation) inquiry recognizes that even if the actor is *a* cause, intervening and/or remote or unforeseeable events sometimes intrude between a defendant's conduct and the ultimate result in such a fashion as to "break the causal chain" between act and result.

> **Actual Causation ("But For") + Legal Causation**
> **= Criminal Causation**

(1) Actual Causation

The actual causation test is the easiest test for the prosecution to satisfy. Normally, it requires proof simply that the defendant was *a* cause of the proscribed result. In the common law and Model Penal Code terminology that is used in most jurisdictions, this means that the result in question, for instance, the death of the victim, would not have occurred "but for" the defendant's conduct.

In most situations, it is not that difficult to establish that a defendant's conduct was the "but for" cause of a death. If, for example, a person shoots his victim twice in the chest and the victim then falls over dead, one can easily conclude that this person was an actual cause of the victim's death. Put another way, but for this shooting, the victim would not have died. Actual causation is established.

Sometimes, even when a defendant shoots at an intended victim and misses, one might still be able to establish that but for that defendant's conduct, a resulting death would not have occurred. Suppose, for example, that the defendant fired six shots in an attempt to kill her intended victim, but missed with all six shots. However, the evidence suggests further that the victim was so badly frightened by the shots that he suffered a heart attack soon after the shooting. Even if that victim suffered from heart disease and might have died soon in any event, under these circumstances, the defendant can nonetheless be regarded as a but for or actual cause of the victim's death—that is, but for this shooting, the victim would not have died when he did. Actual causation is established.

Reliance strictly upon the but for test for actual causation, however, is sometimes an inadequate measure of criminal causation. Suppose that two persons attempt to kill someone with gunfire and both of them shoot and simultaneously inflict *mortal* wounds. Because either person's conduct would have been sufficient, in and of itself, to cause the victim's death, neither of them can be regarded technically as *the* but for cause of the victim's death. Even if one of them had not shot the victim, the victim still would have died from the other actor's gunshots. Nevertheless, few courts would allow either defendant to escape criminal culpability for that reason.[1] Both persons' conduct could be regarded as a substantial factor in the victim's death, and such a conclusion has been deemed in these circumstances to supplant a strict but for analysis. As the Kentucky Court of Appeals concluded in 1955, the "law will not stop, in such a case, to measure which wound is the more serious, and to speculate upon which actually caused the death."[2]

The but for test also presents difficulties in the (more common than you might think) situation where one defendant has inflicted a mortal wound on his victim, and then a second or third person comes along and also wounds the victim while he is already dying. In such a situation one might argue that only the second individual should be criminally responsible for the victim's death, assuming that the wound that he inflicted was either mortal in itself or hastened the victim's death. Although the wound inflicted by the first defendant was mortal, because of the subsequent wound(s), the first wound arguably did not actually cause the victim's death, at least not before the second or third actor intervened.

However, courts usually find that both or all actors in such a situation must bear criminal responsibility for the victim's death, again, at least where the subsequent independent wound was mortal itself or hastened the victim's death. For example, in the classic case of *Henderson v. State*,[3] one defendant stabbed the victim several times with a knife. Following this attack, the other defendant shot the victim, resulting in his immediate death. The Alabama Court of Appeals declined to try to apportion causal responsibility as between the two defendants, concluding instead that "the [first] defendant would be guilty of the homicide, notwithstanding the jury may not have believed that death would have inevitably followed from such knife wound alone, and notwithstanding they may not have believed that there was any preconcert or community of purpose between defendant and his son." Moreover, if both defendants are working together to kill someone, they might well also both be culpable as accomplices[4] or co-conspirators.[5]

---

[1] *See, e.g., Cox v. State*, 305 Ark. 244, 808 S.W.2d 306 (1991).
[2] *Jones v. Commonwealth*, 281 S.W.2d 920 (Ky. App. 1955).
[3] 11 Ala. App. 37, 65 So. 721 (1914).
[4] See Chapter 5.
[5] See Chapter 7.

(2) Legal Causation

The but for test for actual causation just discussed is a necessary but not a sufficient part of a determination of criminal causation. If it were to be used by itself as the *only* test for causation, the but for test would create undesirable and unfair results.

For example, we know that Timothy McVeigh bombed the Federal Building in Oklahoma City on April 19, 1995, resulting in the deaths of 167 people. However, if a court strictly applied the but for causation analysis, it could also conclude that both of McVeigh's parents were a cause of those tragic deaths. Had they never met and had a child, McVeigh would not have been born, and therefore he would not have committed his terrorist acts. In a literal sense, you see, the parents were a but for cause of the deaths. But no rational criminal justice system would impose criminal liability on someone's parents simply because they decided to have a child who subsequently grew up to become a killer. The parents' actions are too remote from the deaths, both in terms of time and analytical correlation, to justify punishment.

Because of this inadequacy of the but for test standing alone, every jurisdiction supplements it with some form of additional **legal sufficiency test** that shifts the causation inquiry from a focus on actual causation to a focus on **legal causation**. In other words, the more difficult to satisfy concept of legal causation focuses on the question whether the defendant's acts are connected *sufficiently* to the ultimate criminal result to justify a finding of criminal responsibility.

Put another way, while the but for test embraces a wide variety of often innocuous activity, sometimes only indirectly related to the ultimate criminal result, a legal sufficiency test narrows that broad sweep to include only actions that are appropriately deemed by a particular jurisdiction to be sufficiently culpable to justify the coercive force of the criminal law.

F   A   Q

Q: How is this criminal law test different from the tort law proximate cause test?

A: Use of a legal sufficiency analysis is not entirely dissimilar from the analysis used in tort law where the legal causation focus is typically termed a "proximate cause" test. However, largely because a violation of the criminal law results in punishment rather than mere damages, the criminal law's use of legal causation can be—and usually is—different from the tort law concept of proximate cause. It is different in that criminal law legal sufficiency tests are usually intentionally crafted to be harder to satisfy than comparable tests used to gauge causation for purposes of tort law analysis.

Often (but not always), the reason that an actor's actions do *not* satisfy the legal sufficiency prong of the criminal causation inquiry is because "the causal chain is broken" (a common metaphor) by an intervening—sometimes called a "supervening"—act. **Intervening acts** can and do arise in many different ways.

Suppose, for example, that a defendant shoots at C with the purpose of killing him. However, C is merely wounded and is rushed off in an ambulance. Unfortunately, the ambulance driver drives recklessly, causing an accident that results in C's death. From the perspective of the criminal law, we know that the defendant was the but for cause of C's death. But so was the ambulance driver and, per the earlier discussion, the ambulance driver's parents. But the question remains whether defendant was the legal cause of C's death. Or whether the ambulance driver's intervening act of reckless driving should be regarded as breaking the causal chain and thus relieving defendant of criminal responsibility. Jurisdictions use a variety of different but related legal sufficiency tests to answer these questions.

(a) The Year and a Day Rule

At common law, a defendant's conduct could not be deemed to be the legal cause of a homicide unless the victim died within a year and a day following the defendant's acts.[6] As a result, if a defendant tried to kill his victim, but the victim managed to survive the attack for a year and two days (or more), the defendant could not be charged with homicide, although she could still be prosecuted for attempted murder assuming that the other elements of that offense were met.

The rule was somewhat arbitrary even at the common law, but it is especially arbitrary today given advances made in medical technology. Suppose that defendant inflicts what would otherwise be a mortal wound on his adversary. However, because of modern life support equipment, a hospital is able to sustain the victim in a persistent vegetative state. Shortly after a year and a day, the victim dies. Can it really be said (and *should* it be said) that defendant was not really the legal cause of the victim's death? Today, most jurisdictions have simply abandoned the year and a day rule as anachronistic. As the Supreme Court has made the point,

> The year and a day rule is widely viewed as an outdated relic of the common law. . . . Suffice it to say that the rule is generally believed to date back to the 13th century, when it served as a statute of limitations governing the time in which an individual might initiate a private action for murder known as an "appeal of death"; that by the 18th century the rule had been extended to the law governing public prosecutions for murder; that the primary and most frequently cited justification for the rule is that 13th century medical science was incapable of establishing causation beyond a reasonable doubt when a great deal of time had elapsed between the injury to the victim and his death; and that, as practically every court recently to have considered the rule has noted, advances in medical and related science have so undermined the usefulness of the rule as to render it without question obsolete. . . . For this reason, the year and a day rule has been legislatively or judicially abolished in the vast majority of jurisdictions recently to have addressed the issue.[7]

(b) Legal Causation Tests

Modern jurisdictions use a variety of legal sufficiency tests attempting to determine whether the actor's actions were tied sufficiently to the proscribed result to justify the imposition of criminal consequences. For example, some jurisdictions focus on the question whether the defendant's conduct was a "substantial factor" in the ultimate result,[8] or whether the ultimate result was "foreseeable,"[9] "reasonably

---

[6]*See, e.g., Rex v. Dyson* [1908] 2 K.B. 454.
[7]*Rogers v. Tennessee*, 532 U.S. 451, 462-463 (2001).
[8]*See, e.g., People v. Tims*, 449 Mich. 83, 534 N.W.2d 675 (1995).
[9]*See, e.g., People v. Acosta*, 284 Cal. Rptr. 117 (Cal. App. 1991); *Marchl v. Dowling & Co.*, 157 Pa. Super. 91, 41 A.2d 427 (1945).

THE *STEPHENSON* DECISION AND THE KLAN

David Curtiss Stephenson, the defendant in *Stephenson v. State*, was Grand Dragon of the avowedly racist Ku Klux Klan in Indiana and in 22 other northern states at the time of his murder conviction. He was also a candidate for the Democratic Party nomination for President of the United States. Madge Oberholtzer, his victim, ran a state program to combat illiteracy. The facts that came out at Stephenson's trial understandably outraged the community. One man who saw Oberholtzer's body after Stephenson's assault described her as looking like she had been "chewed by a cannibal."

The affirmance of Stephenson's conviction by the Indiana Supreme Court was widely viewed as a demonstration of the judicial branch's political independence given his prominence and political power. Stephenson was sentenced to life in prison and, while serving his sentence, was so incensed by the refusal of the governor to grant him clemency or to commute his sentence, that—to pay the governor back—he released lists of public officials who were or had been on the Klan payroll. He was ultimately paroled but then violated his parole, was recaptured, and sentenced as a parole violator to an additional ten years in prison. He was once again paroled in 1956 on the condition that he leave the State of Indiana and never return.

In 1961, Stephenson was arrested for sexually assaulting a 16-year-old girl, but the charges were dropped on grounds of insufficient evidence. Stephenson is said to have been the author of the quote: "Everything is fine in politics as long as you don't get caught in bed with a live man or a dead woman."

foreseeable,"[10] the "proximate result,"[11] a "sufficiently direct cause,"[12] or the "natural and probable consequence"[13] of defendant's conduct. Some inquire instead whether defendant's conduct "contributed" to the ultimate result,[14] or whether the result was "highly extraordinary."[15]

These tests have not always been well defined, and their meaning has developed largely on a case-by-case basis. But, however they are stated, these various tests tend to have one of two different but related characteristics. Either they look to the defendant and ask what *did* he or *should* he have reasonably foreseen, *or* they look at the other actual causes of the victim's death, if any, and ask how unrelated to the defendant's acts were these independent occurrences.

The application of the natural and probable consequence test is best illustrated by the holding in the classic case of *Stephenson v. State*.[16] In *Stephenson*, the defendant kidnapped a young woman at gunpoint and forced her to travel on a train trip with him. During the trip, he attacked her by biting her neck and face, chewing her breasts, and otherwise mutilating her body. When the train stopped, he took her to a hotel. Later that day, she managed to obtain and take some poison. Her eventual death was a result of an infection in a wound that resulted from the original attack that her body could not fight off because she was so weakened by her suicide attempt. In affirming Stephenson's conviction for murder, the court rejected his argument that his victim took her own life by committing suicide and that that act was an intervening act that broke the causal connection between his otherwise criminal conduct and her death. The Indiana Supreme Court held that the "appellant by his acts and conduct rendered the deceased distracted and mentally irresponsible, and that such was the natural and probable consequence of such unlawful and criminal treatment, and that the appellant was guilty of murder in the second degree as charged in the first count of the indictment."

---

[10]*See, e.g., Bailey v. Commonwealth*, 229 Va. 258, 329 S.E.2d 37 (1985).
[11]*See, e.g., People v. Acosta*, 284 Cal. Rptr. 117 (Cal. App. 1991).
[12]*See, e.g., Commonwealth v. Root*, 403 Pa. 571, 170 A.2d 310 (1961).
[13]*See, e.g., People v. Lewis*, 124 Cal. 551, 57 P. 470 (1899).
[14]*See, e.g., Henderson v. State*, 11 Ala. App. 37, 65 So. 721 (1914).
[15]*See, e.g., People v. Acosta*, 284 Cal. Rptr. 117 (Cal. App. 1991).
[16]205 Ind. 141, 179 N.E. 633 (1932).

(c) Dependent and Independent Intervening Causes

Some courts have distinguished between intervening causes based on whether they are *dependent* or *independent*. The California Court of Appeal, for example, has concluded that a dependent intervening cause involves a response to a defendant's actions while an independent intervening cause is unrelated to a defendant's actions and is essentially coincidental.[17]

This distinction may be illustrated by the following examples. Suppose that a defendant attempts to kill someone, but is unsuccessful. Because of the attempt on his life, however, the intended victim is distraught and unable to keep his mind on his driving as he speeds away in his car. As a result of his inattention, he causes an accident resulting in his own death. Under these circumstances, defendant's poor driving may well be viewed as a direct response to the defendant's conduct and, in jurisdictions using this approach, it would likely be regarded as a *dependent* intervening cause of the victim's death.

In contrast, suppose that defendant again tries to shoot at someone and again misses and again the intended victim speeds away in a careless manner, but this time, the victim does *not* have an accident. However, because he still fears for his life, the victim decides not to go home, but instead to spend the night at his mother's house. During the night, a thunderstorm causes an oak tree to come crashing into the mother's house, killing him. Under these circumstances, the intervening cause of death (the fallen oak tree) would likely be regarded as an *independent* intervening cause because the fact that it caused the victim's death is a coincidence, rather than a direct result of the defendant's conduct.

In both of these examples, the defendant's conduct was a but for cause of the victim's death. In the case of the victim who was shot at and thereafter drove erratically and caused an accident resulting in his death, but for causation is clearly satisfied. Had the defendant not shot at the victim, he would not have been upset, presumably would not have driven so erratically, and would not have died. The same can be said for the victim who was killed by the tree that fell into the house. Had the defendant not shot at him, he would presumably have gone home to his own house and would not have been killed by the falling tree. So, but for causation is satisfied even in the case of a coincidence. But legal causation is different, as has been discussed, and may not be satisfied even though but for causation is.

Furthermore, some courts have held that a dependent intervening cause breaks the chain of causation only when the result is abnormal. Or, put another way, some courts have held that an independent intervening cause always relieves defendant of criminal responsibility, unless it was foreseeable. In the examples above, the dependent intervening cause (the shooting victim driving erratically after being shot at) is not likely to be considered an abnormal response, nor would the result (the victim's death), and therefore it would *not* relieve defendant of criminal responsibility. However, in the case of the independent intervening cause (the tree falling on the house and killing the victim), the result would likely be deemed not to have been foreseeable and therefore *would* cut off such responsibility, breaking the causal chain, using the common causation metaphor.

---

[17] *See, e.g., People v. Acosta*, 284 Cal. Rptr. 117 (Cal. App. 1991).

(d) Model Penal Code Approach

The Model Penal Code uses the but for test as the starting point for its causation analysis, providing that "[c]onduct is the cause of a result when: (a) it is an antecedent but for which the result in question would not have occurred; and (b) the relationship between the conduct and result satisfies any additional causal requirements imposed by the Code or by the law defining the offense."[18] However, as with a common law analysis, the Code's but for test is a necessary but not a sufficient condition to establish causation.

In attempting to determine whether defendant's conduct is the legal cause of a proscribed result, the Model Penal Code differs somewhat from common law approaches. In particular, the Code distinguishes between crimes involving the mens rea of purpose or knowledge, and those requiring only a showing of recklessness or negligence.[19] Under the MPC, when a crime requires purpose or knowledge and "a particular result is an element of an offense, the element is not established if the actual result is not within the purpose or the contemplation of the actor."[20] Suppose, for example, that defendant's purpose is to rob X rather than to kill him, but defendant's gun discharges accidentally, killing X. Under these circumstances, assuming that they could be established in court, defendant cannot be convicted of purposeful murder because he did not have the purpose of killing his victim.[21] He might be convicted of other types of homicide, including killing X recklessly "under circumstances manifesting extreme indifference to the value of human life."[22] However, he cannot be convicted of purposeful murder.

The MPC also provides that causation is satisfied for a crime requiring purpose or knowledge if "the actual result involves the same kind of injury or harm as that designed or contemplated and is not too remote or accidental in its occurrence to have a [just] bearing on the actor's liability or on the gravity of his offense."[23] Consider, for example, the situations discussed earlier involving a defendant who tries to kill someone. If the would-be victim drives off at high speed, trying to evade defendant and gets into an accident leading to his death as a result, this causation test would be satisfied. The actual result in that case (death) is the same as that "designed or contemplated," and is not "too remote or accidental in its occurrence to have a [just] bearing on the actor's liability. . . ."

In the other situation, where defendant shot at someone who, terrified, then drove to his mother's house where he was killed by a falling tree, causation could not be established under the MPC. The actual result involves the same kind of injury or harm as that contemplated by defendant. But, significantly, the method of death is coincidental—unrelated to the defendant's actions—and therefore would likely be regarded as "too remote or accidental" to have a just bearing on defendant's culpability.

The Model Penal Code applies similarly to crimes involving results caused recklessly or negligently. Like the provision on results caused by acts committed purposefully or knowingly, the Code provides that when "recklessly or negligently causing a particular result is an element of an offense, the element is not established if the actual result is not within the risk of which the actor is aware or, in the case of

---

[18]Model Penal Code §2.03(1).
[19]See Chapter 3.
[20]Model Penal Code §2.03(2).
[21]Model Penal Code §2.03(2).
[22]Model Penal Code §2.1.2(1)(b).
[23]Model Penal Code §2.03(2)(b).

negligence, of which he should have been aware."[24] Suppose, for example, that defendant drives recklessly down a city street, swerving in and out of traffic. If the streets are icy and the driver runs off the road, killing a pedestrian, one might readily conclude that she is the actual and the legal cause of the pedestrian's death.

By contrast, suppose that another defendant drives carefully down the same street, but suffers a blow-out even though his tires were in good condition, runs off the road, and kills a pedestrian. In this latter situation, because defendant's actions—which were the but for cause of the victim's death—were not within the risk of which the actor was aware or about which he should have been aware, there would be no criminal responsibility for a homicide offense based upon recklessness or criminal negligence.

As with the provision on purposefulness and knowledge, the Model Penal Code also has special causation provisions relating to crimes involving recklessness or negligence, providing that causation is satisfied if "the actual result differs from the probable result only in the respect that a different person or different property is injured or affected or that the probable injury would have been more serious or more extensive than that caused."[25] The MPC further provides that the causal chain will not be broken if "the actual result involves the same kind of injury or harm as the probable result and is not too remote or accidental in its occurrence to have a [just] bearing on the actor's liability or on the gravity of his offense."[26]

As to strict liability offenses, the Model Penal Code—and the jurisdictions that have adopted this part of it—do not impose strict liability as to the results at issue. On the contrary, when "causing a particular result is a material element for which absolute liability is imposed by law," the MPC provides instead that such liability will *not* be imposed "unless the actual result is a probable consequence of the actor's conduct."[27]

B. Specific Applications

Even though the common law tests are usually stated a bit differently than the Model Penal Code test, both types of test often (but not invariably) produce similar results. Causation issues arise in a strikingly wide variety of settings, as some of the following examples illustrate.

(1) Transferred Intent

A recurring theme in criminal law is the situation in which an actor intends to kill one person (X), and attempts to do so, but mistakenly kills another person (Y) instead. In this situation, in truth, the focal issue is not so much one of causation, but rather one of *mens rea*, more specifically "transferred intent." If a defendant pulls out a gun and shoots at X, but kills Y because he is a poor shot, no one would doubt that defendant is the actual and legal cause of Y's death. However, because defendant had the intent to kill X, but did not have the intent to kill Y, it may be difficult to find that she *intentionally* killed Y. In such a situation, the courts have transferred defendant's intent to kill X to Y and concluded that defendant is indeed guilty of intentionally killing Y.

---

[24]Model Penal Code §2.03(3).
[25]Model Penal Code §2.03(3)(a).
[26]Model Penal Code §2.03(3)(b).
[27]Model Penal Code §2.03(4).

The Model Penal Code leads to the same result, providing that the element of causation can be satisfied for a purposeful crime if "the actual result differs from that designed or contemplated, as the case may be, only in the respect that a different person or different property is injured or affected or that the injury or harm designed or contemplated would have been more serious or more extensive than that caused."[28] Under the MPC, because the actual result in our hypothetical differed from that designed or contemplated only in the respect that a different person was injured, defendant would be regarded as having purposely murdered Y, even though her actual purpose was to murder X, not Y.

The common law and the Model Penal Code approaches to transferred intent have been criticized on the ground that they produce an incongruence between a defendant's *actual mens rea* and the ultimate result of her actions. Indeed, in the typical situation of transferred intent—often a homicide—even without such a transfer, the actor would be facing *very* substantial criminal charges, if not murder charges. At the very least, such a defendant could be prosecuted for the *attempted* murder of X.[29] In addition, in jurisdictions that apply the felony-murder doctrine, the killing of Y might well be treated as felony-murder. Nonetheless and despite these criticisms, in the overwhelming majority of instances, the transferred intent doctrine applies.

(2) "Eggshell" Victims

In tort law, an actor must take his victim as he finds him. In other words, if a tortfeasor encounters an "eggshell victim," someone who is particularly susceptible to injury, he accepts the consequences of his poor choice of victims with respect to his tort liability. Is the same thing true in the criminal law? Sometimes.

In some cases, there is a close enough connection between the victim's unanticipated medical condition and his death that the defendant has been held criminally responsible. For example, in the well-known case of *People v. Stamp*,[30] a robbery victim had a heart attack due to the excitement of the robbery and died. The California Court of Appeal held that "[s]o long as life is shortened as a result of the felonious act, it does not matter that the victim might have died soon anyway. In this respect, the robber takes his victim as he finds him."

Similarly, in *State v. Frazier*,[31] defendant struck his victim on the jaw. Unfortunately, the victim was a hemophiliac. The injury would have caused only minor injuries to a non-hemophiliac, since it created only a slight laceration on the inside of the victim's mouth. However, since he was a hemophiliac, it produced a hemorrhage lasting ten days, ending in his death. Defendant had no idea about the victim's condition, but the Supreme Court of Missouri held that this defendant should not be excused on this ground.

Even though the *Frazier* court refused to hold that the victim's hemophilia broke the chain of causation, it still may be difficult to convict such a defendant for murder or manslaughter. In Model Penal Code terms, murder requires proof that the defendant killed purposely or knowingly, or recklessly with extreme indifference to the value of human life. In a case such as *Frazier*, where the actor did nothing more than hit his victim in the jaw, it may be very difficult to persuade a fact finder

[28]Model Penal Code §2.03(2)(a).
[29]See Model Penal Code §5.01.
[30]2 Cal. App. 3d 203, 82 Cal. Rptr. 598 (1969).
[31]339 Mo. 966, 98 S.W.2d 707 (1936).

that defendant purposely or knowingly killed his victim. Indeed, although a closer case, it will probably be difficult even to prove that such a defendant acted recklessly, with extreme indifference to the value of human life. While it is dangerous to hit people on the jaw, such behavior does not usually reflect indifference to the value of human life.

Moreover, in order to convict this defendant of reckless homicide, it would be necessary to show that he consciously disregarded a risk of death. That might not be possible if the defendant had absolutely no reason to know or suspect (making his disregard conscious) that his victim was a hemophiliac. Finally, for negligent homicide, it must be shown that defendant "should have been aware" of a substantial and unjustifiable risk of death. While defendant might be found to have this mens rea, a conviction even on this ground would be by no means certain.

But not all criminal courts agree with the outcomes in *Frazier* and *Stamp*. For example, in *Fine v. State*,[32] the evidence showed that Hodges suffered from high blood pressure when defendant assaulted him by placing both hands on his throat. Even though defendant turned Hodges loose within a few seconds, he never regained consciousness because he suffered a ruptured blood vessel in the brain. The Tennessee Supreme Court concluded that defendant should not be held responsible for Hodges's subsequent death: "It is settled law in all homicide cases that the collateral crime, i.e. the alleged unlawful act antedating death, must be so integrated with and related to the homicide that it can be said to have proximately caused or contributed to it. The related occurrences in the instant case, which immediately preceded the sudden paralysis of the deceased, were so remote in causal effect that his death can only be thought of as a fortuitous circumstance."

(3) Unexpected Acts of the Victim

A number of causation cases have focused on unexpected acts by the victim that contribute to the criminal result. For example, in *Commonwealth v. Cheeks*,[33] defendant stabbed the victim in the abdomen during a robbery. The injury necessitated an operation that resulted in tubes being inserted through the victim's nostrils into his stomach. The victim was disoriented, uncooperative, and confused, and he pulled out the tubes on several occasions. Ultimately, he pulled out one of the tubes, gagged, and asphyxiated. In *Cheeks*, the Pennsylvania Supreme Court concluded that the victim's unexpected act did not relieve the defendant of criminal responsibility, finding that "[t]he fact that the victim, while in a weakened physical condition and disorientated mental state, pulled out the tubes and created the immediate situation, which resulted in his death, is not such an intervening and independent act sufficient to break the chain of causation or events between the stabbing and the death."

A similar result was reached by the District of Columbia District Court in *United States v. Hamilton*.[34] In that case, like *Cheeks,* the victim pulled tubes out of himself resulting in his death. The court held that it "is well established that if a person strikes another and inflicts a blow that may not be mortal in and of itself but thereby starts a chain of causation that leads to death, he is guilty of homicide. This is true even if the deceased contributes to his own death or hastens it by failing to take proper treatment."

---

[32]193 Tenn. 422, 246 S.W.2d 70 (1952).
[33]423 Pa. 67, 223 A.2d 291 (1966).
[34]182 F. Supp. 548 (D.D.C. 1960).

Today, in jurisdictions using the Model Penal Code causation tests, the focal question in cases like those described above would be whether or not the resulting death was "too remote or accidental" to find the defendant responsible.

Sidebar

DEATHS IN HOSPITALS

A 1988 Rand Corporation study concluded that:

If the quality of care provided by a hospital affects its death rate, then some deaths must be preventable. We have developed a new method to investigate this issue and have reviewed 182 deaths from 12 hospitals . . . for three conditions (cerebrovascular accident, pneumonia, or myocardial infarction). The investigators prepared a dictated summary of each patient's hospital course. Then, at least three physicians reviewed each summary and independently judged whether the death could have been prevented. [We] found that 27% of the deaths might have been prevented [and] a 14% rate of probably preventable deaths. Patients whose deaths were probably preventable were younger (74.7 compared with 78.6 years . . .), less often demented (12% compared with 26% . . .), and less severely ill . . . than patients whose deaths were nonpreventable.

R.W. Dubois & R.H. Brooks, *Preventable Deaths: Who, How Often and Why?*, Ann. Intern. Med. 1988 Oct. 1:109(7):582-589.

(4) Negligent Medical Care

A number of causation cases deal with the problem of whether negligent medical care should be regarded as an intervening factor that breaks the causal chain. In general, courts have answered this question in the negative.

Negligent medical care → Does not break the causal chain
Grossly negligent medical care → Breaks the causal chain

Assume, for example, that an actor shoots G, intending to kill him, but inflicts only a serious stomach wound. Unfortunately for G, at the hospital the doctors render negligent—as opposed to "grossly negligent" or "willful and wanton"—medical care, and G dies. The question is whether that negligent medical care, which might well lead to a successful civil action for medical malpractice, is a sufficient intervening cause of death so that it relieves the actor of criminal responsibility for homicide.

At common law, medical care was regarded as a normal and foreseeable response to a gunshot wound and, accordingly, was a superseding cause only if it was so outrageously improper or inappropriate as to be regarded as abnormal. Similarly, most modern decisions have concluded that merely negligent medical care is *not* so abnormal that it relieves a defendant of criminal responsibility. For example, in *People v. Calvaresi*,[35] although defendant shot his victim, severing an artery, he argued that inadequate medical care was the supervening cause of death. The Colorado Supreme Court made clear, however, that mere negligence on the part of an attending physician does not constitute a causal defense because it is "entirely too frequent to be considered abnormal."

Under the Model Penal Code, the same result would obtain. Where defendant had the purpose to kill his victim and the resulting injury was the same as that contemplated, in all likelihood negligent medical care would be regarded as too remote or accidental to break the causal chain.

Significantly, however, when medical care is *grossly* negligent or intentionally harmful to the victim, a different result might well obtain. Courts have often found that grossly negligent care or intentionally harmful care is so abnormal as to break the causal chain and relieve a defendant of criminal responsibility, for homicide, at

---

[35]188 Colo. 277, 534 P.2d 316 (1975).

least, if not for other crimes, such as attempted murder or aggravated assault. For example, in *People v. Calvaresi*,[36] the Colorado Supreme Court ruled that "gross negligence is abnormal human behavior, would not be reasonably foreseeable, and would constitute a defense, if, but for that gross negligence, death would not have resulted."

There is another subcategory of decisions worth noting here. When a victim is near death, and her organs are harvested for donation purposes, the organ taking—which ultimately and necessarily results in death when the victim is removed from life support—is *not* regarded as an intervening act that serves to break the chain of causation.

In *People v. Bonilla*,[37] for example, defendant inflicted a mortal wound on Cronkite, who went into a coma. Cronkite's condition quickly deteriorated, and when he became totally unresponsive to all stimuli and his electroencephalograms went "flat," he was placed on life support. His mother signed a consent form allowing his kidneys and spleen to be removed for donation. After this was done, doctors disconnected Cronkite's life-support systems, resulting in his death. In the ensuing criminal prosecution, defendant claimed that the doctors' actions were the cause of death and that he was not criminally responsible. The court rejected this argument, however, commenting that "[c]riminal liability for homicide requires that the defendant's actions be a sufficiently direct cause of death, but direct does not mean immediate or unaided. It is enough that defendant's conduct forged a link in a chain of events which brought about the death. Intervention of a secondary agency constitutes a defense only if the death is solely attributable to it."

(5) Crimes Involving Recklessness or Negligence

Causation issues also arise in cases involving crimes based on a mens rea of recklessness or negligence. The analysis in these cases is sometimes a bit different from the analysis of intentional, purposeful, or knowing conduct. The following examples demonstrate some of these differences.

(a) Intoxicated Drivers

From time to time, bartenders or bar owners—or private hosts, for that matter—serve their guests too much to drink, resulting in situations where these inebriated guests subsequently leave and cause automobile accidents (or do other stupid, drunken things) that kill other people. Under such circumstances, can the bartender be charged with reckless or negligent homicide? Almost certainly, a bartender would be—at the very least—negligent in continuing to serve alcohol to an intoxicated customer if the bartender had reason to believe that she might try to drive away when leaving the bar. But does the customer's own criminal act of driving while drunk relieve the bartender of criminal responsibility by breaking the causal chain? Is the patron's act of driving while intoxicated a superseding or intervening event?

The answer is "no." In common law terms, the customer's decision to drive while intoxicated is not a mere coincidence, unrelated to the bartender's conduct.

---

[36]188 Colo. 277, 534 P.2d 316 (1975).
[37]95 A.D.2d 396, 467 N.Y.S.2d 599 (1983).

Moreover, while the customer's act of driving while drunk is itself criminal, it can hardly be regarded as an abnormal event under the circumstances. Such drunk driving is all too common, however abhorrent it might be. Similarly, in Model Penal Code terms, the homicidal result would be deemed to be within the scope of the bartender's recklessness or negligence, and the ultimate result cannot easily be regarded as too remote or accidental.

(b) High-Speed Chases

Can a defendant who attempts to flee the police in his car and, in so doing, causes the death of another driver be held criminally responsible for that death? Yes. Under such circumstances, there can be no doubt about his criminal responsibility because it was the defendant who created a reckless or negligent risk of death to others. Moreover, there is no intervening event to cut off criminal culpability. As a result, under both the common law and the Model Penal Code, such a defendant would be held criminally responsible for the resulting death.

But suppose that, rather than causing the death of another driver, the defendant is charged with the death of a pursuing police officer. Suppose further that there is evidence that the deceased officer was negligent because he drove too fast and/or recklessly during the chase and, as a result, skidded off the road into a telephone pole. Should the officer's own negligence relieve the defendant of criminal responsibility for the death? The answer is "no." In driving at high speeds, defendant created a risk of injury or death to those he encountered as well as to pursuing police officers. In addition, even though the deceased officer may have been negligent himself, his actions were a response to the defendant's actions and cannot be regarded as abnormal or sufficiently coincidental to break the causal chain. Under the Model Penal Code, moreover, the officer's death is unlikely to be regarded as too remote or accidental to fail to establish the causation element of a homicide offense.

(c) Omissions

When a case involves a claim that a defendant failed to fulfill a duty imposed by law, the defendant may be criminally responsible for causing a prohibited result, despite the criminal acts of others. For example, in *Palmer v. State*,[38] defendant mother moved in with McCue. McCue brutally whipped and beat Palmers's daughter, Terry, ultimately killing her, and defendant did not stop him. Despite McCue's brutality, the Maryland court concluded that his criminal conduct did not break the chain of causation. "The trial judge found that there was a causal connection between the mother's negligence and the death. . . . There seems to be no doubt that the direct and immediate cause of Terry's death was the violent blow or blows inflicted upon her by McCue. . . . But we do not deem this action upon his part to amount to an 'intervening efficient cause' (as distinguished from one that is concurrent or contributing), as that term is used in the statement of the doctrine of proximate cause. . . . McCue's violent and unrestrained actions were of such a nature as to put any ordinary, reasonable person on notice that the child's life was truly and realistically in immediate peril. The appellant easily could, and should, have removed Terry from this danger. Her failure to do so, under the circumstances previously described, is sufficient to support a finding by the trial judge that her gross and criminal negligence was a contributing cause of Terry's unfortunate death."

---

[38]223 Md. 341, 164 A.2d 467 (1960).

(d) Pursuing Attackers

Some criminal cases deal with the question whether criminal attackers can be held criminally responsible when the person they are pursuing subsequently dies as a result of the pursuit. A poignant illustration is the case of *People v. Kern*,[39] also known as the "Howard Beach" case, which involved several white teenagers who assaulted and threatened three black men. In the course of the assault, several defendants relentlessly chased Griffith, who retreated by jumping a barricade and attempting to cross a six-lane highway. A passing motorist collided with him and killed him. Defendants argued that the evidence on causation was legally insufficient due to the motorist's intervening act. The New York court disagreed, noting that defendants' actions were a "sufficiently direct cause" of Griffith's death as to warrant the imposition of criminal liability. "[T]he only reasonable alternative left open to Griffith while being persistently chased and threatened by the defendants and their friends, several of whom were carrying weapons, was to seek safety by crossing the parkway where he unfortunately met his death."

(e) Drag Racing

A number of causation cases address the question whether one drag racer can be said to have caused the death of another drag racer, of bystanders, or others who are killed as a result of the race. One of the best known of these decisions is *Commonwealth v. Root*.[40] In that case, Root was charged with involuntary manslaughter for the death of his competitor during a drag race that took place on a rural highway. Even though the speed limit was 50 mph, the racers hit speeds of 70-90 mph. The death occurred in a no-passing zone on the approach to a bridge where the highway narrowed to two directionally opposite lanes. Root was leading in the right-hand lane, when the deceased tried to pass in a no-passing zone on the approach to a bridge and was hit by a truck traveling in the opposite direction. While the court did not doubt that Root could be convicted of any number of vehicular offenses, including speeding or reckless driving, it held that he was not the "direct cause" of his co-competitor's death as "the deceased was aware of the dangerous condition created by the defendant's reckless conduct in driving his automobile at an excessive rate of speed along the highway but, despite such knowledge, he recklessly

Sidebar

THE HOWARD BEACH CASE

"*When:* December 20, 1986

The facts: On their way out of a Howard Beach pizzeria, where they'd stopped to grab a slice after their car broke down, Michael Griffith and his friends, all black youths, are accosted and chased by a group of white teenagers from the neighborhood yelling 'Kill the n——s.' Griffith is struck by a car on the Belt Parkway and killed. Mayor Ed Koch calls it a 'racial lynching,' the most horrendous incident in his nine years as mayor. Many New Yorkers meet Al Sharpton, Vernon Mason, and Alton Maddox for the first time. Mason and Maddox represent two of the victims and Charles Hynes leads the prosecution which results in three murder convictions.

"*The protests:* Sharpton works the media and helps arrange a march of 1,200 mostly black demonstrators through the neighborhood. Residents respond by shouting at the protestors and racial tensions grow.

"*Landmark case:* 'For the first time in a race case, to our knowledge, [the Governor appointed] a special prosecutor, Charles Hynes. That was a landmark. Because that was the first time the state conceded there was a problem in how the criminal-justice system responds to racial violence.' —Al Sharpton in the 30th anniversary issue of New York Magazine."

Howard Beach, Crimes & Scandals, New York Magazine, http://www.newyorkmetro.com/news/articles/03/03/35th/crazedcity/crimes/17.htm.

---

[39] 149 A.D.2d 187, 212-213, 545 N.Y.S.2d 4, 20 (1989).
[40] 403 Pa. 571, 170 A.2d 310 (1961).

chose to swerve his car to the left and into the path of an oncoming truck, thereby bringing about the head-on collision which caused his own death."

Not all courts or commentators agree. In *Jacobs v. State*,[41] for example, a drag racer killed the innocent driver of an oncoming vehicle. Jacobs, another racer, was convicted of manslaughter and his conviction was upheld on appeal: "The deaths which proximately resulted from the activities of the three persons engaged in the unlawful activity of drag racing made each of the active participants equally guilty of the criminal act which caused the death of the innocent party."

(f) Games of "Chicken"

Some people have engaged in games of "chicken," driving directly at one another, seeing who will swerve away first, or some variation on that theme, resulting in the death of one of the participants. Can the surviving participant be regarded as the cause of the deceased participant's death? In *Forden v. Joseph G.*,[42] defendant and deceased entered into a suicide pact that was supposed to be carried out by driving a car off a cliff. The cliff was on a curve overlooking a 300- to 350-foot precipice on a country road. The two proceeded up the hill past the cliff, turned around and drove down around the curve and over the steep cliff at speeds in excess of 50 mph. No one saw brake lights flash. The impact of the crash killed deceased and caused severe injuries to defendant, resulting in the amputation of a foot. The State charged defendant with the homicide of the deceased, and the court sustained the charge, noting that "under the common law the survivor of a suicide pact was held to be guilty of murder."

(g) Narcotics Suppliers

Can a supplier of narcotics be held criminally responsible for the death of someone who uses the drugs he supplied? Yes, in some instances at least. In *State v. Wassil*,[43] Groleau, an alcoholic who had previously used depressants, spent the day drinking and "doing pills." By evening, he was visibly inebriated. Defendant injected heroin into his own arm, and then gave some to Groleau, who injected it into his own arm. Approximately 15 seconds later, Groleau lost consciousness, collapsed onto the floor, and died. A jury found defendant guilty of homicide, rejecting the contention that Groleau's action of injecting himself was an intervening cause of death. The conviction was sustained on appeal, the court finding that "[t]he record supports the jury's finding that the defendant's conduct substantially and materially contributed, in a direct manner, to Groleau's death. The actions of the defendant in purchasing and delivering the narcotics led directly to Groleau's injection of those narcotics, and thus, to his death. But for the delivery of the narcotics, moreover, death would not have occurred." The court went on to find that, "because Groleau already was inebriated at the time the defendant delivered the drugs to him, he did not voluntarily, consciously disregard a known risk to himself when he injected the drugs."

---

[41]184 So. 2d 711 (Fla. App. 1966).
[42]34 Cal. 3d 429, 667 P.2d 1176, 194 Cal. Rptr. 163 (in banc 1983).
[43]233 Conn. 174, 658 A.2d 548 (1995).

SUMMARY

■ To establish causation, the defendant must have been an actual but for cause of the criminal result *and* his or her acts must have been connected sufficiently to that result to justify a finding of criminal responsibility.

■ To determine whether a defendant's acts were sufficient to establish causation, jurisdictions use tests that either look to the defendant and ask whether he foresaw or should have reasonably foreseen the criminal result and/or they look at other causes of the criminal result and ask how unrelated to the defendant's acts these causes were.

■ The MPC provides that causation is not established for a crime requiring a mens rea of purpose or knowledge if the result was too remote or accidental.

■ Negligent medical care ordinarily does not break the causal chain between a defendant's acts and a criminal result, but grossly negligent medical care does.

CONNECTIONS

Relationship to Actus Reus
Where an act element of a criminal offense (see Chapter 2) requires the accused's completion of a specified result—for example, the death of a human being for homicide offenses (see Chapter 8)—the criminal offense ordinarily will also require that the State establish that the accused person caused that result.

Relationship to Homicide
One of the traditional elements of homicide offenses (see Chapter 8) is the result element of the death of a human being. Accordingly, criminal causation is also a required element of homicides: A showing is necessary that the person charged actually caused the death.

Relationship to Mens Rea
The situation where an actor intends to kill one person but instead kills another person by mistake is often treated as a causation question, but perhaps should be treated instead as an issue of mens rea (see Chapter 3) and an appropriate application of transferred intent.

Complicity

5

In general, the criminal law is premised on the sensible notions that people should be held responsible for their own actions and that the

OVERVIEW

level of their culpability should be tied to their own criminal intent and their own criminal conduct. But there are two common situations where criminal responsibility attaches based in part on the fact that *someone else* has acted criminally. The first is when a defendant is deemed to be complicit as an accomplice of another person who commits a criminal act. The second situation is when someone is held responsible vicariously for another person's criminal conduct. Such vicarious criminal responsibility might be imposed on an individual or a corporation.

A. ACCOMPLICE CULPABILITY

1. Common Law Restrictions and Modern Approaches
2. Mens Rea Requirement
3. Act Requirement
4. Renunciation
5. Scope of Accomplice Responsibility

B. VICARIOUS LIABILITY

1. Corporate Culpability
2. Criminal Responsibility of Corporate Officers and Agents

The Model Penal Code provides that a "person is guilty of an offense if it is committed by his own conduct or by the conduct of another person for which he is legally accountable, or both."[1] The Code explains further that a "person is legally accountable for the conduct of another person" in the following situations: "(a) acting with the kind of culpability that is sufficient for the commission of the offense, he causes an innocent or irresponsible person to engage in such conduct; or (b) he is made accountable for the conduct of such other person by the Code or by the law defining the offense; or (c) he is an accomplice of such other person in the commission of the offense."[2]

Most commonly, people are held criminally responsible when they are found to be complicit in criminal activity either as an accomplice of another person in the commission of a crime or where they are held vicariously responsible for the acts of another person.[3]

A. Accomplice Culpability

Every jurisdiction has laws on the books that impose criminal sanctions on **accomplices**, sometimes called **accessories** or **aiders-and-abettors**, to criminal conduct. Basically, these laws are designed to punish those who provide aid, assistance, or active encouragement to someone else who commits a crime.

At common law, there were four potential parties to a felony. The first two parties were considered **principals** because they were present physically at the scene of the crime. A "principal in the first degree" was any individual who actually committed the crime. By contrast, a "principal in the second degree" was someone who was actually or constructively present at the scene of the crime and aided or abetted its commission.

The common law also provided punishment for accessories. An "accessory before the fact" was someone who was not present at the crime scene, but rendered aid or encouragement to the perpetrator *before* the fact. An "accessory after the fact" also was not present at the crime scene, but provided aid or encouragement to the perpetrators *after* the crime was completed.[4] For misdemeanors, no distinction was made for accessories. Anyone who aided or encouraged the commission of a misdemeanor was considered to be a principal.

COMMON LAW PARTIES TO A FELONY

Principals in the First Degree
Principals in the Second Degree
Accomplices Before the Fact
Accomplices After the Fact

---

[1]Model Penal Code §2.06(1).
[2]Model Penal Code §2.06(2).
[3]See also Chapter 7(G) (Culpability of Co-Conspirators).
[4]The common law also contained the crime of "misprision of felony" for those situations when an individual was not involved in the commission of the crime either as a principal or as an accessory, but who tried to conceal the offense. Modern statutes are similar in criminalizing "obstruction of justice" offenses.

(1) Common Law Restrictions and Modern Approaches

Because individuals found to be accessories were subject to the death penalty at the common law, common law courts adopted elaborate and byzantine rules to moderate the harsh effects of this broad accessorial net. The most important limitation adopted by these courts was the rule that an accessory's culpability was deemed to follow or "shadow" that of the principal. As a logical result, an accessory could not be convicted absent the prior conviction of the principal. And if the principal died, fled and escaped prosecution, or was acquitted, the accessory's conviction could not stand; it stood or fell with the principal. Similarly, if the principal's conviction was reversed on appeal, the accessory's conviction had to be reversed as well.

However, a principal in the second degree—still a principal—was treated differently than an accessory in that her conviction could be sustained regardless of whatever happened or might happen to the principal in the first degree. As a result, there was much litigation regarding whether a particular defendant should be treated as a principal or as an accessory. In misdemeanor cases, by contrast, all parties were deemed to be principals, hence, a prior acquittal of a principal did not prevent the subsequent conviction of someone who merely offered assistance.

To overcome these seemingly arbitrary judge-made rules relating to accessorial liability, statutes were enacted in England and in the United States amending the common law. In 1848, the British Parliament enacted a statute providing that an accessory before the fact could be "indicted, tried, convicted, and punished in all respects like the Principal."[5] Significantly, however, this statute permitted an accessory to be convicted even though the principal was acquitted.

In the United States, legislatures enacted similar statutes, largely abolishing the common law distinctions between accessories and principals in both felony and misdemeanor cases, and providing that *all parties involved in crimes—whatever their former status under the common law—are to be tried, convicted, and punished as principals.*

Merger

Principals in the First Degree + Principals in the Second Degree + Accomplices Before the Fact = Principals

The only exception to this "merger" (as it is usually termed) of principals and accessories is that accessories *after* the fact do not merge with principals; they are still treated separately as accessories, typically with a lesser punishment.

There are a number of different crimes relating to activities undertaken by individuals after a principal offense has already occurred. Receiving stolen property, for example, is a common example, assuming that the person who received the property was unaware that a theft was to take place beforehand (thus becoming an accessory *before* the fact). One of the most common after-the-fact crimes found in many jurisdictions is the crime of "obstruction of justice." Or, more accurately, the family of crimes relating to obstruction of justice. In federal criminal law, for example, Title 18 of the U.S. Code includes 20 separate obstruction of justice offenses.

Additionally, since accessories before the fact are now merged with principals in most jurisdictions, their culpability no longer turns on what happens to any other party.

---

[5] 11 & 12 Vic. ch. 46, §1.

The Model Penal Code is consistent with this modern merger approach, providing expressly that "[a]n accomplice may be convicted on proof of the commission of the offense and of his complicity therein, though the person claimed to have committed the offense has not been prosecuted or convicted or has been convicted of a different offense or degree of offense or has an immunity to prosecution or conviction or has been acquitted."[6]

F   A   Q

Q: Does the fact of merger mean that the concept of accomplices before the fact no longer exists?

A: No. It simply means that the old common law distinctions no longer exist and a person can be charged and convicted of a crime in the same fashion whether he or she is alleged to have acted as a principal or an accomplice before the fact.

At common law, moreover, when the courts still distinguished between principals and accessories, a defendant might go free if the prosecution charged her as a principal, but the evidence revealed that she had committed acts consistent with an accessory or vice versa. Under the modern approach, however, with principals and accessories merged (except for accessories after the fact), a defendant can be convicted on proof that she functioned *either* as a principal or an accessory.

Criminal defendants sometimes raise notice issues challenging the charges that have been filed against them, arguing that they were given insufficient notice of what the prosecution would try to establish at trial: principal or accessory status. For instance, if the prosecution claims that defendant is guilty of murdering a victim, must she receive notice that she is being charged with being the actual perpetrator (in the sense of the common law definition of a principal in the first or second degree) or as providing aid and assistance to the perpetrator (in the common law sense of an accessory before the fact)?

This is an important question, which has an impact on defense counsel's trial preparation. Depending on all of the facts involved, courts typically look to see whether notice of how the prosecution intends to prosecute the case was provided expressly or impliedly. If no notice was provided, the key question is whether defendant was prejudiced by the prosecution's failure to be clear on this point.

For example, in *Baker v. Alaska*,[7] although defendant and his two friends were all charged with robbing a pizza delivery person, there was uncertainty about whether defendant himself was charged as a principal or as an accessory. As a result, Baker's defense attorney objected to an accomplice instruction that allowed the jury to convict him as an accomplice even though the prosecutor had indicated that he intended to treat Baker as a principal in the first degree because he allegedly struck the victim. The Alaska Court of Appeals concluded, however, that there was no surprise or prejudice to Baker and therefore that he had received adequate notice of the government's theory of the case, and his conviction was, accordingly, affirmed.

---

[6]Model Penal Code §2.06(7).
[7]905 P.2d 479 (Alaska Ct. App. 1996).

Likewise, in *New Hampshire v. Sinbandith*,[8] defendant was charged with selling a controlled substance based on an allegation that it had been sold by his girlfriend and that he had acted in concert with her. Defendant claimed that the prosecution had to show that he had acted purposely with respect to these sales (the standard for accomplices), rather than simply knowingly (the standard for principals). The New Hampshire Supreme Court concluded that "language in an indictment alleging that a defendant acted 'in concert with' another is sufficient to charge the defendant *both* as a principal and as an accomplice."[9] And, the court added, "[t]he indictments provided sufficient notice to the defendant that he was being charged as a principal. That they were captioned as accomplice charges does not alter the explicit language of the indictments that put the defendant on notice that he could be convicted as either a principal or an accomplice. Having sufficiently charged the defendant as a principal, the indictments provided the defendant adequate notice to prepare a defense to principal or accomplice liability."

A second common law limitation on accessorial liability was the notion that an accessory could only be tried in the jurisdiction where he or she rendered assistance to the criminal endeavor. As a result, if a robbery took place in Kansas, but defendant rendered assistance in Missouri, the accessory could be prosecuted only in Missouri, even though the crime itself was committed in Kansas. Most jurisdictions have changed this common law rule as well, so that an accessory can be tried in the jurisdiction where the crime was actually committed rather than solely in the jurisdiction where the accessorial acts were committed.[10]

(2) Mens Rea Requirement

As a general rule, in order to convict an individual as an accessory, it must be shown that he or she had the intent or purpose to serve as an accessory to the crime. More specifically, the mens rea of accomplice liability is often described in the case law as having two separate and independent components: (1) the intent to assist a principal actor in committing a crime and (2) the intent that the principal actually commit that crime. In most jurisdictions, this intent can be, and usually is, implied circumstantially from a person's actions.

The Model Penal Code states that complicity is a crime of purpose: "A person is an accomplice of another person in the commission of an offense if . . . (a) with the purpose of promoting or facilitating the commission of the offense, he [engages in accessorial conduct]."[11] Under the Code, accordingly, the mere fact that a defendant was present at the scene of a crime provides an insufficient basis for establishing a complicit mens rea. The prosecution must show beyond a reasonable doubt that defendant had the actual purpose of promoting or facilitating commission of the offense. When a crime that is defined by reference to a result element is involved, the Model Penal Code provides for accomplice liability when defendant "acts with the kind of culpability, if any, with respect to that result that is sufficient for the commission of the offense."[12]

Even though accomplice liability requires proof (under the MPC) that the defendant acted intentionally or purposely, courts often infer this mens rea

[8]143 N.H. 579, 729 A.2d 994 (1999).
[9]Emphasis added.
[10]*See, e.g., State v. Darroch*, 305 N.C. 196, 287 S.E.2d 856 (1982).
[11]Model Penal Code §2.06(3)(a).
[12]Model Penal Code §2.06(4).

circumstantially from the facts presented. For example, in *New York v. Kaplan*,[13] Kaplan was convicted of selling a controlled substance based on his involvement in narcotics transactions. The evidence revealed that he was present at one sale, introduced the buyer to the sellers, and told the sellers to "take care of the young lady." At another sale, he got off the couch, walked to a file cabinet, removed an envelope that contained narcotics, and placed it on the desk in front of an undercover agent. When the agent then placed money on the table, Kaplan picked it up and began counting it. Kaplan argued that he could not be convicted as an accomplice as there was insufficient evidence that he had the specific intent to sell a controlled substance. But the New York Court of Appeals disagreed, finding adequate evidence of intent circumstantially.

In many instances, evidence of the defendant's intent is less clear. For example, in *State v. Ulvinen*,[14] a woman was murdered by her husband because she refused to have sex with him. After choking her to death, he dismembered her body in the bathtub. The man's mother had strained relations with her daughter-in-law and told friends that she hated her. On the morning of the murder, when the husband told his mother that he was going to "put [his wife] to sleep," then dispose of the body, the mother replied that that would "be for the best." During the actual murder, the mother was asleep. However, after the killing, the mother was adamant about shielding her granddaughter from witnessing the dismembering should she awake. As a result, the mother lay down on a couch near the bathroom to keep watch. The Minnesota Supreme Court concluded that this evidence was *insufficient* to demonstrate complicity on the mother's part: "The evidence presented to the jury at best supports a finding that [she] passively acquiesced in her son's plan to kill his wife. . . . Her response that 'it would be the best for the kids' or 'it will be the best' was not . . . active encouragement or instigation. . . . However morally reprehensible it may be to fail to warn someone of their impending death, our statutes do not make such an omission a criminal offense."

F   A   Q

Q: Can the mens rea of accomplice liability be implied from a person's presence at a crime scene with other criminal actors?

A: No. The prosecution *cannot* convict an individual as an accessory simply by showing that he or she was simply present at the scene of the crime and therefore must have intended to be complicit. Mere presence is not enough to establish accessorial intent.

Can a defendant who is simply shown to know that a crime was being committed be held to have the mens rea necessary to establish accessorial intent? Or put another way, has an actor assisted a criminal act when he knows about it, but does nothing to prevent it from occurring? While some older decisions answer that question in the

---

[13]6 N.Y.2d 140, 556 N.E.2d 415, 556 N.Y.S.2d 976 (1990).
[14]313 N.W.2d 425 (Minn. 1981).

affirmative,[15] most recent decisions answer it in the negative, although some jurisdictions punish the separate and lesser offense of knowing facilitation.

In *People v. Lauria*,[16] for example, defendant Lauria ran a telephone answering
service and some of his customers were prostitutes, as Lauria knew, having availed
himself of such services. The question was whether Lauria, by facilitating this
criminal activity by taking phone messages, was complicit in the acts of prostitution.
The court answered that question in the negative, concluding that a defendant does
not incur accomplice liability simply because he knows that someone may be using
his services for criminal purposes.

But, the court added, there are some occasions in which complicity *can* be
inferred from knowledge. As the court explained:

> [W]e find that sometimes, but not always, the criminal intent of the supplier may be
> inferred from his knowledge of the unlawful use made of the product he supplies.
> Some consideration of characteristic patterns may be helpful.
>   1. Intent may be inferred from knowledge, when the purveyor of legal goods for illegal
> use has acquired a stake in the venture. . . . In the present case, no proof was offered of
> inflated charges for the telephone answering services furnished the codefendants.
>   2. Intent may be inferred from knowledge, when no legitimate use for the goods or
> services exists. . . . [T]here is nothing in the furnishing of telephone answering service
> which would necessarily imply assistance in the performance of illegal activities. Nor is
> any inference to be derived from the use of an answering service by women, either in any
> particular volume of calls, or outside normal working hours. . . .
>   3. Intent may be inferred from knowledge, when the volume of business with the
> buyer is grossly disproportionate to any legitimate demand, or when sales for illegal use
> amount to a high proportion of the seller's total business. In such cases an intent to
> participate in the illegal enterprise may be inferred from the quantity of the business
> done. [No] evidence of any unusual volume of business with prostitutes was presented
> by the prosecution against Lauria.

In a handful of mostly older cases, although an actor tries to provide assistance to
another person in the commission of a crime and therefore has the mens rea for
complicity, the would-be principal lacks the intent to commit the crime, and therefore neither—principal nor accomplice—is guilty of the offense. For example, in the
nineteenth-century case of *State v. Hayes*,[17] defendant Hayes agreed with Hill to
burglarize a store by opening a window and helping Hill slide through it. After he
entered that way, Hill handed Hayes stolen goods through the window, and both men
were captured within a matter of minutes. However, the facts showed that Hill had
participated only to trap Hayes, had alerted the store's owner, and was aware that the
police would be waiting for them. The court held that the jury should have been
instructed that Hayes could not aid and abet a principal who lacked the requisite
criminal intent when he performed the act.

Today, the *Hayes* decision is not good law in most jurisdictions. More commonly,
since the merger of accomplices and principals before the fact, each actor is judged
separately and it would not ordinarily matter to the culpability of an otherwise guilty
accessory that a principal may have lacked the proper mens rea. Indeed, the fact that
we assess culpability based on each individual's *own* acts and intent, explains the
result, even in some older cases, in situations involving the opposite factual scenario

---

[15]*See, e.g., Jindra v. United States*, 69 F.2d 429 (5th Cir. 1934).
[16]251 Cal. App. 2d 471, 59 Cal. Rptr. 628 (1967).
[17]105 Mo. 76, 16 S.W. 514 (1891).

as that described above, where the perpetrator of the crime has the necessary criminal *mens rea*, but the accomplice does not.

For example, in *Wilson v. People*,[18] Wilson and Pierce burglarized a drugstore with Pierce helping Wilson enter the store. While Wilson was inside, Pierce called the police and helped them track Wilson down. The Colorado Supreme Court held that Pierce had the right to have the jury determine whether he lacked the requisite mens rea to be convicted as an accomplice: "One who participates in a felony as a feigned accomplice, in order to entrap the other, is not criminally liable, and he need not take an officer of the law into his confidence to avoid an imputation of criminal intent."

Additionally, the separate issue arises: Can an individual be an accomplice to a crime predicated on recklessness or negligence? Some courts have said "no." In *People v. Marshall*,[19] for example, defendant Marshall loaned his car to a friend who he knew was intoxicated, and then went to bed for the evening. An hour later, while the defendant was sound asleep, the friend caused an accident resulting in a death. The Michigan Supreme Court ruled that Marshall was *not* guilty of involuntary manslaughter as an accomplice since the actual killing "was not counseled by him, accomplished by another acting jointly with him, nor did it occur in the attempted achievement of some common enterprise."

The Model Penal Code appears, in contrast, to permit accomplice liability in these circumstances. The MPC provides that: "When causing a particular result is an element of an offense, an accomplice in the conduct causing such result is an accomplice in the commission of that offense, if he acts with the kind of culpability, if any, with respect to that result that is sufficient for the commission of that offense."[20] In all likelihood, the defendant in *Marshall* had the kind of culpability required for a manslaughter (recklessness) or negligent homicide (negligence) conviction, and therefore could have been be convicted had the MPC approach been the test used in Michigan at the time.

(3) Act Requirement

In addition to proving that an accused acted with the necessary *mens rea*, a conviction for complicity also requires proof that the defendant actually aided, abetted, or encouraged commission of the offense. More specifically, to establish the actus reus of criminal complicity, the prosecution needs to prove beyond a reasonable doubt that the accused actively aided in the commission of the crime—for example, by supplying the means to commit the crime, such as the murder weapon or burglar's tools, or by providing verbal or physical encouragement or support for the perpetrator, or by providing other, more tangible assistance, such as helping to actually plan the crime.

The Model Penal Code provides that an individual is an accessory if, acting with the required mens rea, he commits any of three acts: "(i) solicits such other person to commit it, or (ii) aids or agrees or attempts to aid such other person in planning or committing it, or (iii) having a legal duty to prevent the commission of the offense, fails to make proper effort so to do."[21]

---

[18]103 Colo. 441, 87 P.2d 5 (1939).
[19]362 Mich. 170, 106 N.W.2d 842 (1961).
[20]Model Penal Code §2.06(4).
[21]Model Penal Code §2.06(3).

Significantly, the mere fact that a person was physically present at the scene of a crime does *not* in and of itself establish the existence of a criminal act. As the Texas Court of Appeals has cogently made the point, "[a] person who is merely present at the scene of the offense is not an accomplice; an affirmative act or omission is required."[22] In *Lane v. Texas*,[23] for example, defendant Lane was convicted of the crime of aggravated robbery of an elderly person. Although a key witness against Lane, Patricia, had gone to the crime scene along with the perpetrators, the Texas Court of Appeals held that she was nonetheless *not* an accomplice: "Patricia was present during the entire series of events that night and knew full well what the other three actors were doing. However, Patricia committed no affirmative act in furtherance of the crime. Further, her omission of not stopping the crime and not alerting anyone about the crime was not an omission that our laws have criminalized so that she would become an accomplice by omission."[24]

In some older cases, accomplice liability was established on a showing that a defendant simply encouraged the perpetrator of a crime. In the English case of *Wilcox v. Jeffrey*,[25] a famous American saxophonist was given permission to enter England on the condition that he not work. But he performed anyway at a night club and the court found that an English writer who reviewed the concert for a magazine *was* complicit in the saxophonist's criminal conduct because he paid to go to the concert to report on it, knowing that the saxophonist was performing illegally. Hence, the court concluded, he was "encouraging" the saxophonist's criminal activity.

Today, ordinarily, a greater showing than "mere encouragement" is required in order for the prosecution to establish an act of accessorial liability. Typically, courts look for acts of active assistance. As the California Court of Appeal has made the point, "[a]n aider and abettor is chargeable as a principal only to the extent he or she actually knows and shares the full extent of the perpetrator's specific criminal intent, and actively promotes, encourages, or assists

---

[22]*Lane v. Texas*, 991 S.W.2d 904 (Tex. Ct. App. 1999).
[23]991 S.W.2d 904 (Tex. Ct. App. 1999).
[24]*See also, e.g., Hawaii v. Soares*, 72 Haw. 278, 815 P.2d 428 (1991) (holding that defendants could not be convicted as accessories to an assault absent proof that they acted with the intent of promoting or facilitating the commission of the crime).
[25][1951] 1 All E.R. 464.

the perpetrator with the intent and purpose of advancing the perpetrator's successful commission of the target offense."[26]

Similarly, sometimes an actor is viewed by courts as having simply been helpful, as opposed to being an accomplice. In *State v. Gordon*,[27] for example, an undercover police officer told defendant that he was interested in buying hashish. Defendant told the officer that "Craig deals quite heavily in narcotics." Defendant gave the officer Craig's address, the officer then bought narcotics from Craig, and defendant was charged with criminal facilitation. The argument that defendant made in his defense in this case is called, in some jurisdictions, a "conduit defense." He argued that he was assisting the buyer (the undercover police officer) not the seller (Craig) and was therefore merely a "conduit" for the drugs, rather than an accomplice of the seller. The court in *Gordon* agreed, holding that defendant was not complicit on these bare facts. Other decisions are in accord.[28]

Moreover, an actor might be held criminally responsible as an accomplice even though there is some doubt about whether his assistance actually helped the perpetrator of the crime. For example, in the classic case of *State v. Tazwell*,[29] Tazwell and Kealey were convicted of the burglary of a barn with intent to steal, and Hall was charged as an accessory before the fact. The evidence showed that Hall provided Tarwell and Kealey with burglary tools before they went to the barn, but that the two found and used better tools when they arrived. The court held that Hall could nonetheless be found guilty of accomplice liability, adding that "[i]t would be strange, indeed, if one who had so far counseled, aided, and abetted a burglary as to provide and furnish implements to effect it, could escape because when the burglar reached the place of his crime he found more convenient tools, and did not actually use those furnished him for the purpose by his confederate."

Indeed, most courts hold that the prosecution need not prove that an accomplice's encouragement or assistance actually had a causal effect on the commission of the crime.

(4) Renunciation

An issue that sometimes arises is whether an accomplice can terminate or renounce her participation in a crime in such a way that she is no longer culpable. As a matter of policy, permitting such an effective renunciation makes some sense as we want to encourage accomplices to terminate any continuing role in criminal activity. The less crime we have, the better. On the other hand, there is a competing consideration: Simply put, what's done is done. Certainly a principal is not permitted to undo a criminal act she has already committed (other than an inchoate act, such as attempt or conspiracy), although her desistance might well serve to diminish the severity of the punishment she might ultimately receive for what she has already done. But what about accomplices?

In most jurisdictions, the rule is the same. An accomplice is no more able to terminate her commission of a crime *after* having committed it than a principal is.

---

[26]*People v. Hypolite*, 2005 WL 758440, *10 (Cal. App. 2 Dist. 2005).
[27]32 N.Y.2d 62, 295 N.E.2d 777, 343 N.Y.S.2d 103 (N.Y. App. 1973).
[28]*See, e.g., Commonwealth v. Flowers*, 479 Pa. 153, 387 A.2d 1268, 1272 (1978)("If [defendant] can be said to have assisted anyone, it was the buyer, not the seller . . . [and] an agent of the buyer cannot be convicted of the sale.").
[29]30 La. Ann. 884 (1878).

But, a minority of jurisdictions disagree, and do permit a successful renunciation by an accomplice if it occurs *before* the criminal act in which the accomplice is complicit has actually occurred and if the actor takes steps to keep that criminal act from occurring. The Model Penal Code, for example, specifically provides that an accomplice may effectively terminate her complicity provided that she acts "prior to the commission of the offense," and does one of two things: "(i) wholly deprives it of effectiveness in the commission of the offense; or (ii) gives timely warning to the law enforcement authorities or otherwise makes proper effort to prevent the commission of the offense."[30]

(5) Scope of Accomplice Responsibility

Since the merger of principal and accomplice before the fact, accomplices are held criminally responsible as if they actually committed the crime themselves. In other words, any individual accused of criminal activity—principal or accomplice—can be charged with the committed crime itself.[31] An accomplice need not be charged as an accomplice. Rather, a person who actively assists a murder may be charged as a murderer; a person who actively assists a rape may be charged as a rapist; a person who actively assists in a robbery may be charged as a robber.

However, in an appropriate case, there can be and often is some variance between the charges brought against or proved of the principal and the charges leveled against or proved of an accomplice. Suppose, for example, that A is an accomplice of B in the murder of C. In the jurisdiction in question, the crime of murder is divided into degrees with premeditation providing the principal basis for a finding of first-degree murder. If the accomplice acts with premeditation, but the principal acts in the heat of passion, it is conceivable that the accomplice could be convicted of first-degree murder, while the principal could be convicted only of voluntary manslaughter. Correspondingly, if the principal acted with premeditation, but the accomplice did not and was unaware of the principal's premeditation, the accomplice would not be convicted of first-degree murder even if the principal is convicted of that crime.

What happens when a principal commits crimes other than those that an accomplice actually knew about or foresaw? Some cases have held that an accomplice is criminally responsible for the "natural and probable consequences" of his acts.[32] In such a jurisdiction, although an accomplice may have intended to assist only in the commission of one crime, an armed robbery perhaps, he might nonetheless be found guilty of committing other offenses as well. For example, in jurisdictions applying the felony-murder doctrine, one who is complicit in the crime of armed robbery may be found guilty of murder when the principal kills someone, however unforeseeably, during the course of the robbery.[33] However, the Model Penal Code rejects this approach, as do a number of jurisdictions that hold that an accomplice is only responsible for the crimes that he or she actually intends to aid and abet.

There are some other limits to accomplice liability recognized in various jurisdictions. For example, the Model Penal Code provides that, unless "otherwise provided by the Code or by the law defining the offense, a person is not an accomplice in an offense committed by another person if: (a) he is a victim of that offense;

[30]Model Penal Code §2.06(6).
[31]*See, e.g.,* Model Penal Code §2.06.
[32]*See, e.g., People v. Prettyman,* 14 Cal. 4th 248, 58 Cal. Rptr. 2d 827, 926 P.2d 1013 (1996).
[33]*See, e.g., State v. Carothers,* 84 Wash. 2d 256, 525 P.2d 731 (1974).

or (b) the offense is so defined that his conduct is inevitably incident to its commission"; or he terminates his commission in the crime as earlier provided.[34]

B. Vicarious Liability

Sometimes, a defendant may be found guilty of criminal conduct as a result of the criminal actions of other persons even though the defendant was not involved personally in the criminal conduct. In such instances, culpability is imposed under **vicarious liability** principles. For example, in many jurisdictions, the owner of a bar is held to be vicariously responsible under the criminal law for the acts of his bartender in serving alcohol to underage patrons.

Commonly, principles of vicarious responsibility are employed against corporations and corporate agents. There are, however, some significant limitations on the scope of such vicarious culpability.

(1) Corporate Culpability

In the early common law, English courts refused to impose criminal sanctions on corporations. Although criminal liability could be imposed on the individual corporate officers or employees who participated in criminal conduct, the corporate entity itself was regarded as exempt, largely due to the fact that the corporation was not a person and, therefore, did not have a mind with which to form a criminal mens rea. Nor did a corporation have body or life that could be imprisoned or forfeited. Today, in contrast, it is widely recognized that corporations *can* be held vicariously responsible for the actions of their agents or employees in appropriate cases, assuming the existence of an appropriate statute saying as much.[35] The more pertinent question to be answered is when, and under what circumstances, such criminal responsibility can be (and is) imposed.

Most often, when corporations are held criminally responsible for the commission of crimes, it is for so-called public welfare or regulatory offenses. Most of these offenses are based not only on vicarious liability but on strict liability as well—that is, no mens rea is required. What is more, in the proper circumstances, corporations can be—and have been—prosecuted for the commission of much more serious crimes, even homicide. However, under a common statutory formulation proposed by the MPC, a corporation can only be convicted of a serious criminal offense if it was "authorized, requested, commanded, performed or recklessly tolerated by the board of directors or by a high managerial agent acting in behalf of the corporation within the scope of his office or employment."[36]

The imposition of criminal responsibility on corporations is justified by a variety of considerations. First, it is hoped that if corporations are held criminally responsible for the acts of their officers, directors, or agents, they will be more inclined to supervise those individuals and steer them away from criminal activities.[37] It has also been argued that, to the extent that corporate shareholders benefit from corporate criminality, they should likewise be required to bear the legal consequences.[38]

---

[34]Model Penal Code §2.06(6).
[35]*See, e.g., New York Central & Hudson R.R. v. United States*, 212 U.S. 481 (1909).
[36]Model Penal Code §2.07(4)(C).
[37]Model Penal Code §2.07, Comment.
[38]*Id.*

A MORE SOPHISTICATED TAKE ON CORPORATIONS AND CRIME

Consider the following:

Enron and Arthur Andersen, Kidder Peabody, Salomon Brothers, Ford and its Pinto: each decade brings more examples of businesses gone bad, violating the law and the public trust. Massive fraud, outrageous self-dealing, devious accounting, and other wrongdoing by elite business leaders attract attention and fuel quick reform. [Business] firms' noncompliance with various regulatory programs appears to be pervasive.

[Two] visions of the firm dominate the compliance literature. The first is the firm as a rational profit-maximizer, obeying the law only when it is in the firm's best economic interest to do so. Thus, violations occur when the perceived benefits of noncompliance exceed the anticipated cost of sanctions. This view of the firm is consistent with deterrence theory, which regulators have historically relied upon in developing their enforcement programs.

[The] second vision of the firm is that of law-abiding actor, struggling in good faith to comply with increasingly complicated and contradictory laws and regulations. In this view[,] the act of compliance is not driven by the threat of legal sanctions. Instead, compliance flows from the firm's drive to obey the law, sometimes called the "compliance norm." The compliance norm is fueled by the belief that legitimate regulation—regulation that is developed and implemented fairly—ought to be followed. [Supporters] of the [second] approach . . . support substantial reforms of the traditional enforcement approach including simplified regulations, expanded outreach and education efforts, and increased use of cooperative compliance assistance methods that appeal to the regulated community's law abiding nature.

Timothy F. Malloy, *Regulation, Compliance and the Firm,* 76 Temp. L. Rev. 451, 451-455 (2003).

The decision of the South Dakota Supreme Court in *South Dakota v. Hy Vee Food Stores, Inc.*[39] illustrates aptly the modern approach to corporate criminality. In *Hy Vee Food Stores, Inc.*, a corporation was convicted of selling alcohol to a minor. The company challenged the conviction, contending that its employees—who were not charged—committed the wrongful acts, not the corporation itself, and that the corporation should not be subject to vicarious criminal liability for its employees' acts. Although the court recognized that the law "disfavors statutes which impose criminal liability without fault, much less those enactments which impose such liability vicariously," it concluded nonetheless that "criminal liability for certain offenses may be imputed to corporate defendants for the unlawful acts of its employees, provided that the conduct is within the scope of the employee's authority whether actual or apparent."

The Model Penal Code provides for the imposition of criminal sanctions on corporations only when certain strict requirements are met:

(a) the offense is a violation or the offense is defined by a statute other than the Code in which a legislative purpose to impose liability on corporations plainly appears and the conduct is performed by an agent of the corporation acting in behalf of the corporation within the scope of his office or employment, except that if the law defining the offense designates the agents for whose conduct the corporation is accountable or the circumstances under which it is accountable, such provisions shall apply; or

[39]533 N.W.2d 147 (S.D. 1995).

(b) the offense consists of an omission to discharge a specific duty of affirmative performance imposed on corporations by law; or

(c) the commission of the offense was authorized, requested, commanded, performed or recklessly tolerated by the board of directors or by a high managerial agent acting in behalf of the corporation within the scope of his office or employment.[40]

As is apparent from the text set out above, §2.07(1)(a) applies to regulatory offenses, while §2.07(1)(c) applies to criminal offenses set out in the MPC itself.

The MPC further provides that, when "absolute liability is imposed for the commission of an offense, a legislative purpose to impose liability on a corporation shall be assumed, unless the contrary plainly appears."[41] In addition, the Model Penal Code provides similar rules for unincorporated associations.[42] However, the MPC also establishes a defense for corporate entities and unincorporated associations that exercise due diligence to prevent the commission of crimes.[43]

(2) Criminal Responsibility of Corporate Officers and Agents

Criminal sanctions can also be imposed on corporate directors, officers, and agents in appropriate situations. In some instances, when a corporate employee is, for example, the individual who actually engages personally in criminal conduct, a criminal prosecution might result strictly on the basis of the individual's own conduct. Suppose, for example, that a corporate president signs off on a new automobile even though he is made fully aware that its gasoline tank may explode in a rear-impact collision. If the president is deemed to have acted recklessly in those circumstances, creating a substantial and unjustifiable risk of death to passengers in the vehicle, he might well be guilty of manslaughter—strictly on the basis of his own actions—if the vehicle thereafter explodes and kills someone.

As a general rule, corporate officials are not usually held vicariously liable for the criminal acts of their subordinates. For example, if a subordinate drives a company vehicle recklessly on a highway and causes the death of another motorist, the corporate president will not ordinarily be held criminally responsible for that death. Large companies have too many employees to hold corporate officers liable for independent criminal acts committed by individual employees. On the other hand, if a corporate officer is implicated in the corporate criminality in some more direct way, for instance if he is present in the car at the time of the reckless

[40]Model Penal Code §2.07(1).
[41]Model Penal Code §2.07(2).
[42]Model Penal Code §2.07(3):

An unincorporated association may be convicted of the commission of an offense if:
(a) the offense is defined by a statute other than the Code that expressly provides for the liability of such an association and the conduct is performed by an agent of the association acting in behalf of the association within the scope of his office or employment, except that if the law defining the offense designates the agents for whose conduct the association is accountable or the circumstances under which it is accountable, such provisions shall apply; or
(b) the offense consists of an omission to discharge a specific duty of affirmative performance imposed on associations by law.

[43]Model Penal Code §2.07(5):

In any prosecution of a corporation or an unincorporated association for the commission of an offense included within the terms of Subsection (1)(a) or Subsection (3)(a) of this Section, other than an offense for which absolute liability has been imposed, it shall be a defense if the defendant proves by a preponderance of evidence that the high managerial agent having supervisory responsibility over the subject matter of the offense employed due diligence to prevent its commission. This paragraph shall not apply if it is plainly inconsistent with the legislative purpose in defining the particular offense.

driving and orders his subordinate to drive in excess of the speed limits, he may well bear criminal responsibility.

The Supreme Court, in two important decisions, has affirmed the proposition that, in some instances, assuming a proper statutory basis, corporate officials may be held criminally responsible for some of the actions of their subordinates. The first case, *United States v. Dotterweich*,[44] involved charges that defendants shipped misbranded and adulterated drugs. The Court upheld a corporation's president's vicarious conviction for the acts of the corporation (through its employees) on the ground that he had a "responsible relation" to the criminal acts in question.

Dotterweich was followed, reaffirmed, and further refined by the Court in *United States v. Park*.[45] In *Park*, a retail food chain, Acme, and its CEO, Park, were charged with violations of the Federal Food, Drug, and Cosmetic Act. Specifically, it was alleged that Acme had received food shipped in interstate commerce that, while it was being held in Acme's Baltimore warehouse, was contaminated by rodents. Although the company pleaded guilty, Park pleaded not guilty. For his part, Park testified that he "functioned by delegating 'normal operating duties,' including sanitation, to subordinates," and that he was involved with "the big, broad, principles of the operation of the company." Even though Park admitted that he was ultimately responsible for the entire operation of the company, he nonetheless moved to dismiss the charges against him on the ground that he was not *personally* responsible for the violations at issue.

Relying on *Dotterweich*, the Supreme Court affirmed Park's conviction, concluding that "the only way in which a corporation can act is through the individuals who act on its behalf." As a result, the Court held further that criminal responsibility could be imposed upon "all who [have] a responsible share in the furtherance of the transaction which the statute outlaws." Moreover, criminal responsibility could lawfully be extended, the Court continued, "not only to those corporate agents who themselves committed the criminal act, but also to those who by virtue of their managerial positions or other similar relation to the actor could be deemed responsible for its commission."

As previously noted, the primary policy rationale for enacting such vicarious liability statutes is deterrence: We want to give the *individuals* who have the actual power to prevent criminal conduct from occurring an incentive to make sure that the conduct does not in fact occur. As a result, in cases such as *Park*, courts have ratified the imposition of vicarious—and, most often, strict—liability on anyone who possesses the actual power and control sufficient to keep the criminal conduct in question from taking place. In some respects, punishing high-level corporate officials, such as Park, makes more sense than punishing low-level officials such as janitors. Punishing the janitor in the Acme warehouses because of the presence of rodents is probably less likely to lead to their eradication than punishing those who have more authority over the situation, the higher-ups in the corporate hierarchy.

Significantly, however, the *Park* Court did recognize the unfairness of holding a corporate official criminally responsible vicariously in a situation where he or she lacked the actual power to correct or eliminate the criminal conduct at issue. As a result, the Court concluded that a defendant who is accused of criminal conduct

---

[44]320 U.S. 277 (1943). See also discussion of *Dotterweich* in Chapter 3.
[45]421 U.S. 658 (1975).

based on a vicarious relationship with someone else may defend on the grounds that he or she was powerless to prevent or correct the conduct at issue.

The dissenters in *Park* likened this powerlessness defense to a common law negligence notion—that is, a corporate officer can be held vicariously liable if she had a duty to prevent the criminal conduct and it can be shown that it was caused by her negligent failure to meet the standard of care appropriate to that duty.

Q: Does this mean that the vicarious responsibility of corporate officers for criminal acts of their subordinates is essentially based on negligence?

A: No. While the *Park* decision demonstrates the limited constitutional constraints on the extent of vicarious liability of corporate officers, a number of jurisdictions have, by statute, legislated even higher mens rea requirements that need to be met before criminal responsibility attaches. For example, a Pennsylvania statute imposes a requirement of recklessness as a basis for vicarious corporate criminal responsibility.[46]

The Model Penal Code contains several provisions relating expressly to the criminal responsibility of corporate officers and employees. One section provides for the direct responsibility of corporate supervisors for the acts of employees who engage in criminal conduct: "A person is legally accountable for any conduct he performs or causes to be performed in the name of the corporation or an unincorporated association or in its behalf to the same extent as if it were performed in his own name or behalf."[47] This section provides that an employee who commits a criminal act while in corporate employ is nonetheless individually responsible for his or her actions, whether or not his or her corporate employer bears any fault or responsibility in the matter.

Another Model Penal Code provision deals with vicarious liability generally. It provides that: "Whenever a duty to act is imposed by law upon a corporation or an unincorporated association, any agent of the corporation or association having primary responsibility for the discharge of the duty is legally accountable for a reckless omission to perform the required act to the same extent as if the duty were imposed by law directly upon himself."[48] In other words, if a corporate official has the "primary responsibility" for making sure that food is kept in healthy conditions—away from rats, for example—then that official can be held criminally responsible for a reckless failure to discharge his duty.

Finally, another Model Penal Code simply states that "[w]hen a person is convicted of an offense by reason of his legal accountability for the conduct of a

---

[46]*See* 18 Pa. Cons. Stat. §307(e)(2) ("Whenever a duty to act is imposed by law upon a corporation or an unincorporated association, any agent of the corporation or association having primary responsibility for the discharge of the duty is legally accountable for a reckless omission to perform the required act to the same extent as if the duty were imposed by law directly upon himself.").
[47]Model Penal Code §2.07(6)(a).
[48]Model Penal Code §2.07(6)(b).

corporation or an unincorporated association, he is subject to the sentence authorized by law when a natural person is convicted of an offense of the grade and the degree involved."[49]

SUMMARY

■ Except for accessories after the fact, the common law distinctions between principals and accessories have been largely abolished.

■ Since accessories before the fact are now merged with principals in most jurisdictions, their culpability no longer turns on what happens to any principal.

■ The mens rea of accomplice liability has two components: (1) the intent to assist a principal actor in committing a crime and (2) the intent that the principal actually commit that crime.

■ Mere presence at the scene of a crime is not enough to establish an accessorial act or intent.

■ A conviction for complicity requires proof that the defendant actually aided, abetted, or encouraged commission of the offense, although ordinarily, a greater showing than mere encouragement is required and courts look for acts of active assistance.

■ Some statutes create vicarious liability, criminalizing conduct based on the criminal actions of another person even though the defendant was not involved personally.

■ The Supreme Court has held that a corporate official may not be held criminally responsible vicariously for conduct he or she lacked the actual power to correct or eliminate.

CONNECTIONS

Relationship to Conspiracy

The acts of assistance that can make a person responsible for a crime as an accomplice are often closely connected to the acts of agreement that can make one culpable criminally as a co-conspirator. See Chapter 7. The important difference is that the crime that is the object of the conspiracy does not need to actually occur in order to find a person guilty of conspiracy; it is the unlawful agreement itself that is punished.

---

[49]Model Penal Code §2.07(6)(c).

Relationship to Mens Rea

Many public welfare offenses are not only strict liability offenses (see Chapter 3) but vicarious liability offenses as well.

Relationship to Theft Offenses

Like the concepts of principals and accomplices at the common law that have largely merged in modern crimes codes, the various common law theft offenses have been consolidated into a single, general theft offense in most modern crimes codes (see Chapter 11).

Attempt

6

Attempt is an "inchoate" criminal offense. That is to say that it is a crime where the actor has as his or her ultimate objective another (completed or "choate") criminal offense, but somehow or other fails to achieve that particular criminal end. The most common inchoate offenses punished in most jurisdictions are the crimes of attempt, conspiracy, and solicitation. The act element of attempt has been expanded dramatically in the past few decades, increasing significantly the number of otherwise innocent acts that can now be prosecuted as attempts.

OVERVIEW

A. ACTUS REUS

　1. Traditional Definitions
　2. Model Penal Code Test
　3. Other Attempt-Related Crimes

B. MENS REA

C. ABANDONMENT

D. IMPOSSIBILITY

The crime of attempt is one of three common **inchoate offenses**—attempt, conspiracy, or solicitation—crimes committed while an actor is trying to complete another criminal objective, sometimes called the choate offense.[1] Inchoate offenses are also occasionally referred to as "anticipatory," "incipient," "incomplete," or "preliminary" crimes. The actus reus of attempt is variously defined in different jurisdictions, but usually focuses either on how close the actor has come to completing the choate criminal offense (proximity tests) or how far he or she has already gone toward completion of that offense (substantial step test). The mens rea of attempt is the intent to commit the specific crime that is the actor's criminal object.

Moreover, an attempted crime is a crime that ends in a failure to commit the intended offense. Hence, attempt is not only a crime in and of itself, but it is also a lesser included offense of that intended choate offense, if the latter actually takes place.

The attempt itself must be complete before it is deemed to be criminal. We do not punish individuals criminally, for example, merely for thinking "evil" thoughts—or even for fantasizing about committing crimes.[2] However, when a defendant goes beyond thinking and fantasizing and actually *tries* to commit a criminal act—for example, he makes an effort to kill someone by shooting at them—even if he doesn't succeed, the State has a legitimate interest in punishing and deterring such dangerous, anti-social conduct. Indeed, those individuals who engage in *attempts* to commit criminal acts are arguably every bit as dangerous to us as those individuals who actually succeed. Hence, some commentators argue further, it would be both unjust and irrational to punish only the latter and ignore the former simply because of the mere fortuity of failure.

In most jurisdictions today, attempt is punished pursuant to a "general attempt statute," a criminal statute that makes it an independent criminal offense to attempt to commit *any* another crime. In other jurisdictions, most prominently in our federal criminal law, there is no general attempt statute. Attempt only exists as a crime in such a jurisdiction when it is specifically included in the definition of another specific (choate) criminal offense.

A. Actus Reus

One of the most difficult tasks in dealing with the crime of attempt is the determination of precisely when a defendant's conduct has proceeded just far enough to be so dangerous to us as to constitute the actus reus of attempt. Different jurisdictions have defined this actus reus quite differently. Notably, however, every jurisdiction agrees that to satisfy the actus reus of attempt, an actor has to commit some act that goes beyond **mere preparation**.

(1) Traditional Definitions

Traditionally, most courts faced with the issue of deciding how to gauge the actus reus of attempt have focused on the question of how close the defendant came to actually committing the crime that was his or her criminal object. These sorts of tests

---

[1] See discussion of conspiracy in Chapter 7. Solicitation is the crime of commanding, encouraging, or requesting another person to commit a crime with the intent that the person being solicited actually commit that crime.

[2] See discussion in Chapter 2.

are commonly called **proximity tests** because they attempt to gauge in different ways the proximity of the actor's conduct to the final intended (choate) criminal objective.

The most extreme of these proximity tests was the last proximate act test, which required that an actor be shown to have completed the last possible act before completion of the substantive crime intended before he could be convicted of an attempt to commit that crime.[3] For example, a would-be murderer would have committed the last proximate act of the crime of attempted murder when he shot at his intended victim, but not before. However, an actor's dangerous and anti-social behavior is clear long before that point. Accordingly, very few courts ever utilized such a limiting and crabbed definition of the actus reus of attempt. We do not wait until an assassin has actually shot and missed before finding that an attempted murder has taken place.

Most courts traditionally used a less restrictive variation of the proximity test for the actus reus of attempt while continuing to focus on the question of how close the defendant actually came to committing the ultimate act. One of the best known of these old American cases was *Commonwealth v. Peaslee*,[4] an opinion of the Massachusetts Supreme Judicial Court authored by Oliver Wendell Holmes, later a celebrated Justice of the United States Supreme Court.

In *Peaslee*, defendant Peaslee was charged with attempting to burn a building with intent to injure the insurers. The evidence revealed that he had arranged flammable items in the building in such a way that they were ready to be lighted, and when they were, would have burned the building. Peaslee drove toward the building, but changed his mind about committing the crime when he was about a quarter of a mile away. The question was whether his acts came close enough to the accomplishment of the choate offense to be punishable as an attempt. The court concluded that, since Peaslee had only taken the "first steps" toward the commission of a criminal act, there was always the chance "that the would-be criminal may change his mind."

Justice Holmes added that "[i]f the preparation comes very near to the accomplishment of the act, the intent to complete it renders the crime so probable that the act will be a [crime. The] degree of proximity held sufficient may vary with circumstances, including, among other things, the apprehension which the particular crime is calculated to excite." As a result, the court concluded, there was no attempt in this case because the crime was not close enough to completion.

Another classic example of the proximity approach was the Vermont Supreme Court's 1906 decision in *State v. Hurley*.[5] In *Hurley*, defendant prisoner convinced a former inmate to throw hacksaws to him through a prison window. A guard saw this and ordered defendant to drop the saws, which he did. The court subsequently overturned defendant's conviction for attempted escape, applying a proximity test under which the "preparation must be such as would be likely to end, if not extraneously interrupted, in the consummation of the crime intended." The court ruled that this conduct did not cross that line: "It is true that [Hurley] procured [the hacksaws] with the design of breaking jail. But he had not put that design into execution, and might never have done so."

Similarly and finally, in another classic case, *People v. Rizzo*,[6] defendant Rizzo and three others planned to rob Rao of a payroll that he was to carry from a bank to

---

[3]*See, e.g., Regina v. Eagleton*, 169 Eng. Rep. 826 (Crim. App. 1855).
[4]177 Mass. 267, 59 N.E. 55 (1901).
[5]79 Vt. 28, 64 A. 78 (1906).
[6]246 N.Y. 334, 158 N.E. 888 (1927).

his employer. Rizzo and his pals, two of whom were armed, set out in their car searching for Rao. They went to the bank and to various buildings owned by Rao's employer. Their conduct aroused the suspicions of a police officer who stopped and arrested them. At the time of their arrest for attempted robbery, they had not even found Rao. Although the court found that defendant clearly intended to commit the crime, it struggled to figure out whether defendant's conduct went beyond mere preparation. After observing that acts of preparation are too remote to constitute the crime of attempt, the New York Court of Appeals drew a distinction between acts that "are remote and those which are proximate and near to the consummation." In order to be convicted of attempt, the court held, defendant's "acts must come or advance very near to the accomplishment of the intended crime." The court concluded that Rizzo and his friends had not come near enough: "[T]hese defendants were not guilty of an attempt to commit robbery in the first degree when they had not found or reached the presence of the person they intended to rob."

Proximity tests are not necessarily outdated. Some more recent decisions in some jurisdictions (a minority today) continue to use one variant or another of these tests to assess when an individual accused of an attempt crime has satisfied the actus reus by going beyond mere preparation.

In *People v. Mahboubian*,[7] for example, the New York Court of Appeals applied what it called a "dangerously close" proximity test. In *Mahboubian*, defendant insured his collection of antiquities for $18.5 million. He then arranged, along with a co-defendant, to have two men steal them. The men tried to commit the theft, but were caught. Mahboubian was charged with attempted grand larceny. The court held that that crime was committed despite the fact that Mahboubian never submitted a false claim to his insurer: "Where the boundary line between preparation and attempt should be placed differs with different crimes. Here, it is significant that defendants' conduct went far beyond mere discussion of a crime and beyond agreement to commit a crime, and even beyond arming themselves in preparation for a crime. Defendants hired professional burglars, provided them with tools, and caused them to break into a warehouse and steal property in the dead of night. . . . Defendants' conduct had plainly 'pass[ed] that point where most men, holding such an intention as defendant holds, would think better of their conduct and desist.' " As a result,

Sidebar

CLOSING IN ON PROXIMITY

There are (were) a number of different types of proximity tests:

(1) The *physical proximity doctrine* under which defendant must have committed an overt act that was proximate to the completed crime, or directly tending toward the completion of the crime, or amounting to the commencement of the consummation.

(2) The *dangerous proximity doctrine* under which the court considers the gravity and probability of the offense, and the nearness of the act to the crime.

(3) The *indispensable element test* (similar to the proximity tests) which emphasizes whether an indispensable aspect of the criminal endeavor remains over which the actor has not yet acquired control.

(4) The *probable desistance test* which focuses on whether, in the ordinary and natural course of events, without interruption from an outside source, defendant's conduct will result in the crime intended.

(5) The *abnormal step approach* under which the focus is on whether defendant's conduct has gone beyond the point where the normal citizen would think better of his conduct and desist.

(6) The *res ipsa loquitur or unequivocality test* under which the defendant's conduct manifests an intent to commit a crime.

United States v. Mandujano, 499 F.2d 370, 376 (5th Cir. 1974) (emphasis added).

---

[7]74 N.Y.2d 174, 543 N.E.2d 34, 544 N.Y.S.2d 769 (1989).

defendant was deemed to be dangerously close to the completed crime, resulting in the commission of an attempt.

Notably, the various proximity tests still in use in some states produce different results on the key question of just how close an actor has to come to completing her criminal objective in order to be deemed guilty of an attempt. The answer to this question depends, first, on which proximity test the jurisdiction uses. And it depends, second, on the specific facts involved. In any case, the actor must have done enough to have gone well beyond mere preparatory acts.

(2) Model Penal Code Test

The Model Penal Code rejected all of these traditional proximity tests in favor of a **substantial step test**. Using this newer test, the actus reus of attempt is made out where the actor has taken a "substantial step in a course of conduct planned to culminate in his commission of the crime."[8] The goal of this Code test was to criminalize attempts at an earlier point than the proximity tests did, well *before* a would-be criminal actually got dangerously close to committing the crime in question. Most jurisdictions today follow this substantial step approach.

While this test is focused on action that often would occur before an actor's conduct was proximate to the completion of the intended criminal act, nonetheless, as the Model Penal Code has provided further, "[c]onduct shall not be held to constitute a substantial step . . . unless it is strongly corroborative of the actor's criminal purpose."[9]

criminal idea → mere preparation → substantial step → proximity

The MPC has also helpfully provided that

[w]ithout negativing the sufficiency of other conduct, the following, if strongly corroborative of the actor's criminal purpose, shall not be held insufficient as a matter of law:

(a) lying in wait, searching for or following the contemplated victim of the crime;

(b) enticing or seeking to entice the contemplated victim of the crime to go to the place contemplated for its commission;

(c) reconnoitering the place contemplated for the commission of the crime;

(d) unlawful entry of a structure, vehicle or enclosure in which it is contemplated that the crime will be committed;

(e) possession of materials to be employed in the commission of the crime, that are specially designed for such unlawful use or that can serve no lawful purpose of the actor under the circumstances;

(f) possession, collection or fabrication of materials to be employed in the commission of the crime, at or near the place contemplated for its commission, if such possession, collection or fabrication serves no lawful purpose of the actor under the circumstances;

(g) soliciting an innocent agent to engage in conduct constituting an element of the crime.[10]

---

[8]Model Penal Code §5.01.
[9]Model Penal Code §5.01(2).
[10]*See id.*

F   A   Q

Q: Does the substantial step test eliminate the distinction between attempt and mere preparation?

A: No. Under a proximity or the substantial step test, demonstrating mere preparation on an accused person's part is still not enough to establish the actus reus of attempt. But an actor often will take a substantial step, after mere preparation, before he or she comes close enough to committing the intended crime under a proximity test.

The drafters of the MPC noted that the substantial step test is substantially different from the traditional proximity tests that it replaced in three significant ways:[11]

First, the substantial step test shifts the emphasis from what remains to be done—the chief concern of the proximity tests—to what the actor has already done. This means that an attempt can be committed even if further steps need to be taken before the intended crime could be completed. Accordingly, actions that do not go far enough to establish an attempt under a proximity test may well suffice to establish attempt under a substantial step test.

Second, under the substantial step test, a court does not need to find that the actor would probably have desisted prior to completing the crime in order to establish an attempt.

Third, the requirement of proving a substantial step will usually prove less of a hurdle for the prosecution than other proximity tests that require that the actor's conduct must itself manifest the criminal purpose. Firmness of criminal purpose is intended to be shown by requiring the substantial step itself.

DIFFERENCE IN FOCUS

Proximity Tests:
How close did the person come toward committing
a crime?
Substantial Step Test:
How far did the person go toward committing a crime?

The draftsmen concluded further that, in addition to assuring firmness of criminal design, the requirement of a substantial step precludes attempt liability, with its accompanying harsh penalties, for relatively remote preparatory acts. At the same time, by not requiring a "last proximate act" or one of the other proximity tests, it permits the apprehension of dangerous persons at an earlier stage.

---

[11]Model Penal Code §5.01, Comment at 47 (Tent. Draft No. 10, 1960).

An excellent example of how the substantial step approach works in actual practice can be found in the Second Circuit's decision in *United States v. Jackson.*[12] In *Jackson*, defendants, who planned to rob a bank, went to the bank with a suitcase, a sawed-off shotgun, shells, masks, and handcuffs. But, demonstrating the truthfulness of the old adage, "the early bird gets the worm," the would-be robbers arrived after the bank was closed and decided to postpone the robbery to another time.

The police learned about the postponed robbery plan and staked out the bank. FBI agents observed defendants' car with a cardboard license plate on the rear, moving past the bank. The car circled the block and came to a stop on the side of the bank. When defendants spotted the FBI agents, they drove away. They were subsequently arrested and found in possession of sawed-off shotguns, a revolver, a pair of handcuffs, and masks. In concluding that defendants had committed the crime of *attempted* robbery, the *Jackson* court found that they had engaged in two separate and distinct types of acts, each of which qualified as a substantial step toward commission of the crime: They reconnoitered the place contemplated for the commission of the crime, and they possessed paraphernalia to be employed in the commission of the crime.

Another example of the application of the substantial step test can be found in the Illinois Supreme Court's decision in *People v. Terrell.*[13] The police were informed that two armed men were hiding behind a service station. An officer investigated and saw defendant crouched in the weeds in an empty lot near the station. Defendant then jumped up, threw away a gun, climbed a fence, and ran away holding a black nylon stocking with a knot in the end. Although defendant claimed he went to the station to buy cigarettes, he had no money on him. The court held that defendant's intent to rob was clearly established and that, given the facts just recited, he had taken a substantial step toward the commission of the robbery.

Some jurisdictions use the substantial step test but apply it fairly narrowly. For example, in *State v. Molasky*,[14] defendant, a prison inmate, solicited another inmate

---

[12]560 F.2d 112 (2d Cir. 1977).
[13]99 Ill. 2d 427, 459 N.E.2d 1337, 77 Ill. Dec. 88 (1984).
[14]765 S.W.2d 597 (Mo., en banc, 1989).

to help him murder three people. The other inmate, who turned out to be an under-cover agent, claimed that he could arrange for "Joe" to do the killings for $5,000. Defendant agreed to the price, and stipulated the time when the killings could be done, how he wanted the bodies disposed of, and stated that nothing was to be done in front of his son. The Missouri Supreme Court held that defendant could not be convicted of attempted murder on these facts because he had not taken a substantial step toward commission of the crime. The court concluded that his "solicitation was not accompanied by any other corroborative action. True, there was talk about the killings, [but defendant] had made no concrete arrangements for payment, no money changed hands, and Holt never received a picture or similar identification of the victims. Testimony also showed conversations of this type are an everyday event in prison, discussed freely. [A] substantial step is evidenced by actions, indicative of purpose, not mere conversation standing alone."

The Illinois Supreme Court also took a restrictive view of the application of the substantial step test in *People v. Smith*.[15] In *Smith*, defendant directed a cab driver to take him to Genesee Street to a jewelry store. The driver pointed out a jewelry store, but defendant told him that it was "not the one." The driver then noticed a police car and asked defendant if they should ask for directions. Defendant declined and quickly left the taxi. The suspicious driver notified the police, who apprehended defendant. He then admitted that he intended to rob another jewelry store on Gen-esee Street. The court concluded that, on these facts, defendant had *not* committed an attempt even though he had committed a number of acts that the MPC lists as "substantial steps" because, the court held, they were not "strongly corroborative of the actor's criminal purpose." The court found no corroboration because the store was never identified, suggesting that there was no "contemplated victim of the crime." In addition, it was difficult to argue that defendant was "reconnoitering the place" since the store was not identified by name, location, or physical description.

(3) Other Attempt-Related Crimes

In addition to the crime of attempt, many crimes codes also prohibit related crimes—e.g., crimes involving possession of burglar's tools or other items that might be used in the commission of a crime. For example, in *Moore v. State*,[16] defendant was con-victed of such an offense when he was found to be carrying a "screwdriver-like utensil" that he had used to make pry marks on the front door of a residence.

B. Mens Rea

The mens rea of the crime of attempt is the intent to commit the specific crime that is the actor's criminal objective. If a person is charged with the crime of attempted rape, for example, the prosecution must show that the accused's intention was in fact to rape his victim, not simply to assault or otherwise harm her.

[15]148 Ill. 2d 454, 593 N.E.2d 533, 170 Ill. Dec. 644 (1992).
[16]197 Ga. App. 9, 397 S.E.2d 477 (1990).

F A Q

Q: Can someone be convicted of the crime of attempt *generally*?

A: No. There is no crime of just plain attempt. It must be attempt *to do a specific thing*—for example, attempted burglary, attempted robbery, attempted murder. And the mens rea that must be established, similarly, must be the intent to commit that specific crime that is the object of the attempt.

In *People v. Miller*,[17] for example, defendant threatened to kill Jeans, who was annoying his wife, and went to a field where Jeans was working. Carrying a rifle, defendant walked directly toward Jeans, who was 250 yards away. When defendant was 100 yards away, he stopped to load his rifle, but he did not take aim. Jeans then saw the defendant and fled. The California Supreme Court reversed defendant's conviction for attempted murder, holding that defendant's intent was ambiguous because he might have entered the field in an attempt to kill Jeans, or he might have been there simply to demand Jeans's arrest. The court explained: "The wrong-doer must specifically contemplate taking life; and though his act is such as, were it successful, would be murder, if in truth he does not mean to kill, he does not become guilty of attempt to commit murder."

The Model Penal Code defines the crime of attempt as a crime ordinarily requiring proof of the mens rea of "purposely." If, however, causing a particular *result* is an element of the intended crime, then the actor's mere belief that his or her actions will cause that result is sufficient to establish the mens rea.

More specifically, the MPC provides that a

> person is guilty of an attempt to commit a crime if, acting with the kind of culpability otherwise required for the commission of the crime, he:
> (a) *purposely* engages in conduct that would constitute the crime if the attendant circumstances were as he believes them to be; or
> (b) when causing a particular result is an element of the crime, does or omits to do anything *with the purpose* of causing or with the belief that it will cause such result without further conduct on his part; or
> (c) *purposely* does or omits to do anything that, under the circumstances as he believes them to be, is an act or omission constituting a substantial step in a course of conduct planned to culminate in his commission of the crime.[18]

Proof problems relating to mens rea are inevitable in attempt cases. Sometimes the prosecution will have clear and direct evidence of the defendant's intent to commit a specific crime. For example, if defendant pulls a revolver, points it at his intended victim's head, and screams "Die, you worthless scum," one might readily conclude that defendant had the intent or purpose to kill and that, if the gun failed to fire when he pulled the trigger, that he had committed the crime of attempted murder.

---

[17]2 Cal. 2d 527, 42 P.2d 308 (1935).
[18]Model Penal Code §5.01(1) (emphasis added).

But in most cases, the State does not possess such direct or clear-cut evidence of intent. Instead, the prosecution is forced to establish the accused's intent circumstantially.

For example, in *State v. Maestas*,[19] defendant was fleeing after committing a bank robbery when he passed a police officer standing in the middle of the street. The officer fired a shot at defendant's van, and defendant fired back at the officer and missed. In upholding defendant's conviction for attempted murder, the court held that the jury could reasonably have inferred defendant's intent to murder circumstantially from his actions: "It is . . . well settled that such specific intent [to take the life of the person assaulted] may be proved by circumstantial, as well as direct, evidence, and that it may be inferred from the acts and conduct of the accused, the nature of the weapon used by defendant and manner in which it was used, taken together with all the other circumstances in the case. [T]he jury might have [considered] evidence concerning [defendant's] conduct and the circumstances surrounding the alleged gunshot, including testimony that he had just committed a bank robbery, that he had attempted to avoid capture by throwing money out of the van window and that he had demonstrated an indifference to the safety of others by driving erratically and on the wrong side of the traffic divider in his efforts to elude pursuers."

The California Court of Appeal's decision in *People v. Gibson*[20] illustrates similarly that the intent to commit an attempt can be—and often is—inferred from the circumstances. In *Gibson*, defendant was charged with attempted burglary. After midnight, defendant crossed a dark alley carrying a 14-foot ladder, which he placed by the fence in the rear of a department store. When stopped by a police officer, he told the officer that he was thinking about stealing the ladder to use it at his home. Defendant was wearing gloves and was in possession of two flashlights, wire cutters, and a coil of copper wire. At the scene, the officer also found a sack that contained burglar's equipment, including a sledge hammer, bits, braces, flashlights, gloves, and 30 feet of quarter-inch rope ladder. The court concluded that there was sufficient evidence of defendant's intent: "[If] a man traveled 25 miles [to] find a store to burglarize and thereafter was detected by an officer at midnight bearing a ladder down a dark alley and placing it at the rear of a department store and if he is equipped with all the tools commonly used by burglars, there could be no doubt that he was attempting to commit a burglary. [It] could not reasonably be said that he was out to improve his health. . . . [His] criminal purpose was clearly evident."

Finally, even in a jurisdiction with a general attempt statute, it may not be possible to establish an attempt for every crime in the crimes code. The mens rea for some choate offenses may be established by means of transferred intent where the intent to commit the crime is inferred from the actor's intent to commit a different crime. But this concept does not apply to attempt crimes that require proof of the mens rea to commit the specific crime that is the object of the attempt.

For this reason, there is no cognizable crime of attempted felony-murder in most (but not all) states. Under the felony-murder doctrine, adopted in some states,[21] a defendant who causes a death during the commission of a specified felony is guilty of felony-murder. But a defendant who commits one of those specified felonies

---

[19]652 P.2d 903 (Utah 1982).
[20]94 Cal. App. 2d 468, 210 P.2d 747 (1949).
[21]See Chapter 8.

and does *not* cause a death, even if defendant threatens to kill a victim or wounds her, is *not* guilty of attempted felony-murder.

For example, in *Bruce v. State*,[22] during a robbery of a shoe store, defendant's gun accidentally discharged, wounding but not killing the store owner. Although defendant had threatened to kill the victim, the Maryland Court of Appeals concluded that defendant could *not* be convicted of attempted felony-murder because "the criminal intent requisite to proving a felony murder is the specific intent to commit the underlying felony. Because a conviction for felony murder requires no specific intent to kill, it follows that because a criminal attempt is a specific intent crime, attempted felony murder is not a crime in Maryland."

C. Abandonment

One of the recurrent issues in attempt cases is the effect of a defendant's decision to abandon her planned course of criminal action before its completion; the question that arises is whether such an **abandonment** constitutes a good defense to a charge of attempt. Most (but not all) jurisdictions accept such an abandonment defense on a "locus penitentiae" theory, which is the belief that the criminal law should encourage defendants to abandon their criminal endeavors prior to the time the choate offense intended is actually accomplished. Or, to put it another way, if defendants are held criminally responsible whether or not they abandon an attempted crime in progress, there is less reason—or none at all—for them to desist.

F   A   Q

Q: What happens in the minority of jurisdictions that do not accept an abandonment defense?

A: In those jurisdictions, inchoate offenses are treated just like choate offenses. You cannot abandon an armed robbery after it has occurred. Similarly, in those jurisdictions, you cannot abandon an *attempted* armed robbery after that attempt has already occurred. For example, in *State v. Workman*, defendants decided to rob a gas station. They parked in an alley and took a rifle and masks and walked behind the station and waited. The attendant saw them hiding and called the police. When police arrived, they were walking away. Tried for attempted first-degree robbery, defendants claimed abandonment unsuccessfully: "Once a substantial step has been taken, and the crime of attempt is accomplished, the crime cannot be abandoned." 90 Wash. 2d 443, 584 P.2d 382 (en banc 1978).

How does the abandonment defense work in jurisdictions where it is an accepted defense, whether by statute or court decision? Consider the Pennsylvania Superior Court's decision in *Commonwealth v. McCloskey*.[23] In that case, a prison guard heard an alarm indicating that someone was attempting to escape. Guards immediately checked the prison population, but found no one missing. They did find, however,

---

[22]317 Md. 642, 566 A.2d 103 (Md. App. 1989).
[23]234 Pa. Super. 577, 341 A.2d 500 (1975).

that a piece of barbed wire had been cut in the recreation area, and they also found a prison laundry bag filled with civilian clothing. The next morning, without prompting, defendant told a guard that he was going to make a break the night before, but that he changed his mind "because I thought of my family, and I got scared of the consequences." The superior court held that defendant's claim of abandonment dictated a reversal of his conviction: "[A]ppellant was still within the prison, still only contemplating a prison breach, and not yet attempting the act. He was thus in a position to abandon the criminal offense of attempted prison breach voluntarily, thereby exonerating himself from criminal responsibility."

Sidebar

ABANDONING ABANDONMENT

Should abandonment be a complete defense? Consider the following:

The defense is permitted only if the defendant renounces because he or she has had a purely internal change of heart and was not caused to abandon the criminal conduct by fear of detection or the like. But the action that the agent has already done is no less culpable because the agent later "gets religion." [The] moral evaluation of an action is complete at the time of the action, independently of an agent's later action. We might more favorably evaluate the character of a criminal who later tries to mitigate the harm, but the character of the original criminal act is not changed by later conduct, no matter how admirable it may be.

Stephen J. Morse, *Reason, Results and Criminal Responsibility*, 2004 U. Ill. L. Rev. 363, 392-393.

In some instances, however, even in jurisdictions where an abandonment defense exists, a defendant's conduct may have gone too far to permit abandonment. A good illustration is the decision of the Indiana Court of Appeals decision in *State v. Smith*.[24] In *Smith*, defendant stabbed his uncle following an argument and then became remorseful about what he had done. So he dragged his uncle to his car, and sped him to the hospital. The uncle survived, although he suffered stab wounds between his ribs and close to his heart that collapsed both lungs. On these facts, the court rejected defendant's claim of abandonment: "[A]bandonment must occur before the crime is completed or the harm is done. . . . The offense here was completed with the first thrust of Smith's knife. This was followed by a second stabbing and further pursuit of the uncle with the knife. Two attempts were completed and Smith abandoned the third attempt. Remorse, common to many who are imprisoned for crime, is not abandonment. Here, abandonment came too late."

The Model Penal Code recognizes the defense of abandonment, but places strict conditions upon its invocation. The MPC provides that when conduct would otherwise constitute an attempt, "it is an affirmative defense that [the actor] abandoned his effort to commit the crime or otherwise prevented its commission, under circumstances manifesting a complete and voluntary renunciation of his criminal purpose."[25]

If one participant in a crime abandons the enterprise, but others do not, the others can still be held criminally responsible.[26] However, in order to take advantage of the defense, the abandonment cannot be "motivated, in whole or in part, by circumstances, not present or apparent at the inception of the actor's course of conduct, that increase the probability of detection or apprehension or that make more difficult the accomplishment of the criminal purpose."[27] In addition, the

---

[24]409 N.E.2d 1199 (Ind. App. 1980).
[25]Model Penal Code §5.01(4).
[26]*Id.*
[27]*Id.*

Code provides that renunciation "is not complete if it is motivated by a decision to postpone the criminal conduct until a more advantageous time or to transfer the criminal effort to another but similar objective or victim."[28]

Consistent with the Model Penal Code approach, many courts have rejected abandonment claims when defendants discontinued their intended criminal conduct strictly out of an increased fear of apprehension.

In *People v. Staples*,[29] for example, defendant, a would-be bank robber, rented an office directly over a bank vault and put drilling tools there. Subsequently, he drilled holes in the floor above the vault. At some point, defendant's landlord became aware of his activities and notified the police. Defendant later testified that he had planned to rob the bank, but that he "began to realize that, even if I were to succeed, a fugitive life of living off of stolen money would not give me enjoyment of life. I still had not given up my plan however. . . . I came back several times thinking I might slowly drill down." The California Court of Appeal held, on this record, that "[t]he inference of th[e] nonvoluntary character of defendant's abandonment was a [proper] one for the trial judge to draw."

Other courts have, similarly, upheld the rejection of abandonment claims because they found that the defendant did not renounce his criminal purpose or did so only because accomplishment of the criminal objective had become more difficult. For example, in *People v. Acosta*,[30] defendant attempted to purchase cocaine, but ultimately did not go through with the purchase because of the inferior quality of the product. Under these circumstances, the court rejected defendant's claim of abandonment: "[W]hile it may be true that there was an abandonment 'with respect to [that] particular quantity of cocaine,' this is immaterial for purposes of the . . . renunciation defense. Rather, there must be an abandonment of over-all criminal enterprise, which on this record plainly was not the case."

Likewise, in *People v. McNeal*,[31] defendant entered a woman's trailer at gunpoint, told her to undress, and shoved her onto the couch. The victim testified that: "I started crying and talking about my daughter, that I was all she had because her daddy was dead, and he said if I had a little girl he wouldn't do anything, for me just to go outside and turn my back." Defendant then left. However, the court rejected defendant's claim of abandonment: "Based on her testimony, a fact-finder could legitimately infer that defendant abandoned his attempt in response to the victim's use of her wits in keeping defendant talking and in convincing him to let her go. While we find it to be a close question, we hold that a victim's entreaties or pleadings may constitute 'unanticipated difficulties' or 'unexpected resistance.'" Thus, the fact finder could and did conclude reasonably that the abandonment was not voluntary.

D. Impossibility

The question has often arisen whether a defendant can be convicted of an attempt offense when it was impossible for him to actually accomplish the crime that was his criminal objective. For example, is an actor guilty of attempted murder if he shoots at a bed, thinking incorrectly that the person he meant to kill was sleeping under the covers? Is an actor guilty of attempted possession of marijuana if she is puffing away

---

at what she thinks is a marijuana cigarette, but she has actually been sold oregano that she then rolled and smoked?

Traditionally, courts distinguished between **factual impossibility**, which was deemed *not* to be a defense to an attempt crime, and **legal impossibility**, which was deemed to be a complete defense to an attempt crime. However, at this point, it is exceedingly difficult to explain what that really means, more difficult still to attempt to explain why a factual impossibility was not legal . . . and vice versa. Indeed, the degree of confusion created by this supposed distinction between legal and factual impossibility is virtually unrivaled in any other area of criminal law.

Suffice it to say that some jurisdictions found a factual impossibility to exist where facts present at the time of the attempt, but unknown to the actor, made actual commission of the intended substantive crime impossible. Oft-cited examples of factual impossibility found in older cases include: attempting to perform an abortion on a woman who was not in fact pregnant,[32] striking an empty bed with the intent to murder the person who usually slept there,[33] and reaching into an empty pocket with the intent to pickpocket.[34]

In contrast, an attempt was deemed to be a legal impossibility when an actor committed acts that, taken together, did not constitute substantive crimes. Oft-cited examples of legal impossibility found in older cases include: bribing a person assumed to be a juror who was in fact not a juror,[35] receiving stolen goods that were in fact not stolen at all.[36] The common thread in these legal impossibility cases, it is sometimes said, is that the actor made a factual mistake about a legal status, such as whether a person was a juror or whether goods were stolen.

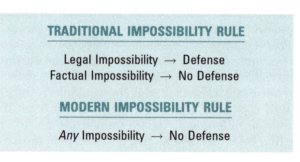

TRADITIONAL IMPOSSIBILITY RULE

Legal Impossibility → Defense
Factual Impossibility → No Defense

MODERN IMPOSSIBILITY RULE

Any Impossibility → No Defense

It does not take much thought to realize, however, that the primary difference between these two supposed categories of impossibility turned in fact on whether the court focused on what the actor intended to do (but did not do because of the impossibility) or what the actor actually did (although he intended to do something different). The former category was treated as a factual impossibility; the latter as legal impossibility. But—*and this is the important point*—if the focus was changed, the result changed as well.

For example, take the case of the pickpocket who picked an empty pocket, and who was convicted of an attempt crime because that was deemed to be a factual

---

[32]*People v. Huff,* 339 Ill. 328, 171 N.E. 261 (1930).
[33]*State v. Mitchell,* 170 Mo. 633, 71 S.W. 175 (1902).
[34]*People v. Twiggs,* 223 Cal. App. 2d 455, 35 Cal. Rptr. 859 (1963); *People v. Moran,* 123 N.Y. 254, 25 N.E. 412 (1890).
[35]*State v. Taylor,* 345 Mo. 325, 133 S.W.2d 336 (1939).
[36]*People v. Jaffe,* 185 N.Y. 497, 78 N.E. 169 (1906).

impossibility. It was a factual impossibility because the actor intended to pickpocket but facts present at the time of the attempt—nothing in the pocket—unknown to the actor, made actual commission of the intended substantive crime impossible. And as the California Court of Appeal has said, "[i]t would seem to be quite absurd to hold that an attempt to steal property from a person could not be predicated of a case where that person had secretly and suddenly removed the contents of one pocket to another and thus frustrated the attempt, or had so guarded his property that it could not be detached from his person."[37]

But, that said, if we instead focus upon the outcome of the actor's actions rather than the actor's intent, the same factual scenario could easily be viewed as legal impossibility, a defense, because the actor could be said to have committed acts that, taken together, did not constitute the substantive crime of theft. Or put another way, it is not the crime of theft to pick an empty pocket.

The point is, again, that it is relatively easy to take the same facts and find them to be a factual impossibility (no defense to an attempt crime) or legal impossibility (traditionally, a defense to an attempt crime). A comparison of two factually similar decisions reaching different results—both involving defendants who tried to shoot at deer out of season, but who in fact shot only at a fake deer or decoy—further illustrates this point.

In *State v. Guffey*[38] the Missouri Court of Appeals concluded that defendant could not be convicted of various provisions of the Wildlife Code, including attempt, as the "hide of a doe long since deceased, filled with boards, excelsior and rods with eyes made of a reflective scotch tape, was not a deer within the meaning of the statute. . . ." The court noted that "[t]he State's evidence shows that one of the defendants did shoot the dummy but did they pursue, chase or follow a deer by shooting this stuffed defunct doe hide? It was not a deer. If the dummy had been actually taken, (it could not be pursued) defendants would not have committed any offense. It is no offense to attempt to do that which is not illegal." Legal impossibility served as a complete defense.

But, in contrast, consider *State v. Curtis*,[39] which also involved an attempt to take a deer decoy. In *Curtis*, however, the court rejected the argument that "impossibility" precluded defendant's conviction, emphasizing that "defendant's behavior demonstrated an intent to take a wild deer out of season. He performed an overt act toward the commission of the intended crime. His conduct went as far as it could in achieving the goal of taking a wild deer out of season." In the court's view, defendant's "failure to actually take a live wild deer is of no consequence. . . . There was no testimony that defendant thought the decoy was not a live deer." Factual impossibility served as no defense at all.

In an attempt to eliminate these inconsistencies and unfairness, most jurisdictions no longer distinguish between supposed cases of legal impossibility and factual impossibility at all. Most jurisdictions have accomplished this reform simply by eliminating the defense of impossibility altogether. The Model Penal Code takes this position as well, eliminating the impossibility defense entirely. In other words, provided that defendant's intended criminal objective would have constituted a crime, neither a showing of factual nor legal impossibility insulates a defendant from criminal responsibility for her actions.

---

[37]*People v. Twiggs*, 223 Cal. App. 2d 455, 35 Cal. Rptr. 859 (1963).
[38]262 S.W.2d 152 (Mo. App. 1953).
[39]157 Vt. 629, 603 A.2d 356 (1991).

The Nevada Supreme Court's decision in *Van Bell v. State*[40] illustrates the modern approach rejecting any defense of impossibility. In *Van Bell*, defendant paid an undercover agent to procure a young girl for him for purposes of sexual intercourse. He chose his victim from photographs, represented to him to be girls five or six years old. He also prepared for sex by arranging for a room and buying a lubricant to use in the sex act. When defendant was arrested and charged with attempted sexual assault, he tried to defend himself on the ground that the undercover agent did not really have a young girl available to have sex with him, essentially an impossibility defense.

But the court rejected this defense out of hand: "In the present case, we have the clearest evidence of appellant's intent to commit sexual assault on the young girl. [Given] the unequivocal evidence of appellant's intent to commit the crime, we hold that his acts of driving toward the apartment where the girl was allegedly waiting and purchasing Vaseline to use as a lubricant sufficed for attempt liability." Under the old impossibility regime, in contrast, the defense of legal impossibility may well have been made out by the defendant arguing that he could not have committed the crime of sexually assaulting a child who did not exist.

SUMMARY

■ Attempt is an "inchoate offense," like conspiracy and solicitation, a crime committed while an actor is trying to accomplish another criminal objective.

■ To commit an attempt, an actor has to perform an act that goes beyond mere preparation.

■ Traditionally, the actus reus of attempt gauged proximity—that is, how close the defendant came to committing the crime that was his or her criminal object.

■ Today, the actus reus of attempt in most jurisdictions is the more inclusive substantial step test—that is, how far the defendant went toward committing the crime that was his or her criminal object.

■ The mens rea of the crime of attempt is the intent to commit the specific crime that is the actor's criminal objective.

■ Most jurisdictions accept an abandonment defense to attempt, excusing otherwise criminal conduct where the actor completely and voluntarily abandoned his effort to commit a crime prior to its completion.

■ Traditionally, factual impossibility was not a defense to an attempt crime and legal impossibility was a defense, the tenuous distinction being that factual impossibility existed where facts unknown to the actor made commission of the intended crime impossible and legal impossibility existed when an actor committed acts that did not constitute substantive crimes.

■ Due to the difficulty in distinguishing between factual and legal impossibility, most jurisdictions today have simply eliminated any impossibility defense at all.

---

[40]105 Nev. 352, 775 P.2d 1273 (1989).

CONNECTIONS

Relationship to Actus Reus

Attempts have their own actus reus, different from the actus reus of the criminal offense that the actor tried but failed to commit. See Chapter 2. Defined differently in different jurisdictions, that actus reus might focus on the actor's proximity to completion of the intended criminal act or simply on the question whether the actor took a substantial step toward his or her criminal goal.

Relationship to Assault and Battery

In many jurisdictions today, the crime of simple assault includes *both* the common law offenses of assault *and* battery (see Chapter 9); hence, in these states, an attempted battery is an assault.

Relationship to Conspiracy

The most common inchoate offenses punished in most jurisdictions are attempt, conspiracy (see Chapter 7), and solicitation. By "inchoate," what is meant is that these are criminal offenses where the actor has as his or her ultimate objective a completed (choate) criminal offense.

Conspiracy

7

The existence of the crime of criminal conspiracy is a response to the perceived special danger to society posed by group criminal activity. A group

OVERVIEW

is viewed as more likely to succeed in its criminal endeavors than a single, individual criminal acting alone. The fact that co-conspirators can divide the preparation for the criminal objective among themselves may encourage them to engage in more elaborate criminal schemes and might well increase the likelihood that those schemes will succeed. Moreover, since co-conspirators may provide moral support to one other, they may also strengthen their collective perseverance, reducing the chance that the criminal objective will be abandoned. Like the crimes of attempt and solicitation, conspiracy is an inchoate offense.

A. UNILATERAL-BILATERAL CONSPIRACIES

B. MENS REA

C. THE ACT OF AGREEMENT

D. OVERT ACT

E. RENUNCIATION OR WITHDRAWAL

F. NO MERGER

G. CULPABILITY OF CO-CONSPIRATORS: *PINKERTON* DOCTRINE

H. WHO IS A CO-CONSPIRATOR AND WITH WHOM?

I. HOW MANY CONSPIRACIES ARE THERE?

The crime of conspiracy is one of three common **inchoate offenses**—attempt, conspiracy, and solicitation—crimes committed while an actor is trying to complete another criminal objective, sometimes called the choate offense.[1] The actus reus of conspiracy is the act of agreeing with another person to accomplish a criminal end, although, in some jurisdictions, that other person need not agree back. The mens rea of conspiracy is the intent to agree with another person to commit a criminal objective and the intent to commit the criminal act itself. Since the actus reus of conspiracy—agreement—is different from the actus reus of the criminal act that is the aim of the conspiracy, conspiracy is *not* a lesser included offense of that target offense. Hence, it does not merge with a completed criminal act.

Most (but not all) criminal codes contain a "general" conspiracy offense, a statute that prohibits individuals from agreeing with another person to commit any other criminal offense.[2] However, some commentators argue that the conspiracy offense, as it is currently defined in modern criminal codes, no longer serves a useful or sensible function—if it ever did—given the overlap between conspiracy offenses and other inchoate or substantive offenses.[3] Indeed, some jurisdictions do not criminalize the crime of conspiracy at all; some jurisdictions limit the conspiracy offense to agreements to commit only particular crimes.

A conspiracy prosecution places a criminal defendant in a very awkward position. In most instances, co-conspirators are tried together and there is a risk that jurors will not sufficiently distinguish between the various individuals who, it is sometimes said, are all caught up in the same "net." In other words, in conspiracy prosecutions,

Sidebar

BIG FISHES, LITTLE FISHES, AND THE SIZE OF THE NET

Very large conspiracy trials are becoming more common. In *United States v. Posada-Rios*,* for example, 35 defendants were charged in a 134-page indictment with various drug offenses arising out of an alleged conspiracy. Ten of these defendants were subsequently convicted after 84 days of trial. The resulting appellate opinion took more than 50 pages to dispose of the numerous arguments involving the length of the trial and the "tense atmosphere created by the high security required."

Is it fair for someone to be tried in a setting like this? With this many co-defendants? Isn't it possible, maybe even likely, that a jury might mix up the big fish and the little fish that have been snared in the prosecutor's net?

*158 F.3d 832 (5th Cir. 1998).

---

[1]See discussion of attempt in Chapter 6. "Solicitation" is the crime of commanding, encouraging, or requesting another person to commit a crime with the intent that the person being solicited actually commit that crime.

[2]In federal criminal law, a similar "RICO" offense also exists, prohibiting other group criminal activity. "The Racketeer Influenced and Corrupt Organizations Act (RICO) prohibits participation and conspiracy to participate in a pattern of 'racketeering activity,' 18 U.S.C. §§1962(c), (d), and defines 'racketeering activity' to include 'any act which is indictable under . . . section 1341,' §1961(1)." *Cleveland v. United States*, 531 U.S. 12 (2000). *See also Boyle v. U.S.,* ___ U.S. ___, 129 S. Ct. 2237, 2244, 173 L. Ed. 2d 1265 (2009) ("From the terms of RICO, it is apparent that an association-in-fact enterprise must have at least three structural features: a purpose, relationships among those associated with the enterprise, and longevity sufficient to permit these associates to pursue the enterprise's purpose."); *U.S. v. Turkette*, 452 U.S. 576, 101 S. Ct. 2524, 69 L. Ed. 2d 246 (1981). Moreover, another federal criminal statute forbids any person from engaging in a continuing criminal enterprise (CCE). 21 U.S.C. §848(a). Some states also have similar state versions of the RICO or CCE statutes.

[3]*See, e.g.*, Philip E. Johnson, *The Unnecessary Crime of Conspiracy*, 61 Cal. L. Rev. 1137 (1973); Neal Kumar Katyal, *Conspiracy Theory*, 112 Yale. L.J. 1307 (2003); Paul Marcus, *Criminal Conspiracy Law: Time to Turn Back from an Ever Expanding, Ever More Troubling Area*, 1 Wm. & Mary Bill of Rts. J. 1 (1992).

there is a worrisome possibility that some defendants may be convicted based on "guilt by association." It is certainly possible that someone may be convicted of criminal conspiracy (*swept into the net*, metaphorically) simply because he or she associated previously with one or more of the co-conspirators, however innocent that association was in actual fact.

In addition, although criminal defendants must be tried in the district or county where the alleged crime was committed,[4] in conspiracy prosecutions, that formula often covers a number of jurisdictions because it permits prosecution, for example, in any venue where one co-conspirator engaged in an overt act in furtherance of the conspiracy, even if the other alleged co-conspirators were never present in that jurisdiction.[5]

Moreover, in conspiracy cases, there is an exception to the hearsay rule for statements made by co-conspirators in furtherance of the conspiracy,[6] meaning that hearsay statements of co-conspirators can be used to establish the existence of a conspiratorial agreement,[7] thereby increasing the chances that the jury will find that a conspiracy exists. Finally, proof of the existence of a conspiracy need not be direct, but can be and often is proved entirely by circumstantial evidence. In the final analysis, therefore, a conspiracy charge can be very difficult to defend. No wonder that the crime of conspiracy is often called, in Judge Learned Hand's oft-quoted words, "that darling of the modern prosecutor's nursery."[8]

A. Unilateral-Bilateral Conspiracies

At common law, a conspiracy consisted of an agreement between two or more persons to commit, by concerted action, an unlawful act or a lawful act by unlawful means. This has been deemed the **bilateral** approach to conspiracy because there must be at least two people in actual agreement (bi = two). As a result, in a bilateral jurisdiction, if a person thought that he was agreeing to commit a crime with another person, but that other person was really a government agent who was simply feigning agreement, there could be no conviction for conspiracy. The necessary requirement of *two or more persons* actually agreeing to conspire together would not have been satisfied.

Similarly, for the same reason, if two individuals conspired to commit a crime, and one of them was acquitted, the remaining defendant could not be convicted either, unless there are other co-conspirators who were convicted. Conviction might be possible if one of the conspirators died, so long as the prosecution could establish the existence of the conspiracy. The bilateral approach is still used in federal criminal law.

Today, however, most (but not all) state jurisdictions with conspiracy statutes on the books have abandoned the bilateral approach and have instead followed the approach taken by the Model Penal Code, which focuses on the act of a *single* individual who is or believes that he or she is agreeing with another person to commit a criminal act: "A person is guilty of conspiracy with another person or persons to commit a crime if with the purpose of promoting or facilitating its commission

---

[4]U.S. Const., amend. VI.
[5]*See, e.g., Krulewitch v. United States*, 336 U.S. 440 (1949).
[6]*See, e.g., Lutwak v. United States*, 344 U.S. 604 (1953).
[7]*See, e.g., Bourjaily v. United States*, 483 U.S. 171 (1987).
[8]*Harrison v. United States*, 7 F.2d 259, 263 (2d Cir. 1925).

he: (1) agrees with such other person or persons that they or one or more of them will engage in conduct that constitutes such crime or an attempt or solicitation to commit such crime; or (2) agrees to aid such other person or persons in the planning or commission of such crime or an attempt or solicitation to commit such crime."[9] This is called the **unilateral** approach to conspiracy.

The unilateral approach is justified on the basis that a person who believes he is conspiring with another to commit a crime is a danger to the public regardless of whether the other person has in fact agreed to commit that crime. Given the extensive use of undercover agents by law enforcement agencies, the trend toward adoption of a unilateral—*broader and more inclusive*—conspiracy offense has resulted in harsher punishment for many individual defendants who are accused and convicted of conspiracy in addition to other inchoate and/or substantive offenses, even though these individuals did not actually act in concert with someone else.

In a unilateral jurisdiction, when a co-conspirator dies or is acquitted or is never charged with a crime at all, nothing happens. Unlike the bilateral test, in a unilateral jurisdiction, it does not matter what happens to other real or feigned co-conspirators. Instead, the criminal responsibility of each person charged with conspiracy is evaluated on the basis of that person's own actions and intent.

BILATERAL APPROACH

Actor + Undercover Agent = *No* Conspiracy

UNILATERAL APPROACH

Actor + Undercover Agent = Conspiracy

The unilateral approach to conspiracy analysis is reflected in the Wyoming Supreme Court's decision in *Miller v. Wyoming.*[10] In *Miller*, defendant Miller was imprisoned and solicited another inmate, Ingersoll, to arrange for a purchase of weapons. An agreement was reached to provide the firearms through a man named Powell in exchange for a payment of $2,500. Miller also decided to pay Powell to kidnap Miller's ex-wife and children for $50,000. Miller offered to allow Ingersoll to escape from prison with him in exchange for Ingersoll's help with the kidnapping. But, as it turned out, Powell was acting as a government agent.

The court applied the unilateral approach to conspiracy to these facts and concluded that Miller could be convicted of the crime of conspiracy to commit a kidnapping, even though Powell was acting for the government and had no intent to actually conspire: "The focus under the unilateral theory is on the culpability of the defendant, without any necessity to establish the guilty mind of one or more co-conspirators. . . . Miller's guilty mind was not diminished by the fact that Powell had made an agreement to serve as a law enforcement informant. It is true that Miller's chance of succeeding in kidnapping his family under the circumstances was minimal, but Miller has 'nonetheless engaged in conduct which provides unequivocal evidence of his firm purpose to commit a crime.'"

---

[9]Model Penal Code §5.03(1).
[10]955 P.2d 892 (Wyo. 1998).

As previously mentioned, not every court or legislature has moved to the unilateral approach to conspiracy—the federal courts still use a bilateral approach, for example. And even where the conspiracy statute is the same as in a unilateral jurisdiction, the result might be different. In *Washington v. Pacheco*,[11] for example, Pacheco conspired with a government agent, and the Washington Supreme Court interpreted a statute similar to the one applied in *Miller*. The court concluded— unlike *Miller*—that a "conspiratorial agreement necessarily requires more than one to agree because it is impossible to conspire with oneself." The court declined to follow the unilateral approach, noting that the "increased danger" that comes from group criminal activity is not present when a person "conspires" with a government agent who pretends agreement. Moreover, the court added, there is "no increased chance the criminal enterprise will succeed, no continuing criminal enterprise, no educating in criminal practices, and no greater difficulty of detection."[12]

Finally, in a bilateral jurisdiction, **Wharton's Rule** limits the permissible scope of conspiratorial liability. That rule provides that, in the absence of contrary legislative intent, two individuals may *not* be convicted for conspiracy where they have committed a crime that necessarily requires the participation of two individuals— for example, conspiracy to commit incest.[13] While Wharton's Rule is infrequently applied today in any jurisdiction, it is entirely inapplicable in a unilateral conspiracy jurisdiction.

B. Mens Rea

The mens rea of conspiracy is often described in the case law as having two separate and independent components: (1) the intent to agree with another person to commit the target act and (2) the intent to commit the target act itself. If co-conspirators agree to murder one of the conspirator's spouses, for example, the two elements are satisfied. Not only have they intentionally *agreed* to commit the target act, they also have the intention to commit that act (murder).

In the ordinary case, conspiracy charges involve crimes of intent or, in Model Penal Code terms, purpose or knowledge. Indeed, in most jurisdictions, defendants *cannot* conspire to commit crimes involving recklessness or negligence as it is an oxymoron to intend to be reckless . . . or negligent. Put another way, if someone intends to be reckless or negligent in order to

[11]125 Wash. 2d 150, 882 P.2d 183 (1994).
[12]*See also United States v. Valigura*, 50 M.J. 844 (Army Ct. Crim. App. 1999).
[13]*See, e.g., Iannelli v. United States*, 420 U.S. 770, 782-783 (1975) ("This Court's prior decisions indicate that the broadly formulated Wharton's Rule does not rest on principles of double jeopardy. . . . Instead, it has current vitality only as a judicial presumption, to be applied in the absence of legislative intent to the contrary. The classic Wharton's Rule offenses—adultery, incest, bigamy, duelling—are crimes that are characterized by the general congruence of the agreement and the completed substantive offense. The parties to the agreement are the only persons who participate in commission of the substantive offense, and the immediate consequences of the crime rest on the parties themselves rather than on society at large.").

accomplish a criminal result, he or she is actually acting intentionally (purposely or knowingly in MPC terms).

For example, in *Palmer v. Colorado*,[14] defendant Palmer was convicted of conspiracy to commit reckless manslaughter for firing his gun at several people. The court held that no such crime could logically exist as conspiracy "is a specific intent crime that requires the defendant to intend to agree, and to intend specifically to achieve the result of the crime." As a result, the court concluded, the "state of mind required for reckless manslaughter is irreconcilable with the specific intent required for conspiracy. Logic dictates that one cannot agree in advance to accomplish an unintended result."

As a general rule, one who merely interacts with co-conspirators, even armed with knowledge of the existence of the conspiracy, does not thereby join the conspiracy as a result of this incidental contact. For example, in *United States v. Falcone*,[15] the Supreme Court held that someone who sold sugar to bootleggers, knowing that it would be used in producing criminal contraband, is not thereby converted into a co-conspirator, at least not without further proof of conspiratorial activity: "[O]ne who without more furnishes supplies to an illicit distiller is not guilty of conspiracy even though his sale may have furthered the object of a conspiracy to which the distiller was a party but of which the supplier had no knowledge." Similarly, in *United States v. Baker*,[16] the Seventh Circuit held that someone who buys marijuana does not thereby become a co-conspirator with the sellers: "Substantial evidence does not support the conclusion that [the buyer] joined the [sellers'] conspiracy. He was a buyer, no more."

It is possible, however, for a seller—or a buyer for that matter—to become part of a conspiracy under the right circumstances. The holding in *Direct Sales Co. v. United States*[17] is illustrative. In that case, a pharmaceutical house sold huge quantities of morphine to a physician over a seven-year period. Given the quantity and the controlled nature of the product, the Supreme Court held that the defendant had conspired with the physician to distribute the drug illegally. As the Court explained, "[s]elling a camera to a spy does not make one a traitor—but selling camera and film, developing the prints, enlarging the detail in the critical areas, and collecting half of the payment for the secret information would assuredly land one in prison."

But, these decisions are highly fact specific. A simple change in one or two key facts can make all the difference in the world. In *United States v. Blankenship*,[18] for example, defendant Lawrence rented a house trailer to drug co-conspirators knowing that it would be used to manufacture methamphetamine. One of the conspirators told defendant what he planned to make and offered him $1,000 or one ounce of methamphetamine. Lawrence preferred the cash and took $100 as a down payment. He covered the floor of the trailer with plastic for protection. A few days later, he changed his mind and told Bland, one of the conspirator's assistants, that he wanted the chemicals and equipment removed and Bland complied. When the conspiracy was uncovered, Lawrence was indicted and ultimately convicted.

The Seventh Circuit reversed the conviction, concluding that Lawrence had not joined the broad conspiracy that had been charged: "If providing assistance to a criminal organization were the same thing as conspiracy, then Lawrence would be

---

[14]964 P.2d 524 (Colo. 1998).
[15]311 U.S. 205 (1940).
[16]905 F.2d 1100 (7th Cir. 1990).
[17]319 U.S. 703 (1943).
[18]970 F.2d 283 (7th Cir. 1992).

guilty. Yet there is a difference between supplying goods to a syndicate and joining it, just as there is a difference between selling goods and being an employee of the buyer. . . . Lawrence knew what [the conspirators] wanted to do in the trailer, but there is a gulf between knowledge and conspiracy. [There] is no evidence that Lawrence recognized, let alone that he joined and promoted, the full scope of the [corrupt] organization's activities. He may have joined, or abetted, a more limited agreement to manufacture a quantity of methamphetamine, but he was not charged with that offense."

Finally, jurisdictions take different positions on the question whether or not someone can conspire to commit an attempt (a so-called double inchoate). You would think that one could not—logically—conspire to commit an attempt for reasons similar to the reason why one cannot conspire to be reckless: It's ordinarily illogical to suppose that someone would agree to commit a failed criminal act. However, there are a handful of federal decisions that have permitted such a charge and conviction on the theory that the conspiracy failed to accomplish an intended criminal offense where the statutory definition of the crime prohibited both the attempt and the substantive crime.[19]

C. The Act of Agreement

The actus reus of conspiracy is the conspiratorial agreement—that is, the agreement to commit a criminal offense. All too often, however, co-conspirators have multiple criminal objectives, raising the question just how many conspiracies exist . . . one or more? Generally, the answer to that question is simple: If co-conspirators make a single agreement to accomplish a number of criminal objectives, even if it is a continuing agreement, there is a single conspiracy. If, in contrast, co-conspirators make two or more separate agreements, each to accomplish one or more criminal objectives, there are two or more conspiracies.[20] The point is that since the actus reus of conspiracy is the agreement, each *new* agreement creates a new conspiracy.

F   A   Q

Q: What if co-conspirators add a new criminal objective at a later point? Is that a new conspiracy?

A: No. It is still just one conspiracy as long as the new objective is part of one agreement, even a continuing agreement. As the Supreme Court has made the point, "a single agreement to commit an offense does not become several conspiracies because it continues over a period of time, [and] there may be such a single continuing agreement to commit several offenses." *Braverman v. United States*, 317 U.S. 49, 52 (1942).

---

[19]*See, e.g., United States v. Dearmore*, 672 F.2d 738 (9th Cir. 1982); *United States v. Mowad*, 641 F.2d 1067, 1074 (2d Cir. 1981); *United States v. Clay*, 495 F.2d 700, 710 (7th Cir. 1974). *See also New Mexico v. Villalobos*, 120 N.M. 694, 905 P.2d 732 (1995), discussed in the Merger section of this chapter, *infra*.

[20]*See, e.g., Braverman v. United States*, 317 U.S. 49, 53 (1942) ("Whether the object of a single agreement is to commit one or many crimes, it is in either case that agreement which constitutes the conspiracy which the statute punishes. The one agreement cannot be taken to be several agreements and hence several conspiracies because it envisages the violation of several statutes rather than one.").

It should come as no surprise that it is relatively uncommon for the prosecution to be able to present *direct* proof of a conspiratorial agreement. Most conspiratorial agreements are clandestine; they are not made in front of witnesses nor are they made in the presence of video or audio surveillance, and, in the absence of a plea agreement, it is not in the interest of individual co-conspirators to testify to the existence of such incriminating matters. As a result, the *actus reus* element of conspiracy—the conspiratorial agreement—may be and often is established inferentially and/or circumstantially.

The facts in *United States v. Barnes*[21] illustrate just how circumstantial evidence can be used in conspiracy cases. In *Barnes*, defendant Barnes and D repeatedly assaulted S. The Court of Military Appeals found that the assault occurred after S testified against Barnes at a court-martial. In deciding whether defendant and D had conspired with one another, the court concluded that the conspiratorial agreement "need not take any 'particular form or be manifested in any formal words,'" that it could be "tacit[,] or [only a] mutual understanding among the parties," and that it could be established by "circumstantial evidence and is usually manifested by the conduct of the parties themselves." On the facts, the court held that "there was sufficient evidence of an implied agreement . . . which could, and did, lead a rational trier of fact to conclude that there was a conspiracy to commit kidnapping." The court noted that the victim overheard Barnes tell D, "Don't let her leave. I'm not done with her yet." In addition, the conspirators made statements suggestive of conspiracy: "We're teaching her a lesson" and "We're beating the shit out of her for . . . what she did to us." The court concluded, from these facts, that a "trier of fact could infer [that] the conspirators held a common purpose and intent to hold and harm . . . S, and to seek revenge against her. These statements suggest a tacit agreement to kidnap the victim."

In some instances, the circumstantial evidence of a conspiratorial agreement will not be conclusive. For example, in *Commonwealth v. Mercado*,[22] a Pennsylvania Superior Court decision, defendant Mercado was observed leaning out of a third-floor window and observing crack cocaine sales (all to undercover police officers) made on different occasions by his co-defendant and alleged co-conspirator, Colon. The government argued that Mercado was operating as a "lookout." When the apartment was searched, no drugs were found on Mercado, but officers found a great deal of cocaine sitting out in the open on a tabletop, as well as numerous clear plastic vials, caps, and packets, as well as a spoon and a razor, each containing cocaine residue. The court found that Mercado's mere presence at the scene could support an inference of knowledge of the criminal activity, but not an inference of agreement: "A bright line test to distinguish between cases which give rise to an inference of conspiratorial agreement and those which present merely conjecture does not exist. [But, in this case, Mercado] was not observed handling any money or communicating in any way with Colon. After the police searched the premises, they found no drugs on [Mercado], nor was [he] in the room where the drugs were found. [Mercado]'s mere presence at the location of the drug transaction is not sufficient to implicate him in a criminal conspiracy."

[21]38 M.J. 72 (Ct. Mil. App. 1993).
[22]420 Pa. Super. 588, 617 A.2d 342 (1992).

As previously mentioned, in establishing the existence of a conspiratorial agreement, prosecutors may and often do use testimony by one co-conspirator about what another co-conspirator said, even though such testimony would ordinarily be inadmissible as hearsay. This so-called co-conspirator hearsay exception is justified on the ground that co-conspirators are acting as agents of one another. Under that exception, declarations made by one co-conspirator during and in furtherance of the conspiracy are admissible in court, assuming that there has been a substantial and independent showing that a conspiracy existed and that the individuals in question were a part of that conspiracy.

D. Overt Act

Unlike the common law, most (but not all) jurisdictions with general conspiracy statutes require proof of a so-called **overt act** on the part of one of the co-conspirators in order to establish the existence of a conspiracy. The overt act is *not* the actus reus of the conspiracy. Rather, this element is required to demonstrate the firmness of the co-conspirators' criminal purpose—that is, it transforms the conspiracy from the realm of ideas or "bad thoughts" to concrete action. However, some commentators—and the Model Penal Code—take the position that the overt act requirement should not apply to very serious crimes.[23]

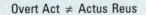

Overt Act ≠ Actus Reus

Courts disagree about the extent of the act that will suffice to meet the overt act requirement. Some jurisdictions—a minority—require that one of the co-conspirators take a "substantial step" toward commission of the crime. Most jurisdictions, however, do not require that significant an act to satisfy this requirement.

Frequently, even a relatively insignificant action on the part of one of the co-conspirators will suffice to establish an overt act. Indeed, in applying the overt act requirement, few courts require—as they frequently do in cases of attempt—that the defendant go beyond acts of preparation and commit acts of perpetration. For example, in *Pennsylvania v. Finnegan*,[24] an undercover police officer, Ralph, called defendant Finnegan and arranged for him to send a prostitute to the officer's motel room. She arrived, identified herself as "Dee Dee," stated that she had been sent by "John," and inquired if defendant was Ralph. After discussing various fees and sexual services, she disrobed and was immediately placed under arrest. In finding that Finnegan and Dee Dee were guilty of conspiracy to commit prostitution, the court concluded that the overt act requirement as to both co-conspirators was satisfied simply by Dee Dee's act of removing her clothes.

---

[23] *See, e.g.*, Model Penal Code §5.03(5) (exempting felonies of the first or second degree from the overt act requirement).
[24] 280 Pa. Super. 584, 421 A.2d 1086 (1980).

F   A   Q

Q: What happens if only one co-conspirator takes an action that can be viewed as an "overt act," but the other co-conspirators do absolutely nothing?

A: The requirement is still met. The theory is that each member of a conspiracy acts for the other members. As a result, the actions of one of the co-conspirators, including an overt act, are chargeable to the other co-conspirators.

Some courts have held, however, that the overt act requirement is not satisfied by mere conversations tending toward establishment of a conspiracy. For example, in *Kansas v. Crockett*,[25] defendant was charged with conspiracy to commit first-degree murder under a statute requiring proof of an overt act. The charging document alleged that defendant engaged in the following overt acts: "planning on the time, location and manner of killing" his intended victim. The court concluded that the overt act requirement demands more, namely proof of an "open, manifest act from which criminality may be implied." The court ruled that the act must be "something apart from conspiracy and is an act to effect the object of the conspiracy, and need be neither a criminal act, nor crime that is object of conspiracy, but must accompany or follow agreement and must be done in furtherance of object of agreement." The court held that defendant's comments relating to planning, tending toward establishment of the conspiracy, did not establish the necessary overt act. Similarly, in *People v. Flood*,[26] the New York Supreme Court explained that "it is 'hornbook' law that conversations among co-conspirators in forming and planning the conspiracy are not overt acts in furtherance of the conspiracy."[27]

As previously mentioned, venue for a conspiracy trial is typically deemed to be appropriate in any jurisdiction in which an overt act took place, even if that jurisdiction is not the jurisdiction in which most of the conspiratorial acts took place.

E. Renunciation or Withdrawal

Unlike acts leading to the commission of completed (choate) criminal offenses, acts leading toward the commission of inchoate offenses such as conspiracy, solicitation, and attempt, may, under the proper circumstances, be "taken back" by appropriate acts of withdrawal, contrition, and by assisting law enforcement officers in their efforts to terminate or prevent whatever related criminal activities may be continuing by others.

Consider the California Court of Appeal's decision in *California v. Sconce*.[28] In *Sconce*, defendant was charged with conspiracy to commit murder. The evidence revealed that he plotted to kill a woman's husband in order to collect on a life

---

[25] 26 Kan. App. 2d 202, 987 P.2d 1101 (1999).
[26] 277 N.Y.S.2d 697 (1966).
[27] *See also People v. Russo*, 393 N.Y.S.2d 435 (App. Div. 1977) (the court characterized the alleged overt acts as "nothing more than words" tending toward establishment of the conspiracy and, hence, that they were not overt acts).
[28] 228 Cal. App. 3d 693, 279 Cal. Rptr. 59 (1991).

insurance policy and that he offered two men $10,000 to commit the murder. Both men refused. Eventually, defendant found someone, Garcia, who promised that he would find someone to commit the murder or do it himself. Later, defendant went with Garcia and pointed the victim out. Defendant also gave Garcia the victim's home address. Garcia then contacted Dutton about committing the murder and they drove to the victim's house to look it over. On the way there, they discussed whether to blow up the victim's car or to shoot him. They settled on blowing up his car because they had explosives and no one would have to pull the trigger. However, later, defendant called the plan off. The court held that withdrawal from a conspiracy requires "an affirmative and bona fide rejection or repudiation of the conspiracy, communicated to the co-conspirators." But, the court added, "once an overt act has been committed in furtherance of the conspiracy, the crime of conspiracy has been completed and no subsequent action by the conspirator can change that." Since an overt act had already occurred, defendant's attempted withdrawal from the conspiracy was ineffective.

Whether the *Sconce* decision makes sense is debatable. The rationale in favor of excusing criminal responsibility in the case of a voluntary withdrawal—encouraging abandonment and thereby weakening the conspiratorial group and the chances of success—certainly would appear to apply even after the commission of an overt act.

As a result, most jurisdictions *do* permit co-conspirators to withdraw from a conspiracy without criminal consequence. However, for such a withdrawal or renunciation to be effective, in most jurisdictions, it must be "voluntary and complete."[29] An actor who desists because of the fear of apprehension, for example, is not acting *voluntarily*. And an individual who simply gives up one of his or her criminal objectives, but not others, has not effected a *complete* withdrawal or renunciation of the criminal enterprise.

F. No Merger

Since the actus reus of conspiracy—a conspiratorial agreement—is entirely different from the actus reus of the target crime itself, for instance, a killing or the sale of narcotics, the rule in most (but not all) jurisdictions is that a conviction for conspiracy to commit a specific crime does *not* merge with a conviction for the crime itself.

Consider, for example, the Supreme Court's decision in *Pinkerton v. United States*.[30] In that case, Walter and Daniel Pinkerton were convicted of tax violations and of conspiracy to commit those violations. The Court noted that the general rule is clear, namely that a substantive offense does not merge with a conspiracy to commit that offense: "It has been long and consistently recognized by the Court that the commission of the substantive offense and a conspiracy to commit it are separate and distinct offenses. A conviction for the conspiracy may be had though the substantive offense was completed."

However, in many (but not all) jurisdictions, there are statutory provisions mandating that multiple inchoate offenses aimed at the same target, such as attempted

---

[29]*See, e.g.*, Model Penal Code §5.03(6) ("It is an affirmative defense that the actor, after conspiring to commit a crime, thwarted the success of the conspiracy, under circumstances manifesting a complete and voluntary renunciation of his criminal purpose.").
[30]328 U.S. 640 (1946).

murder, conspiracy to murder, and solicitation to murder the same person, merge into one another.[31]

G. Culpability of Co-Conspirators: *Pinkerton* Doctrine

If individuals are found to be co-conspirators, one consequence that follows is that because each co-conspirator is viewed as an agent for each of the others, in most (but not all) jurisdictions, each can be held criminally responsible for the criminal actions of his or her co-conspirators committed in furtherance of the conspiracy.

The most notable decision on this point is *Pinkerton v. United States*,[32] discussed in the previous section. Walter and Daniel Pinkerton were convicted both of tax violations and conspiracies to violate the tax laws. There was no evidence, however, that Daniel participated directly in the substantive offenses. Indeed, he was in prison when some of them were committed. But Daniel was nonetheless convicted of these offenses on the theory that they were committed by his co-conspirator, Walter, in furtherance of the unlawful agreement existing between them.

The Supreme Court agreed with this approach, holding that Daniel was indeed responsible for Walter's actions because, "having joined in an unlawful scheme, . . . so long as the partnership in crime continues, the partners act for each other in carrying it forward." This proposition is often called, naturally enough, the **Pinkerton** **Doctrine**. It does have its limits, however. As the *Pinkerton* Court noted, "[a] different case would arise if the substantive offense committed by one of the conspirators was not in fact done in furtherance of the conspiracy, did not fall within the scope of the unlawful project, or was merely a part of the ramifications of the plan which could not be reasonably foreseen as a necessary or natural consequence of the unlawful agreement. But as we read this record, that is not the case."

> ### PINKERTON DOCTRINE
>
> A co-conspirator is responsible for the actions
> of other co-conspirators acting within the scope of
> the conspiracy.

What does it mean to act "in furtherance of the conspiracy"? There are some important limits on the breadth of this element of the *Pinkerton* Doctrine. Consider the Georgia Supreme Court's decision in *Everritt v. Georgia*.[33] In that case, defendant was charged with the murder of a co-conspirator, Cox, who was killed by another co-conspirator in order to keep a separate conspiracy (to commit arson) secret. The court articulated traditional conspiratorial liability principles: "[I]f two or

---

[31]*See, e.g.*, 18 Pa. C.S. §906 (1986) ("A person may not be convicted of more than one of the inchoate crimes of criminal attempt, criminal solicitation or criminal conspiracy for conduct designed to commit or to culminate in the commission of the same crime."). *Cf.* Model Penal Code §5.05(3) ("A person may not be convicted of more than one offense defined by this Article [relating to attempt, conspiracy and solicitation] for conduct designed to commit or to culminate in the commission of the same crime.").
[32]328 U.S. 640 (1946).
[33]277 Ga. 457, 588 S.E.2d 691 (2003).

more persons enter into a conspiracy, any act done by any of them pursuant to the agreement is, in contemplation of law, the act of each of them and they are jointly responsible therefor." *But*, the court added, "a defendant can be held criminally responsible for such collateral acts only if it can be said that they are a *natural* and *probable* consequence of the conspiracy." In this case, the court held, "it cannot be said that the murder of Cox could be reasonably foreseen as a necessary, probable consequence of the conspiracy to commit arson. [Simply] put, a conspiracy to commit arson, without more, does not naturally, necessarily, and probably result in the murder of one co-conspirator by another."

The Model Penal Code rejects the *Pinkerton* Doctrine of conspiratorial liability. A person is not accountable for the conduct of another person solely because he conspired with that person to commit an offense. The Code provides that a "person is guilty of an offense if it is committed by his own conduct or by the conduct of another person for which he is legally accountable, or both."[34] And, as the Code explains further, a "person is legally accountable for the conduct of another person" only in the following situations: "(a) acting with the kind of culpability that is sufficient for the commission of the offense, he causes an innocent or irresponsible person to engage in such conduct; or (b) he is made accountable for the conduct of such other person by the Code or by the law defining the offense; or (c) he is an accomplice of such other person in the commission of the offense."[35]

H. Who Is a Co-Conspirator and with Whom?

A major difficulty in conspiracy cases is defining the scope of the conspiracy and determining just who qualifies as a co-conspirator. The Model Penal Code provision on the scope of conspiratorial liability provides, for example, that "[i]f a person guilty of conspiracy . . . knows that a person with whom he conspires to commit a crime has conspired with another person or persons to commit the same crime, he is guilty of conspiring with such other person or persons, whether or not he knows their identity, to commit such crime."[36]

Q: Is it possible for a co-conspirator to be involved in a conspiracy with people he does not even know?

A: Absolutely. As long as a person knows that there are other persons involved in the conspiracy, that person is part of a conspiracy with them even if he doesn't know who they are. Indeed, this sort of situation is relatively common in conspiracies to import or distribute narcotics, for example.

Courts must still decide who is part of a conspiratorial agreement. In some instances, determining the parties to an agreement will not be difficult. For example,

---

[34]Model Penal Code §2.06(1).
[35]Model Penal Code §2.06(2).
[36]Model Penal Code §5.03(2).

A agrees with B to murder C. In that situation, the scope of the agreement—the murder of C—is obvious, and the parties are defined (A and B). In other cases, however, the scope of the agreement is less well defined, and it may be arguable who is part of the agreement.

Suppose, for example, that defendant, a street dealer of narcotics in Louisville, routinely purchases those narcotics from X, who lives in Miami and imports them from abroad. One might argue that there is a conspiratorial agreement between defendant and X. But has defendant also conspired with X's foreign suppliers? Has he also conspired with others all around the country to whom X also sells drugs?

Whether a conspiracy is deemed to exist between defendant and X, or for that matter between defendant and X's suppliers, can have dramatic ramifications. Since a conspirator is liable for the criminal acts of co-conspirators committed in further-ance of the conspiracy, defendant might potentially be criminally responsible for the acts of not only X, but the foreign suppliers as well. It might also be argued that, if defendant knows that X is selling drugs to others here in the United States, he is also involved in a conspiracy with those others and is responsible for their criminal acts as well. In other words, defendant might potentially be responsible for hundreds of criminal acts committed all over the United States, as well as in other countries.

In an attempt to answer these questions, some courts have used metaphors such as wheels and chains to describe the operation of common types of conspiratorial arrangements. A *wheel conspiracy* involves separate conspiracies (the spokes) linked to each other through a common individual (the hub).

In the hypothetical above, X, the Miami supplier of drugs, would be the hub in that conspiracy. The street dealers in the various cities would be the spokes. Would defendant, a drug dealer in Louisville, be involved in a wheel conspiracy with other buyers from X who are located all over the country? Never a satisfactory answer, we know . . . *but*, it depends. If defendant knows that these other buyers exist—even though he doesn't know who they are—and if he is, in essence, relying on them to keep his narcotics supplier in business, then the answer is probably yes, they are part of the same conspiratorial agreement.[37] Accordingly, one could view the spokes on this metaphorical wheel as connected in that regard.

---

[37]*See, e.g., United States v. Bruno*, 105 F.2d 921, 923 (2d Cir.), *rev'd on other grounds*, 308 U.S. 287 (1939) (Defendant "knew that he was a necessary link in a scheme of distribution, and the others, whom he knew to be convenient to its execution, were as much parts of a single undertaking or enterprise as two salesmen in the same shop. We think therefore that there was only one conspiracy. . . .").

If however, the defendant in this hypothetical did not have knowledge that the other sellers existed, one could view the spokes on this wheel as unconnected, simply spokes, to carry the metaphor further, and the answer to the question whether defendant, a drug dealer in Louisville, was involved in a wheel conspiracy with other buyers from X, who are located all over the country, would probably be no.[38]

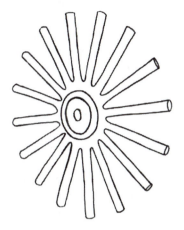

In addition to wheel conspiracies, there are also *chain conspiracies*. By contrast with a wheel conspiracy, a chain conspiracy involves a single conspiracy where individual members—the links in the chain—interact only with the next link in the chain, and may not know about any of the other links farther up or down the chain. Narcotics importation and distribution schemes are common examples of chain conspiracies.

In the hypothetical discussed in the prior paragraphs, the foreign suppliers could possibly be regarded as a "link" with X, the Miami distributor, and with defendant, in

---

[38] *See, e.g., Kotteakos v. United States*, 328 U.S. 750 (1946) (no wheel conspiracy existed where spokes not connected, e.g., through knowledge by the separate conspirators of the existence of other conspirators or conspiracies).

Louisville. Under the Model Penal Code and similar law in many states, "[i]f a person guilty of conspiracy . . . knows that a person with whom he conspires to commit a crime has conspired with another person or persons to commit the same crime, he is guilty of conspiring with such other person or persons, whether or not he knows their identity, to commit such crime."[39] Whether they are or are not co-conspirators depends largely on what the prosecution can establish about each of the conspirators' knowledge about whether a person with whom he is conspiring "has conspired with another person or persons to commit the same crime."

Some courts have, furthermore, declined to extend conspiratorial liability to a simple "buy-sell" transaction. In *United States v. Mercer*,[40] for example, defendant Mercer was convicted of conspiracy to distribute cocaine base. The government argued that since "cocaine comes from out of the country, Mercer must know he is buying from conspirators involved in the importation and distribution of drugs, and therefore he is a member of the conspiracy." The court rejected this argument, holding that there is a "critical distinction between a conspiratorial agreement and a buyer-seller transaction. 'We punish conspiracy because joint action is, generally, more dangerous than individual action.' While a sale, by definition, requires two parties, the agreement is to exchange drugs for money. 'The buy-sell transaction is simply not probative of an agreement to join together to accomplish a criminal objective beyond that already being accomplished by the transaction.' On the other hand, '[c]onspiracies, which are really "agreements to agree" on the multitude of decisions and acts necessary to successfully pull off a crime, pose an additional risk that the object of the conspiracy will be achieved, and so warrant additional penalties.' The essence of the conspiracy, then, is an agreement, not the commission of the substantive offense. 'Where the buyer's purpose is merely to buy and the seller's purpose is merely to sell, and no prior or contemporaneous understanding exists between the two beyond the sales agreement, no conspiracy has been shown.'"[41]

The *Mercer* Court conceded that evidence of a conspiracy might still be found, however, where there is a "continuing relationship that results in the repeated transfer of illegal drugs to the purchaser." For example, in *United States v. Beasley*,[42] the evidence established more than a single buy-sell transaction between defendant and seller. The seller testified that defendant had purchased crack cocaine from him on several occasions and that he knew that defendant was selling cocaine on a particular street corner, and that defendant once "split up" three kilograms of cocaine for resale with him. From this evidence, the court inferred that a continuing course of conduct existed between the parties designed to result in the distribution of cocaine from that particular street corner, thus creating a cognizable conspiracy. Similarly, in *United States v. Bascaro*,[43] defendants were the seller's best buyers, they purchased from the selling group on numerous occasions, and they maintained a close relationship with them. As a result, the Eleventh Circuit Court of Appeals ruled that the evidence was more than sufficient to sustain a conspiracy conviction.

---

[39]Model Penal Code §5.03(2).
[40]165 F.3d 1331 (11th Cir. 1999).
[41]165 F.3d at 1335, quoting *United States v. Townsend*, 924 F.2d 1385, 1394 (7th Cir. 1991) and *United States v. Toler*, 144 F.3d 1423, 1426 (11th Cir. 1998).
[42]2 F.3d 1551 (11th Cir. 1993).
[43]742 F.2d 1335 (11th Cir. 1984), *cert. denied*, 472 U.S. 1017 (1985).

I. How Many Conspiracies Are There?

In *Braverman v. United States*,[44] the Supreme Court made clear that the "precise nature and extent" of a conspiracy must be determined "by reference to the agreement which embraces and defines its objects." As a result, in *Braverman*, when the agreement involved a conspiracy to violate several laws, the Court concluded that there was a single conspiracy notwithstanding the fact that it extended to the violations of multiple laws. The Model Penal Code is consistent with this approach.[45] In short, there are as many conspiracies as there are conspiratorial agreements; but a single conspiracy can and often does have numerous criminal aims.

SUMMARY

- Conspiracy is an inchoate offense, like attempt and solicitation, a crime committed while an actor is trying to accomplish another criminal objective.

- The actus reus of conspiracy is the act of agreeing with another person to accomplish a criminal end, although, in some jurisdictions, that other person need not agree back.

- The mens rea of conspiracy is the intent to agree with another person to commit a criminal objective and the intent to commit the criminal act itself.

- Since the actus reus of conspiracy is different from the actus reus of the criminal act that is the aim of the conspiracy, conspiracy is not a lesser included offense of that target offense and does not merge with a completed criminal act.

- At common law and under current federal law, a conspiracy must be bilateral—it must include an agreement between two or more persons to commit an unlawful act or a lawful act by unlawful means.

- Most states today use a unilateral approach to conspiracy, criminalizing the act of a single individual who is or believes that he or she is agreeing with another person to commit a criminal act.

Sidebar

CONSPIRING TO ELIMINATE CONSPIRACY

Consider the following:

Standing alone, the criminal conspiracy doctrine casts a very wide net, indeed. Increasingly, though, it does not stand alone, but instead it becomes an even more potent force when combined with substantive crimes and new statutory devices such as RICO.

[Certain] features today . . . make the conspiracy offense a matter of intense concern. The crime now is charged quite often. It allows for joinder of offenses and parties into giant "mega-trials." To some it now appears easier to gain convictions of individual, nonessential parties. And the punishment for the convicted conspirator has become severe in terms of both the agreement itself and other crimes allegedly committed in furtherance of it.

[It] is time to refocus attention on the crime of conspiracy, particularly on the reason for having such a joint endeavor offense. The offense exists, as the Supreme Court and many others have stated repeatedly, because of a deep concern with the danger created by the joint activity of serious and determined criminals. To that end, let us go beyond the somewhat trivial arguments concerning individual culpability and responsibility with theories such as the unilateral approach and the elimination of the consistency rule; instead let us concentrate on deterring and punishing group conduct. Let us develop a heightened need for government showings of intent for individuals to join together and of combined efforts of individuals to become a true danger to the community.

Paul Marcus, *Criminal Conspiracy Law: Time to Turn Back from an Ever Expanding, Ever More Troubling Area*, 1 Wm. & Mary Bill of Rts. J. 1, 44-45 (1992).

---

[44]317 U.S. 49 (1942).
[45]Model Penal Code §5.03(3).

- Most jurisdictions with conspiracy statutes require proof of an overt act on the part of one of the co-conspirators in order to establish the existence of a conspiracy because it demonstrates the firmness of the co-conspirators' criminal purpose.

- Most jurisdictions permit co-conspirators to withdraw from a conspiracy without criminal consequence if the withdrawal is voluntary and complete.

- The *Pinkerton* Doctrine provides that a co-conspirator is responsible for the actions of other co-conspirators who are acting within the scope of the conspiracy.

- As long as a person knows there are other persons involved in a conspiracy, that person is part of a conspiracy with them even if she doesn't know who they are.

- The number of conspiracies that exist is determined by the number of conspiratorial agreements that exist, although a single conspiracy may have numerous criminal aims.

CONNECTIONS

Relationship to Attempt

The most common inchoate offenses are attempt (see Chapter 6), conspiracy, and solicitation. An inchoate offense is a criminal offense committed while the actor has as his or her ultimate objective a completed (choate) criminal offense.

Relationship to Complicity

The acts of assistance that can make a person responsible for a crime as an accomplice (see Chapter 5) are often closely connected to the acts of agreement that can make one culpable criminally as a co-conspirator. Of course, the important difference is that the crime that is the object of a conspiracy does not need to actually occur in order to find a person guilty of conspiracy; it is the unlawful agreement itself that is punished.

Homicide

8

Murder. Manslaughter. No one needs to be told that these crimes are among the most heinous offenses that a person can commit. Collectively,

OVERVIEW

these and similar offenses involving the killing of a human being are called "homicide offenses." Whether or not they are the result of intentional or unintentional conduct by an accused, homicide offenses are the quintessential examples of result crimes—that is, they are crimes where the actus reus includes an act resulting in a specified result: the death of another human being. Given the seriousness and the horrific nature of such offenses, as well as the severe potential punishment (including the death penalty in some jurisdictions), it is not surprising that there is a vast and elaborately nuanced body of law relating to homicide in every American jurisdiction.

A. INTENTIONAL KILLINGS

1. Murder
2. Voluntary Manslaughter

B. UNINTENTIONAL KILLINGS

1. Unpremeditated Murder
2. Felony-Murder
3. Involuntary Manslaughter and Negligent Homicide

At common law, the crime of homicide consisted of two separate and distinct offenses: **murder** and **manslaughter**. To establish the crime of murder, a killing had to be committed with **malice aforethought**. In reality, however, the crime of murder did not always require actual proof either of malice or forethought, as those elements could sometimes be implied from the circumstances. Indeed, murder could traditionally be established by a killing that occurred in any of the following four ways: (1) with the "intent" to cause the death or serious bodily injury of another person, (2) with "knowledge" that the action would cause the death or serious bodily injury of another person, (3) when the death occurred during the commission of a felony, or (4) when the accused intended to oppose, by force, an officer or justice of the peace in the performance of his or her duties.

Killings *not* committed with malice aforethought were treated as manslaughter—that is, if they were deemed to be criminal homicide at all.

While a good deal of this traditional treatment of homicide offenses persists in modern criminal law, much of it does not. *It is important to recognize that—today—the various homicide offenses in each jurisdiction are set forth in a number of significantly different ways.*

The crime of homicide in most jurisdictions today includes a number of criminal offenses made up of both intentional and unintentional killings of human beings. Murder in the first degree is traditionally premised on the actor's premeditation and deliberation about a killing and is the classic—and most severe—form of intentional homicide. Voluntary manslaughter is also an intentional killing that has been mitigated from murder, usually because the actor was reasonably provoked and therefore lacked malice. Second-degree murder is a malicious killing, like first-degree murder. It may be intentional, although lacking in premeditation; or it may be unintentional, sometimes referred to as an "abandoned and malignant heart" killing. Involuntary manslaughter is always an unintentional killing where the actor lacks the malice necessary to make out the crime of murder and is, accordingly, a less serious form of unintentional homicide. Each of these offenses presupposes the death of a human being.

Fortunately, however defined, the rate of commission of homicide crimes has been declining.[1]

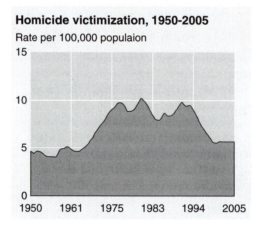

Homicide victimization, 1950-2005
Rate per 100,000 populaion

[1]Federal Bureau of Investigation, Uniform Crime Reports, 1950-2005, Homicide Victimization, 1950-2005, http://bjs.ojp.usdoj.gov/content/homicide/hmrt.cfm.

In this chapter, we examine some *typical* characterizations of modern homicide offenses—principally versions of murder and manslaughter—in an effort to illustrate the customary ways in which the common law has changed and also to demonstrate the way modern crimes codes define the homicide offenses today. But, once again, it is essential to bear in mind that every jurisdiction's crimes code is different; the following discussion reflects simply one—albeit a common—way in which homicide offenses are constructed and defined today.

First-Degree Murder	=	*Intentional Killing*: Malice and Premeditation and Deliberation
		Unintentional Killing: Felony-Murder
Second-Degree Murder	=	*Intentional Killing*: Malice but No Premeditation and Deliberation (impulse)
		Unintentional Killing: Malice and Recklessness (abandoned and malignant heart)
Voluntary Manslaughter	=	*Intentional Killing*: Provocation-Mitigated Murder *or* Murder with an Imperfect Defense
Involuntary Manslaughter	=	*Unintentional Killing*: No Malice but Criminal Negligence or Recklessness

A. Intentional Killings

In general, intentional killings are regarded as the most serious form of homicide. Accordingly, intentional murder usually carries the most severe punishment. When an actor plans to kill intentionally, there is in theory a greater chance of deterring him than there is with unintentional killings. Unintentional killings are, by definition, not intended, and it is not easy to prevent someone from doing something he or she has not intended to do. An unpremeditated act, in particular, is an act that cannot easily be deterred since, again by definition, the actor has not thought about it much or at all. Moreover, those who kill intentionally are generally regarded as in greater need of restraint. In addition, although the premise might not be sound, many believe that those who kill intentionally are more deserving of retribution than those who kill unintentionally because intentional homicides are viewed as more heinous and intentional killers more deserving of severe punishment.

(1) Murder

(a) Murder by Degrees

In many states, the crime of murder is divided into degrees: first-degree murder, second-degree murder, and so on. All murders continue to require, as at common law, proof of malice. In addition to malice, however, murders that are committed intentionally, for instance by poison or ambush or willfully, with **premeditation and deliberation**, are generally classified as first-degree murders, as are felony-murders in many (but not all) jurisdictions. Other intentional murders—malicious but lacking premeditation and deliberation, sometimes called "impulse" killings—are often classified as second-degree murders.

As mentioned previously, first-degree murders are punished more severely than second-degree murders. Indeed, in jurisdictions with capital punishment as a possible penalty, *only* those actors who are convicted of first-degree murder are potentially subject to the death penalty.

Whether it actually makes sense to aggravate murder from second-degree murder to first-degree murder based on the presence or absence of premeditation and deliberation is debatable. While society might have a better chance of deterring a homicide that is committed after it has been premeditated, there may in fact be sensible reasons to punish the premeditator more lightly than the impulsive killer.

For example, suppose that a man's wife is dying from cancer and is in great pain. Even though she begs him to help her end her life by providing her with poison, he repeatedly refuses. After much soul-searching, he decides to provide her with the poison. She drinks it and dies. Although his soul-searching clearly indicates premeditation, it is difficult to believe that this man requires restraint.[2] Even if he is released, there is little likelihood that he will ever be faced with a comparable situation or that he would kill again. In addition, there is little basis for believing that retribution is appropriate. Moreover, under the extreme circumstances of a case such as this, it is not clear that punishing such a defendant severely will have the effect either of deterring others in comparable situations or of expressing the community's strong feelings about the moral wrongfulness of his behavior.

Sidebar

MURDER IN CALIFORNIA

A good illustration of a "murder by degrees" statute is California's:

Cal. Penal Code §189. Murder; degrees

All murder which is perpetrated by means of a destructive device or explosive, a weapon of mass destruction, knowing use of ammunition designed primarily to penetrate metal or armor, poison, lying in wait, torture, or by any other kind of willful, deliberate, and premeditated killing, or which is committed in the perpetration of, or attempt to perpetrate, arson, rape, carjacking, robbery, burglary, mayhem, kidnapping, train wrecking, . . . , or any murder which is perpetrated by means of discharging a firearm from a motor vehicle, intentionally at another person outside of the vehicle with the intent to inflict death, is murder of the first-degree. All other kinds of murders are of the second-degree. . . .

To prove the killing was "deliberate and premeditated," it shall not be necessary to prove the defendant maturely and meaningfully reflected upon the gravity of his or her act.

Like California, most states that divide the crime of murder into degrees specifically provide that homicide constitutes first-degree murder when it is committed "willfully," "deliberately," and/or with "premeditation." Defining and applying the key element of "premeditation" has caused courts a good deal of consternation over the years.

Certainly the premeditation element requires a period of actual thought and reflection by the accused before this element—which essentially distinguishes first-degree from second-degree murder—is satisfied. However, courts disagree about whether the premeditation required for first-degree murder must be truly "mature and meaningful," or, in contrast, whether even a "momentary reflection" is sufficient. A majority of jurisdictions today appear to take the latter approach, finding that no time is too short for a person acting maliciously to actually premeditate and deliberate about a killing sufficiently to make out the crime of first-degree murder.

---

[2]See discussion of the justifications for punishment in Chapter 1.

In *State v. Davis*,[3] for example, defendant and his friends decided to drive around and find someone to "jack." They found their victims unloading groceries from their car in their apartment parking lot. One of defendant's friends approached one of the victims, brandished a knife, and demanded her purse. She resisted. Defendant said to the other victim, a man, "I want your money. Give me your wallet." The woman then heard what sounded like defendant and the other victim wrestling, then three shots were fired and the male victim was shot and killed. Defendant was charged with first-degree murder. The Missouri Court of Appeals concluded that the homicide was premeditated, because defendant was carrying a gun and the jury "could have concluded that the defendant had formed a deliberate purpose of using the gun during his criminal enterprise if necessary to accomplish his ends. The defendant therefore made a decision to use the weapon he was carrying when he was confronted by his intended robbery victim. This demonstrates deliberation." In the court's view, the "deliberation essential to a conviction of first-degree murder need only be momentary."

The holding in *Davis* can be seen as questionable in that it can be argued that there simply was not enough evidence in that case that the defendant had *actually* premeditated and deliberated about the killing, as opposed to acting impulsively and committing a lesser degree of murder. The Missouri court's focus on the defendant's mere decision to use his gun—again, arguably—does not establish premeditation and deliberation in and of itself. The point is that in jurisdictions where no time is too short to support a finding of actual thought and reflection sufficient to establish premeditation, the dividing line between first- and second-degree murder is extremely murky, to put it mildly.

Moreover, if the requirement of premeditation is to mean anything in a literal sense, it necessarily requires a significant if brief period of deliberation. And, again, it is thought that an individual who *actually* premeditates and deliberates about whether to commit a killing is more likely to be deterred than someone who commits a murder on the spur of the moment. First-degree murder is distinguished from second-degree murder largely on that basis. As a result, some (but by no means all) courts require significantly more proof of *actual* thought and deliberation than the *Davis* Court did to establish the premeditation element of first-degree murder.

For example, in *State v. Ramirez*,[4] there was a history of bad relations between defendant and David. Defendant saw David's brother, who looked just like David, walking toward him. Defendant went up to the brother, shook hands with him, and then, for no apparent reason, pulled out a gun and shot and killed him. The killing was totally and completely senseless. Defendant was convicted of first-degree murder, but the Arizona Court of Appeals reversed.

The court concluded that defendant had not committed first-degree murder because of the absence of a proper instruction on premeditation: "[Defining] premeditation as a length of time (which can be instantaneous as successive thoughts in the mind) obliterates any meaningful difference between first- and second-degree murder—other than the penalties." The court noted further that the time sequence here made premeditation difficult or impossible to establish as, "after defendant formed the knowledge that he would kill, he could not possibly pull the gun, and aim it, and pull the trigger faster than he could form a successive thought in his mind. Therefore, if the State's argument prevails, any murder is premeditated [unless]

---

[3]905 S.W.2d 921 (Mo. Ct. App. 1995).
[4]190 Ariz. 65, 945 P.2d 376 (Ct. App. 1997).

defendant acted faster than he could have a second thought." The court concluded that "the first-degree murder statute has never been aimed at those who had time to reflect but did not; it has always has been aimed at those who actually reflected—and then murdered. If the difference between first- and second-degree murder is to be maintained, premeditation has to be understood as reflection."

Finally, in establishing premeditation, there are any number of facts *other than the amount of time involved* that are regularly considered relevant by courts and juries. For example, evidence about how and what defendant did prior to the killing that would show that he was engaged in *planning activity* is relevant. As are facts about the defendant's *prior relationship* and/or conduct with the victim from which the jury could reasonably infer a motive to kill the victim. Also relevant are facts about the *nature of the killing* from which the jury could infer that the manner of killing was so particular and exacting that the defendant must have intentionally killed according to a preconceived design. In fact, in most jurisdictions, the fact finder can also consider what the killer did *after* the killing if such facts shed light on whether the killing may have been planned—he had a getaway car waiting for him, for example.

(b) The Model Penal Code Formulation

The Model Penal Code does not divide the crime of murder into degrees. Instead, it distinguishes between purposeful or knowing homicides on the one hand, and reckless or negligent homicides on the other. In general, except when a defendant acts "recklessly under circumstances manifesting extreme indifference to the value of human life," unintentional homicides are not treated as murder. Instead, they are treated as manslaughter or as negligent homicide and are subject to lesser penalties. The MPC murder section provides as follows:

> (1) Except as provided [elsewhere], criminal homicide constitutes murder when:
> (a) it is committed purposely or knowingly; or
> (b) it is committed recklessly under circumstances manifesting extreme indifference to the value of human life. Such recklessness and indifference are presumed if the actor is engaged or is an accomplice in the commission of, or an attempt to commit, or flight after committing or attempting to commit robbery, rape or deviate sexual intercourse by force or threat of force, arson, burglary, kidnapping or felonious escape.
> (2) Murder is a felony of the first-degree [but a person convicted of murder may be sentenced to death].[5]

(2) Voluntary Manslaughter

The offense of **voluntary manslaughter** is an intentional killing, just like first-degree murder. But it is mitigated from murder to manslaughter due to the presence of adequate and sufficient provocation or other appropriate mitigating excuses for engaging in a killing act. Or, to put it another way, voluntary manslaughter is an intentional murder that includes additional circumstances that serve to negate the requisite element of malice needed to establish murder.

---

[5]Model Penal Code §210.2.

Q: What's the difference between a "complete defense" and a "mitigating defense"?

A: A complete defense is one that, if established, excuses an accused person completely from the criminal charges at issue. A mitigating defense is one that, if established, excuses an accused person from a more serious charge but establishes his or her culpability for a lesser charge, such as from murder to voluntary manslaughter.

Given its mitigating status, voluntary manslaughter is usually raised as a defense by the accused: "I did kill the victim, but the killing was the result of circumstances that mitigate the severity of the offense from murder to manslaughter." Less frequently, the prosecution simply accepts the existence of these mitigating circumstances and actually charges the accused with voluntary manslaughter. In most (but not all) jurisdictions, there are two distinct types of voluntary manslaughter: (1) a provocation or "heat of passion" defense and (2) imperfect defenses.

(a) Provocation or Heat of Passion Defense

The classic way to mitigate an intentional homicide to manslaughter is for the defendant to demonstrate that he was provoked or that he otherwise acted in the heat of passion. While the existence of provocation or heat of passion is not a complete defense and does not excuse the homicide, in the sense of making it noncriminal, it does mitigate the crime from murder to the less serious crime of voluntary manslaughter. Used in this manner, this is called the **provocation defense**.

In most jurisdictions, in order to establish voluntary manslaughter, the accused must show that she was acting under a sudden and intense passion resulting from provocation so serious that it would excite such a passion in a reasonable person. Additionally, most jurisdictions have provided further that such a provocation defense is only cognizable where the accused has either killed her provoker or someone else negligently or accidentally in an attempt to kill the provoker. Provocation, even in a mitigating fashion, does not excuse a generalized killing spree of everyone in sight.

At common law, there were a limited number of provoking acts that were deemed legally sufficient to establish provocation. Catching your spouse committing an adulterous act was one. Today, in most jurisdictions, provocation or heat of passion mitigation can arise out of a myriad of different types of provocative acts. However, many (but not all) jurisdictions continue to hold that "words alone" are *not* sufficient to mitigate murder to manslaughter on the theory that actors must show greater resolve than is demonstrated by responding to insults with a killing act. This rule of law is sometimes called the **sticks and stones doctrine**, taken from the old childhood verse: "Sticks and stones may break my bones, but words will never hurt me."

Even where the sticks and stones doctrine is in force, courts often find that something more than mere words was at play in provoking a defendant's behavior. For example, in *State v. Redmond*,[6] defendant Redmond was washing his car in front

---

[6]937 S.W.2d 205 (Mo. 1996).

of his house when Johnson walked by with the mother of Redmond's child, Sherwood. Johnson and defendant began to argue when Johnson claimed that defendant treated Sherwood badly. Redmond claimed that Johnson then reached into his pocket for a gun and that he thought Johnson was going to kill him. (No gun was found.) So Redmond grabbed a baseball bat and hit Johnson in the head, killing him. After his arrest, Redmond stated, "I can't believe this happened. . . . It just made me mad, so mad. We just had this baby. I can't believe I hit him. . . ." The trial court rejected Redmond's request for a voluntary manslaughter instruction and he was convicted of murder. The Missouri Supreme Court reversed, however, conceding that "words alone, no matter how opprobrious or insulting, are not sufficient to show adequate provocation," but finding nonetheless that there was sufficient evidence demonstrating that those words were accompanied by the victim's threatening manner and the possible display of a deadly weapon. Accordingly, Redmond was held to be entitled to a voluntary manslaughter instruction.

The Model Penal Code also contains a heat of passion provision, although it does not refer to the provision in that way and does not limit the application strictly to "passion" situations. It provides simply that manslaughter can be committed in the following manner: "Criminal homicide constitutes manslaughter when . . . a homicide which would otherwise be murder is committed under the influence of extreme mental or emotional disturbance for which there is reasonable explanation or excuse. The reasonableness of such explanation or excuse shall be determined from the viewpoint of a person in the actor's situation under the circumstances as he believes them to be."[7]

Furthermore, the traditional provocation defense to a murder charge negates the element of malice aforethought that is a required element of murder, thus mitigating the offense to voluntary manslaughter. And, as a matter of due process, the prosecution has the burden of proving the existence of all of the elements of a crime beyond a reasonable doubt.[8] As a result, in jurisdictions that retain this traditional provocation defense, the Supreme Court has held that— when provocation is adequately raised by the accused—the subsequent burden of proof is on the prosecution to prove beyond a reasonable doubt that the defendant was *not* provoked.[9]

Sidebar

NYAH NYAH! NYAH NYAH!

Most courts recognize today that mere words can—and do—hurt people. Some courts have also recognized that hurtful words hurled at someone are often accompanied by other provocative actions, such as offensive gestures and contacts. Modern behavioral research has demonstrated the powerful impact of hate speech. Consider these comments about the work of Stanford professor Laura Leets:

Epithets directed to Jews, homosexuals and ethnic groups, subtle put-downs delivered with a smile, even anti-government rhetoric delivered on talk radio and the Internet catch her attention. "I look at how harmful speech impacts people and how they cope with it," she says. [In] her research, Leets finds that targets of deprecating speech react to the trauma in a pattern similar to the response of victims of crimes. Like crime victims, their first reaction is strongly emotional, followed by feeling the need to change their attitudes in order to understand the incident. Some crime victims and harmful-speech victims report a third phase, in which they change their own behavior as result of the incident.

"[Deprecating] speech is the most commonly reported hate crime and can contribute to ethnic unrest, discrimination and acts of violence," she notes, but laws may not be the most effective way of dealing with it.

News Release, Stanford University (March 4, 1998), http://www.stanford.edu/dept/news/pr/98/980304leets.html.

---

[7]Model Penal Code §210.3.
[8]*See, e.g., In re Winship*, 397 U.S. 358 (1970).
[9]*Mullaney v. Wilbur*, 421 U.S. 684 (1975).

However, in jurisdictions where a version of the provocation defense has been enacted in such a way that it does *not* serve to mitigate a finding of malice necessary to establish murder, the burden of proof of establishing provocation may be and sometimes is placed on the defendant.[10]

(b) Imperfect Defense

Many (but not all) jurisdictions also mitigate intentional murders to voluntary manslaughter by means of a so-called **imperfect defense**.[11] An imperfect defense is a traditional protective defense—like self-defense—where the actor's belief in the need to take protective action is honest but unreasonable. In short, in those jurisdictions that recognize this defense, when a complete defense is imperfectly established— that is, every element is met except the reasonableness of the actor's belief—the crime is mitigated from murder to voluntary manslaughter.

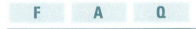

Q: Can an accused raise the defenses of self-defense and imperfect self-defense at the same time?

A: Absolutely. Defendants can and often do argue that a killing was justified as legitimate self-defense, but if the jury doesn't believe that the reasonableness element of that defense was made out successfully, then the defendant hopes to mitigate the homicide from murder to voluntary manslaughter.

In *State v. Ordway*,[12] however, the Kansas Supreme Court ruled that an imperfect defense does not apply where the defendant's unreasonable belief is based on a psychotic delusion. Defendant Ordway was charged with murdering his parents with a shotgun. He argued unsuccessfully at trial that a voluntary manslaughter instruction should have been given to the jury because he killed them with an honest but unreasonable belief that circumstances existed that justified the use of deadly force in the defense of his children. While an imperfect defense exists in Kansas, the court concluded that defendant was not entitled to an instruction on this basis as "[t]he evidence adduced at trial was that defendant was either insane or that he had a longstanding mental illness, neither of which is a mitigating factor under the statute. An unproved insanity defense was not intended to be a mitigating factor in the crime of second degree murder. [Hence, the imperfect defense statute] has no application where a defendant raises the defense of insanity, and more specifically, the 'unreasonable but honest belief' necessary to support the 'imperfect right to self-defense manslaughter' cannot be based upon a psychotic delusion."

---

[10]*See, e.g., Patterson v. New York*, 432 U.S. 197 (1977) (upholding New York's "extreme emotional disturbance" mitigating defense, which placed the burden of proof on the defendant where that defense served to mitigate second-degree murder that did not have malice aforethought as an element).
[11]See also the discussion in Chapter 12 (Justification Defenses).
[12]261 Kan. 776, 934 P.2d 94 (1997).

B. Unintentional Killings

Criminal homicide includes not only intentional killings, but unintentional killings as well. Traditionally, unintentional killings consist of the offenses of second-degree murder (which might also include some intentional, "impulse" killings, as previously discussed), felony-murder, and involuntary manslaughter.

Again, it is very important to remember that there is great variability in each state's homicide provisions. In some states, for example, the residual category of murder—sometimes called second-degree or, in some states, third-degree murder—is treated entirely as an intentional killing, usually a lesser included offense of first-degree murder. In some states, furthermore, there is no felony-murder offense. And, in some states, there are additional homicide offenses such as negligent homicide or homicide by vehicle that are deemed in terms of moral culpability to be equivalent to, or less serious than, involuntary manslaughter.

(1) Unpremeditated Murder

At common law and today as well, the crime of murder—whether intentional or unintentional—is a homicide committed with malice aforethought, as previously discussed. (If the murder is also intentional—that is, premeditation and deliberation are also proved—the offense is first-degree murder.) The element of malice necessary to prove murder can be established expressly or impliedly. By implied malice, what is usually meant is that the malice element can be inferred from an actor's gross recklessness and/or extreme indifference to the value of human life.

> Killing with malice   = **Second-degree murder**
> Killing with malice + *Premeditation and Deliberation* = **First-degree murder**

The unpremeditated, unintentional murder offense is called different things in different jurisdictions. Most often, it is called second-degree murder. Sometimes, it is referred to instead as depraved heart murder or abandoned and malignant heart murder. And sometimes it is simply denominated murder, with no preceding adjective, implying the absence of premeditation and deliberation found in first-degree or premeditated murder.

This residual category of murder—whatever it is called in a particular jurisdiction—sometimes involves a subtle balancing of risk and utility. In some instances, the risk of death to the victim is so great and the utility of the conduct so low that defendant's conduct constitutes unpremeditated murder when it results in a homicide. For example, when teenage kids decide to play Russian roulette, and one of them dies as a result, it is usually held to be murder.[13] The social utility of the teenagers' conduct is so low, because they are simply amusing themselves, in relation to the high risk of death that it cannot be justified and constitutes murder.

The New Hampshire Supreme Court's decision in *State v. Burley*[14] also illustrates how the offense of what is usually called second-degree murder is established. In that

---

[13]*See, e.g., Commonwealth v. Malone*, 354 Pa. 180, 47 A.2d 445, 447 (1946).
[14]137 N.H. 286, 627 A.2d 98 (1993).

case, defendant Burley admitted that he occasionally "dry-fired" his gun by aiming it—unloaded—at various objects in his house. On this occasion, the gun discharged, killing his ex-wife in the next room. Burley was charged with the crime of second-degree murder for causing a death "under circumstances manifesting an extreme indifference to the value of human life, by shooting her in the head with a pistol. . . ." The court concluded that the jury was warranted in convicting him on this basis: "The evidence here showed . . . that the defendant was familiar with the operation of a semi-automatic handgun, that he knew he had loaded the .22, and that he knew his ex-wife was in the next room. [At] the time of the shooting, he was sitting with his elbows resting on raised knees with the barrel of a gun he knew to be loaded pointing into the kitchen where his ex-wife was located. The gun was cocked and ready to fire, and the defendant's finger was in the trigger housing. A firearms expert testified that due to its safety features the gun could not have fired without simultaneously gripping the safety on the back of the handle and squeezing the trigger. The defendant, who had told the police he knew not to point a gun at anyone, finally admitted that he had been 'fooling around' with it after consistently lying by saying he had been cleaning it. On all the evidence the jury was warranted in finding that the defendant's conduct occurred under circumstances manifesting extreme indifference to the value of human life and in thereby finding him guilty of second degree murder."

Analysis under the Model Penal Code would produce the same result on these facts. The MPC provides that "criminal homicide constitutes murder when . . . it is committed recklessly under circumstances manifesting extreme indifference to the value of human life."[15] In *Burley*, the court concluded expressly that Burley manifested extreme indifference to the value of human life. There is a significant risk of death when one points a loaded gun in the direction of another person and "dry-fires" it. Moreover, the risk of death is not offset by any social utility associated with the conduct.

(2) Felony-Murder

At common law, one of the ways in which murder could be established was to demonstrate that the accused committed a homicide in the process of committing or attempting to commit a felonious act. Today, most (but not all) jurisdictions continue to recognize **felony-murder** as a distinct homicide offense, either as a separate component of first-degree murder or as an entirely distinct crime, sometimes deemed second-degree murder. Felony-murder can usually be proved by establishing an unintended killing in the course of the commission of certain specified felonies. Or, put another way, felony-murder is actually an intentional killing where the intent to kill is imputed or transferred from the accused's intent to commit the dangerous felony that is the felony-murder predicate.

In another sense, the felony-murder doctrine imposes what is essentially a form of strict responsibility. If it can be shown that defendant had the mens rea required for the underlying felony and that defendant caused a death during the commission of that felony, then the defendant is guilty of felony-murder without any further showing of homicidal intention. The intent to kill is not an element of the crime. The only mens rea required is the mens rea to commit the underlying felony.

As a result, if A and B decide to rob a liquor store, and happen to cause the death of the clerk during the robbery, they are potentially guilty of felony-murder. A and B cannot defend by showing that they did not intend to kill the clerk or even that they

---

[15]Model Penal Code §210.2.

hoped that no death would occur. They also cannot defend by showing that the death was purely accidental, for instance if A accidentally dropped his gun, which caused it to discharge, killing the clerk. If they caused the death during the commission of a felony, then the felony-murder doctrine applies.

F   A   Q

Q: If someone kills a victim during a felony, is that always felony-murder or could it be another form of murder instead?

A: As an initial matter, some jurisdictions do not criminalize felony-murder. More important, even if a jurisdiction punishes felony-murder, it is still possible that a killing committed during the course of a felony might otherwise be first-degree murder, because the killer premeditated the killing act, or second-degree murder, because the killer acted with reckless disregard of the value of human life.

A good illustration of the application of the felony-murder doctrine is the Wyoming Supreme Court's decision in *Mares v. Wyoming*.[16] In *Mares*, defendant Mares broke into a house with the intent only to commit a burglary. However, unbeknownst to Mares, a resident of the house was present. Also unbeknownst to Mares, one of his fellow burglars was carrying a weapon. Against Mares's wishes, the occupant of the house was murdered. Nevertheless, Mares was convicted of felony-murder: "The felony murder statute imposes a form of strict responsibility on those perpetrating the underlying felony for killings occurring during the commission of that felony; the intent to kill is not an element of the crime."

Many jurisdictions limit felony-murder convictions to situations where the victim's death occurred during the commission, attempt to commit, flight after committing, or flight after attempting to commit enumerated, serious felonies. For example, in Pennsylvania, the enumerated felonies are "robbery, rape, or deviate sexual intercourse by force or threat of force, arson, burglary or kidnapping."[17]

Some other states do not enumerate an exclusive list of triggering felonies (predicates) for application of the felony-murder doctrine, but instead apply the doctrine in any situation where the facts are sufficiently dangerous to human life to justify its application.[18] The Model Penal Code exemplifies this approach. The MPC rejects the felony-murder rule formally, but nonetheless allows a homicide to be treated as murder under the following circumstances: "(1) . . . criminal homicide constitutes murder when . . . it is committed recklessly under circumstances manifesting extreme indifference to the value of human life. Such recklessness and indifference are presumed if the actor is engaged or is an accomplice in the commission of, or an attempt to commit, or flight after committing or attempting to commit robbery, rape or deviate sexual intercourse by force or threat of force, arson, burglary, kidnapping or felonious escape."[19] Thus, the Model Penal Code imposes a presumption of reckless indifference if a killing occurs during the commission of various enumerated, serious crimes.

---

[16]939 P.2d 724 (Wyo. 1997).
[17]Pa. Cons. Stat. §2502(b) and (d).
[18]*See, e.g., Roary v. State*, 385 Md. 217, 867 A.2d 1095 (2005).
[19]Model Penal Code §210.2.

In the examples discussed earlier, the result under the Model Penal Code is likely to be similar to the result reached under the common law. When A and B enter a liquor store with guns drawn, intending to commit a robbery, it is easy to argue that they have recklessly created a risk of death. In such circumstances, there is always a risk that the robbery will go awry and that someone will be killed.

Moreover, one can argue that A and B have manifested extreme indifference to the value of human life simply by carrying weapons, pointing them at others, and using them to force their victims to turn over their money. The Model Penal Code supports this analysis by imposing the presumption that A and B manifested an extreme indifference to the value of human life in committing the robbery.

Likewise, in the *Mares* case, one can argue that Mares also created a reckless risk of death. When one attempts to burglarize a house, there is always a risk that one of the occupants will be present, that struggle will ensue, and that someone might be killed. That is much of the reason why the Model Penal Code presumes extreme indifference to the value of human life in these situations.

However, because of the potential harshness of the felony-murder doctrine, allowing defendants to be convicted of murder for unplanned and unintended killings, some courts and legislatures have placed significant restrictions on the doctrine. In *Mares*, defendant argued that, because the stabbing in that case was a "purely independent act of a co-felon," it would be unduly harsh to apply the felony-murder doctrine and impose a life sentence on him. In rejecting this argument, the court noted that several jurisdictions had enacted statutes establishing a "no-culpability-as-to-the-homicide" defense to felony-murder that applies when the defendant: (1) did not commit the homicidal act or in any way cause, solicit, or aid the commission thereof, (2) had no reason to believe that any other participant would engage in conduct likely to cause death or serious bodily injury, (3) was not armed with a deadly weapon, and (4) had no reason to believe that any other participant was armed with such a weapon.

The court also noted that other limitations had been placed on the doctrine in other jurisdictions: "Adopting an affirmative defense is but one of many mechanisms that other jurisdictions have utilized to mitigate the potential harshness of the rule. For example, the rule has been limited by permitting its use only as to certain types of felonies, by strictly interpreting the requirement of proximate or legal cause, by narrowly construing the time period during which the felony is committed, by downgrading the offense to a lesser degree crime, and by requiring a mens rea of malice."

At common law, a **misdemeanor-manslaughter rule** also existed, imputing the offense of manslaughter to actors who committed an unlawful act not amounting to a felony that nonetheless resulted in the death of a victim. The misdemeanor-manslaughter rule was rejected by the draftsmen of the Model Penal Code. It has also been abolished in most states. Moreover, in those states that still retain the rule, either by common law or by statute, typically the unlawful act needs to be "malum in se," inherently wrong and immoral in nature, in contrast to "malum prohibitum" offenses that are wrong simply because a legislature says so in order to suffice to establish manslaughter.

(3) Involuntary Manslaughter and Negligent Homicide

The crimes of **involuntary manslaughter** and **negligent homicide** also involve unintentional killings. Involuntary manslaughter is distinguished from unintentional murders by the absence of malice aforethought. In modern jurisdictions, the crime is defined by statute and generally requires a showing that defendant killed someone through gross negligence or criminal negligence. Some courts ask further whether defendant acted in a wanton manner. A few jurisdictions provide that an involuntary manslaughter conviction can be founded on *ordinary* rather than criminal or *gross* negligence.

The Model Penal Code definition of manslaughter includes homicide committed recklessly or, as previously noted, "a homicide which would otherwise be murder is committed under the influence of extreme mental or emotional disturbance for which there is reasonable explanation or excuse."[20] The MPC also contains the crime of negligent homicide, which involves a homicide committed negligently.[21] The two crimes are similar in that both require proof that the defendant has disregarded a substantial and unjustifiable risk of death. However, manslaughter (based on recklessness) is distinguished from negligent homicide (which requires proof of criminal negligence) because recklessness requires that defendant *consciously* disregard the risk of death in question, so that recklessness contains a subjective element that criminal negligence does not.

The difference between recklessness and negligence in this setting is illustrated by the decision of the Vermont Supreme Court in *State v. Brooks*.[22] In *Brooks*, Brooks sold his home with a faulty driveway heating system. After defendant's friend and her baby became sick from the system's fumes, it was determined that the heater had a gas leak that produced dangerous levels of carbon monoxide. Nonetheless, Brooks sold the house without making repairs and without mentioning the defect in the heater. Subsequently, the purchaser's family died of carbon monoxide poisoning due to the defective heater.

On these facts, it would be easy to conclude that Brooks negligently caused these deaths by failing to disclose the defect. There was clearly a substantial and unjustifiable risk of death of which he *should have been* aware. But Vermont law required a showing of recklessness in order to establish involuntary manslaughter. The *Brooks* court concluded that Brooks acted recklessly as he had *consciously disregarded* a substantial and unjustifiable risk of death. The court emphasized that Brooks knew the heater was defective and that it presented a substantial risk of death. The court concluded that, under these circumstances, there "was sufficient evidence [of] a conscious disregard of a substantial and unjustifiable risk."

Involuntary manslaughter prosecutions arise out of a wide variety of situations. Suppose, for example, that an actor is driving on a city street when she suffers a blow-out in a tire. Although she makes a valiant attempt to safely bring her car to a halt, she nonetheless veers off the road, killing a pedestrian. Whether her conduct constitutes involuntary manslaughter—or negligent homicide, for that matter—depends heavily on all of the factual circumstances. If she was driving at or near the speed limit on new tires, and if she had no reason to believe that there was any problem with the tires, she is unlikely to have committed involuntary manslaughter, negligent homicide, or any other form of homicide because she was neither reckless nor negligent. There is no indication that she took a substantial and unjustifiable risk or that she deviated in a gross fashion from the standard of care that a reasonable person would have observed in her situation.

---

[20]Model Penal Code §210.3(1).
[21]Model Penal Code §210.4.
[22]163 Vt. 245, 658 A.2d 22 (1995).

F A Q

Q: Which is it? Is involuntary manslaughter a recklessness or criminal negligence offense?

A: It depends entirely on the jurisdiction. In most jurisdictions, involuntary manslaughter requires proof of criminal or gross negligence. But in some other jurisdictions, recklessness is required. And in yet other jurisdictions, ordinary or civil negligence suffices.

In some circumstances, an actor may be acting recklessly or negligently even if she is driving in her vehicle at or below the speed limit. Suppose, for example, that the circumstances dictate that one cannot reasonably drive at the speed limit. This might happen if there is a lot of snow or ice on the road or if there is a heavy fog or even if there are people or animals on the roadway. Under such circumstances, an actor's decision to keep driving at the speed limit may well create a substantial and unjustifiable risk that the driver was deviating in a gross fashion from the standard of care that a reasonable person would observe in her situation.

In addition, if the facts show that a defendant was driving at a high rate of speed—for example, 55 mph in a 35 mph zone—or that she was traveling on tires that were old and bald, a much stronger argument can be made for the proposition that she has taken a substantial and unjustified risk and that she consciously disregarded that risk. For example, in *People v. McCoy*,[23] defendant McCoy was charged with involuntary manslaughter under a statute requiring a showing of gross negligence in order to obtain conviction. The evidence showed that McCoy was traveling at a speed of 50 to 55 mph in a 35 mph zone when he struck and killed two women. While the court acknowledged that a violation of the speed limit, by itself, is not adequate to establish *gross* negligence, the court added that "under certain circumstances, a violation of the speed limit can be gross negligence."

In this case, the court found that there was heavy traffic and McCoy was traveling at a speed significantly in excess of the speed limit. Moreover, even though the women had been standing stationary for some time, he was moving so fast that he did not have time to swerve or take evasive

> **Sidebar**
>
> **SPEED KILLS**
>
> Speeding resulting in highway accidents and fatalities is a serious and—apparently—growing problem. The National Highway Traffic Safety Association (NHTSA) reports that:
>
> Speeding is one of the most prevalent factors contributing to traffic crashes. The economic cost to society of speeding-related crashes is estimated by NHTSA to be $40.4 billion per year. In 2004, speeding was a contributing factor in 30 percent of all fatal crashes, and 13,192 lives were lost in speeding-related crashes. Motor vehicle crashes cost society an estimated $7,300 per second. The total economic cost of crashes was estimated at $230.6 billion in 2000. In 2000, the cost of speeding-related crashes was estimated to be $40.4 billion—$76,865 per minute or $1,281 per second.
>
> [For] drivers involved in fatal crashes, young males are the most likely to be speeding. The relative proportion of speeding-related crashes to all crashes decreases with increasing driver age. In 2004, 38 percent of the male drivers age 15 to 20 who were involved in fatal crashes were speeding at the time of the crash.
>
> NHTSA, National Center for Statistics & Analysis, Traffic Safety Facts 2004—Speeding, http://www-nrd.nhtsa.dot.gov/pdf/nrd-30/NCSA/TSF2004/809915.pdf.

---

[23]223 Mich. App. 500, 566 N.W.2d 667 (1997).

action. There was also evidence suggesting that McCoy did not slow down even after he struck the women. As a result, the court concluded that "defendant engaged in a single, continuous pattern of grossly negligent driving. Accordingly, the trial court did not err in denying defendant's motion for a directed verdict."

A similar analysis might apply to an epileptic driver who drives knowing that he is subject to periodic seizures.[24] One day, while driving on an interstate highway, he has a seizure, and while he is unconscious, his car runs into another car, killing a passenger. In general, the social utility of having an individual drive, knowing that he is subject to epileptic seizures, is very low. In addition, the risk (in this case, of death) is quite high. More to the point, given the fact that the driver consciously disregarded a substantial and unjustifiable risk that a death might result from his conduct, and given the fact that the risk is of such a nature and degree that, as discussed, considering the nature and purpose of the actor's conduct, and the circumstances known to him, its disregard involves a gross deviation from the standard of conduct that a law-abiding person would observe in the actor's situation, recklessness exists sufficient to make the driver responsible for any form of reckless homicide. Even clearer, the driver would most certainly be guilty of negligent homicide, including involuntary manslaughter if it is based on criminal negligence in that particular jurisdiction.

In some jurisdictions, moreover, such homicides may be prosecuted under a vehicular homicide statute focused entirely on deaths caused by negligent or reckless driving. Where these statutes exist, they generally supplement more traditional homicide statutes and often provide for lesser penalties.

Nonetheless, it is well to bear in mind that if a speeding or reckless driver kills someone, neither involuntary manslaughter nor a vehicular homicide crime is necessarily the highest homicide offense that can be proved. Indeed, a death resulting from a speeding motorist's actions may not be criminal at all. Or, it may be involuntary manslaughter—or vehicular homicide—if the requisite criminal negligence or recklessness required in that jurisdiction exists. But it might also be second-degree murder if malice is present impliedly due to a reckless disregard of the value of human life. For that matter, if a speeding motorist aims her car at another person and runs him over, such an act could constitute first-degree murder, assuming the requisite premeditation and deliberation are present.

SUMMARY

■ Homicide crimes include a number of criminal offenses made up of both intentional and unintentional killings of human beings.

■ Most states that divide the crime of murder into degrees provide that homicide constitutes first-degree murder when it is committed willfully, deliberately, and/or with premeditation.

■ Jurisdictions disagree about whether the premeditation required for first-degree murder must be mature and meaningful or whether a momentary reflection is sufficient.

■ The Model Penal Code distinguishes between purposeful or knowing homicides and reckless or negligent homicide.

---

[24]See also discussion of involuntary acts in Chapter 2.

- Voluntary manslaughter is an intentional killing mitigated from murder to manslaughter due to the presence of adequate and sufficient provocation or other appropriate mitigating excuses for engaging in a killing act.

- The provocation defense mitigates murder to voluntary manslaughter when a defendant establishes that he was provoked into acting or otherwise acted in the heat of passion.

- An imperfect defense mitigates murder to voluntary manslaughter where the actor's belief in the need to take protective action is honest but unreasonable. Imperfect self-defense is an example.

- Murder is a killing committed with malice aforethought, and the element of malice can be established expressly or impliedly.

- By implied malice, what is usually meant is that the malice element can be inferred from an actor's gross recklessness and/or extreme indifference to the value of human life.

- Most jurisdictions punish the crime of felony-murder, providing that murder can be established by proving that a killing occurred during the course of certain specified felonies.

- Involuntary manslaughter is an unintentional homicide in the absence of malice aforethought that generally requires a showing that defendant killed someone while acting with gross or criminal negligence.

CONNECTIONS

Relationship to Actus Reus
Homicide is a criminal offense where the actus reus (see Chapter 2), in addition to a killing act, includes the accused's completion of a specified *result*, the death of a human being.

Relationship to Assault and Battery
Most homicides result from assaultive conduct (see Chapter 9) that is taken too far. In fact, it is often the case that an actor simply intends to engage in assaultive conduct but the unintended consequences of such acts is the death of the victim, resulting in charges of second-degree murder or involuntary manslaughter.

Relationship to Causation
One of the traditional elements of homicide offenses is the result element: death of a human being. Accordingly, criminal causation (see Chapter 4) is also a required element of homicides, meaning the prosecution must establish that the accused person actually caused the resulting death in question.

Relationship to Justification Defenses

In most jurisdictions, an imperfect justification defense (see Chapter 12)—for example, an honest but unreasonable belief on the part of the actor who killed another person that she was acting in self-defense—will mitigate the offense of intentional murder to voluntary manslaughter.

Relationship to Mens Rea

In most jurisdictions, each of the basic mens rea concepts adopted by the Model Penal Code—purposefully, knowingly, recklessly, and negligently (see Chapter 3)—can be found as a component of a different homicide offense.

Assault and Battery

9

OVERVIEW

One of the most common and pervasive forms of criminal conduct in the United States is assaultive crime. At common law, there were several criminal offenses that fit broadly into an overarching "assault and battery" category. In addition to the traditional crimes of assault and battery themselves, which were distinct and separate crimes, the crime of "mayhem" also existed. Many modern crimes codes have merged the common law offenses of assault and battery, and distinguish instead between simple and aggravated forms of assaultive conduct.

A. Traditional Assaultive Crimes

   1. Battery
   2. Assault
   3. Mayhem
   4. The Model Penal Code and Merged Assault Formulations

B. Aggravated Assaultive Crimes

C. Consent Defense

D. Modern Variations on Assault Crimes

Simple **assault** exists when a person causes another person to fear that unlawful force is about to be used against him or her or when a person actually uses or attempts to use such force on another person. Aggravated forms of assault encompass more violent forms of assaultive conduct and/or assaultive conduct that has resulted in injury. **Battery** traditionally was the intentional application of force to another person inflicting an injury, or an "offensive touching."

Assault and battery were separate crimes at common law. Today, in contrast, the crimes codes in many jurisdictions typically contain a general assaultive criminal offense, often called "simple assault" or "common assault," and one or more forms of more serious assaultive offenses. These more serious offenses often include "aggravated assault" and/or offenses focused on specific types of assaultive conduct (e.g., sexual assaults or assault with a deadly weapon) and/or they focus on specific categories of victims (e.g., assault on a law enforcement officer or assault on a child).

A. Traditional Assaultive Crimes

Even though the criminal offenses of assault and battery are conceptually distinct in most jurisdictions, they are nonetheless commonly referred to collectively—in one breath—as "assault-and-battery." In some respects, this amalgamation makes sense because a battery is usually preceded by an assault in the sense that an assault requires that defendant place the victim in fear of an imminent battery. Today, however, at least in jurisdictions where the separate offense of battery still exists and has not merged formally with assault, the two crimes are often defined in such different ways that a practical amalgamation is untenable.

(1) Battery

At common law, a defendant committed a battery when he or she intentionally applied physical force to another person and either inflicted an injury or an "offensive touching" on that person.[1] In terms of the actus reus element, battery was a "result crime."[2] The defendant needed to cause an injury or an offensive touching. However, establishing the crime of battery also required proof of the necessary mens rea and the accused's act of actually causing the offensive touching or injury.

At common law, the crime of battery was a crime requiring proof of intent. The offender must have intended to actually apply physical force to his victim, thereby inflicting injury or an offensive touching. The actus reus of battery at common law included the infliction of physical injury or the offensive touching. Of course, the former tends to assume the latter. In other words, when one thinks of a battery inflicting a physical injury, one envisions first an initial physical assault—for example, A attacks B with his fists intending to inflict a battery or C hits D with a baseball bat.

Indeed, in a battery case or any other assaultive prosecution today where an actual physical injury must be demonstrated, that element must be established clearly. In *State v. Gordon*,[3] for example, defendant Gordon kicked his victim, leaving a red mark on his chest. While it is clear that the kick *could* have caused physical injury, the Iowa Supreme Court nonetheless reversed Gordon's conviction because

---

[1] *See, e.g., Johnson v. U.S.*, ____ U.S. ____, 130 S. Ct. 1265, 1270, 176 L. Ed. 2d 1 (2010) ("[T]he common-law crime of battery . . . consisted of the intentional application of unlawful force against the person of another. The common law held this element of 'force' to be satisfied by even the slightest offensive touching.").

[2] See Chapter 2.

[3] 560 N.W.2d 4 (Iowa 1997).

the trial judge had assumed (and instructed the jury) that "[a] red mark or bruise on the skin would constitute an impairment of physical condition, and therefore an injury." The supreme court held, however, that the prosecution was required to produce more evidence to establish *actual* bodily injury—that the victim suffered pain or illness from the kick, for example: "Bodily injury ordinarily 'refers only to injury to the body, or to sickness or disease contracted by the injured as a result of injury.' Injury includes 'an act that damages, harms, or hurts: an unjust or undeserved infliction of suffering or harm. . . .' The red mark or bruise on [the victim's] chest was not a physical impairment per se but only evidence of such impairment."

A battery can be committed either directly (e.g., the defendant uses her fist to strike her intended victim) or indirectly. The Florida Court of Appeals' decision in *Clark v. State*[4] illustrates indirect battery. In *Clark*, defendant, a supervisor, ran his truck into the victim's truck to prevent him from removing materials from a construction site. Defendant was convicted of aggravated battery. Battery in Florida was defined as occurring "when a person either 'actually and intentionally touches or strikes' another person against that person's will or intentionally causes bodily harm or injury to another person." Aggravated battery occurs in Florida when "a person commits battery either causing great bodily harm, permanent disability or permanent disfigurement or using a deadly weapon." The Florida court held that defendant's truck was a "deadly weapon," and—more to our point—added that striking the victim's truck qualified as an indirect attack on the victim's person because of the "unpermitted and intentional invasion of the inviolability of his person." In this instance, the court affirmed defendant's conviction because he "was more than jostled" when his truck was hit.

Historically, as previously noted, a battery could also be committed through infliction of physical injury *or* through an act of offensive touching. For example, in the classic case of *Wood v. Commonwealth*,[5] defendant was charged with battery for placing his hand on his victim's neck and then running it down inside her dress onto her breasts. The court upheld defendant's battery conviction, ruling that "[n]ot every touch is a battery, nor is it necessary that the touch should result in injury to the corporeal person. It is sufficient if it does injury to the mind or feelings."

F A Q

Q: Is offensive touching battery still a criminal offense today?

A: Today conduct of this sort is still punished, but more often than not, it is punished as a form of sexual assault with offenses such as indecent assault, indecent contact, sexual battery, and so on, rather than under a generic battery offense. See Chapter 10 (Rape and Sexual Assault).

In addition to the two types of battery discussed above—infliction of injury and offensive touching—some jurisdictions also criminalize a third type of battery, sometimes referred to as "unlawful-act battery." This form of battery is similar to

[4]746 So. 2d 1237 (Fla. App. 1999).
[5]149 Va. 401, 140 S.E. 114 (1927).

the misdemeanor-manslaughter rule,[6] in that a defendant who caused an injury while engaged in an unlawful act—usually an act that was *malum in se* rather than *malum prohibitum*—is held to be guilty of battery, even if he or she lacked the requisite mens rea for battery. The great majority of jurisdictions reject this form of battery today, as does the Model Penal Code.[7]

(2) Assault

Assault, in contrast to battery, was originally defined as an attempted battery that failed. Traditionally, in order to convict an accused of assault, the prosecution was required to prove that the defendant intended to commit a battery, came close to completing it, and had the present ability to do so. However, over time, the crime of assault was extended to include situations where a defendant intentionally placed someone else in fear of an imminent battery. In other words, the offense of assault eventually included acts that were simply intended to frighten an anticipated victim, even if no actual touching or contact occurred or even was intended to occur.

The assault crime, in this "frightening-another-person" sense, arises in any number of diverse situations. For example, suppose that a defendant points a gun at his victim and threatens to kill him, but the gun is unloaded. Under these circumstances, defendant may still be prosecuted for assault. In other words, the frightening aspect of this branch of assault made it possible to prosecute those actors who did not come close enough to committing a battery or did not even have the present ability to commit it—that is, pointing an unloaded gun.

However, you should also bear in mind that in many questionably assaultive situations, an actor's intent or lack thereof may also be highly relevant. If an actor swerves off the road, for example, and nearly hits A, placing A in fear of physical injury, the crime of assault is not committed if the driver did not intend to place A in fear or apprehension. There are lots of reasons why the driver might have acted as he did but still not have had the intent to assault A. Perhaps he absentmindedly lost control of his car, causing it to swerve, and then regained control before striking A, but after scaring her.

The assault offense in this menacing or frightening sense is also illustrated by the District of Columbia Court of Appeals' holding in *Robinson v. United States*.[8] In *Robinson*, an off-duty police officer, Monroe, driving to work in his own car, heard gunshots and decided to investigate. He was subsequently confronted by defendant Robinson, who pointed a pistol at him. Monroe identified himself as a police officer and told Robinson to drop the gun. Robinson ultimately dropped his gun and walked away. The court held that the critical question in determining whether Robinson was guilty of simple assault was whether "the assailant acted in such a manner as would under the circumstances portend an immediate threat of danger to a person of reasonable sensibility." Because, the court added, Robinson's "act of pointing a gun at . . . Monroe constituted 'a menacing threat[,]' [i]t is irrelevant whether [he] had a specific intent to injure Monroe. An intent to frighten is sufficient, and that intent can be inferred from the pointing of a gun." The court affirmed the jury conviction of assault.

---

[6]See Chapter 8 (Homicide).
[7]Model Penal Code §211.1.
[8]506 A.2d 572 (D.C. App. 1986).

(3) Mayhem

The crimes of assault and battery are designed to protect an individual's right to bodily integrity. The common law also included the crime of mayhem, which was more specifically calculated to protect the State's interest in having men available to fight on its behalf. Mayhem at common law made it a criminal offense for anyone to permanently impair a person's body parts in ways that would affect his ability to fight for the Crown. While mayhem was a felony, assault and battery were usually treated as misdemeanors. Some (but only a few) jurisdictions retain the offense of mayhem.

(4) The Model Penal Code and Merged Assault Formulations

The Model Penal Code's drafters initially sought to simplify the crimes of assault and battery by merging them into a single crime. As the drafters stated, "[S]ucceeding generations have so blurred the ancient categories [of mayhem, battery, and assault] that it more closely accords with modern understanding to deal with them under a single label."[9] The drafters' original proposal would have eliminated the common law definitions of assault and battery altogether and replaced them with the crimes of "bodily injury" and "reckless conduct."

However, it was subsequently decided to abandon this approach in favor of creating two crimes: assault (encompassing, roughly, *both* the common law offenses of assault *and* battery); and aggravated assault (involving assaults committed with deadly weapons). The new assault crime still served to merge the traditional offenses of assault and battery into a single, unified criminal offense.

F A Q

Q: What does it mean that these common law offenses "merged"?

A: In essence, the MPC essentially but not completely merged the separate offenses of assault and battery into one—*more inclusive*—assaultive offense. Although not necessarily using the MPC language, many jurisdictions today use this merged approach to simple assaultive conduct, eliminating a separate battery offense, but including the elements of battery in the assault offense.

The Model Penal Code merger, however, did not completely merge the separate offenses of assault and battery because it did not include in this formulation conduct

[9]Model Penal Code §211(1), Comment (1), at 174 (1980).

punished at common law that resulted in offensive touching. (As noted previously, most jurisdictions today punish these acts in separate sexual offenses.) In addition, the Model Penal Code defined the mens rea for its general assault offense broadly enough to include all four MPC mental states—purposely, knowingly, recklessly, and negligently—at least when the assault is committed with a deadly weapon.[10]

For the basic crime, the Model Penal Code provides that an individual commits an assault if he does one of three things: "(a) attempts to cause or purposely, knowingly or recklessly causes bodily injury to another; or (b) negligently causes bodily injury to another with a deadly weapon; or (c) attempts by physical menace to put another in fear of imminent serious bodily injury."[11]

As a result, under the Model Penal Code, assault can be committed either when one attempts to cause bodily injury to another, or when a person purposely, knowingly, or recklessly causes such injury.[12] The Model Penal Code does not require that the defendant come very close to committing the completed crime, but only that he or she take a substantial step, as that term is defined in the law of attempt.[13]

However, many jurisdictions do not follow the MPC approach, and some impose a much stricter proximity requirement to establish this type of assaultive offense.[14] Under the Code, the term "bodily injury," as used above, is defined as "physical pain, illness or any impairment of physical condition."[15] The Model Penal Code also differs from the common law in that one who attempts to commit an assault can be guilty even if the intended victim is wholly unaware of the attempt.

Assault can also be committed by physical menace when one places another "in fear of imminent serious bodily injury."[16] This Model Penal Code provision is similar to the common law notion of an assault offense made out by frightening another person. Serious bodily injury, as used in this provision, is defined as "bodily injury which creates a substantial risk of death or which causes serious, permanent disfigurement, or protracted loss or impairment of the function of any bodily member or organ."[17] As a result, if a defendant pulls out a knife and waves it menacingly in front of her intended victim, an assault is made out even if the defendant does not actually strike her victim. However, if she simply waves her fist in front of the intended victim, there may or may not be an assault depending on whether the threat of her use of her fist can be regarded as creating a risk of serious bodily injury. Does she have a black belt in martial arts? If so, then the risk of serious bodily injury might exist.

Finally, assault can be committed when one negligently causes bodily injury to another with a deadly weapon. Under the Code, deadly weapon refers to "any firearm or other weapon, device, instrument, material or substance, whether animate or inanimate, which in the manner it is used or is intended to be used is known to be capable of producing death or serious bodily injury."[18] In short, anything capable of causing death or serious bodily injury can qualify as a deadly weapon under the Model Penal Code.

---

[10]Model Penal Code §2.02(2)(a), (b), (c), & (d).
[11]Model Penal Code §211(1).
[12]*Id.*
[13]*See* Model Penal Code §211.1, Comment (2), at 184 (1980).
[14]See Chapter 6 (Attempt).
[15]Model Penal Code §210(2).
[16]*Id.*
[17]Model Penal Code §210(3).
[18]Model Penal Code §210(4).

For example, suppose that defendant routinely speeds while driving his car through a residential neighborhood. One day, a dog runs out in front of him and defendant swerves off the road, seriously injuring a pedestrian. Had the defendant not been speeding, he could have stopped in time to prevent any harm to others. Under these circumstances, defendant is likely guilty of assault. His car was certainly a "deadly weapon," capable of producing death or serious bodily injury. Indeed, in many jurisdictions, legislatures have enacted special statutes imposing criminal responsibility for fatalities arising out of automobile accidents.[19] The Model Penal Code, in contrast, rejects this approach, and specifically permits coverage of this type of conduct under its assault statute.[20]

B. Aggravated Assaultive Crimes

Over time, most states began to abolish their mayhem statutes, supplement their assault statutes, and to replace their battery provisions with aggravated assault or aggravated battery statutes. The goal of these "aggravated" statutes was to punish more violent or targeted forms of assaultive behavior more severely. In some instances, for example, more severe penalties were reserved for situations where the defendant committed his assault while using a deadly weapon. Other statutes imposed more severe penalties on those who assaulted law enforcement officers, and some punished assaultive crimes more severely when they were committed as a predicate to the intention to commit other, more serious criminal acts, such as assault with intent to rob or assault with intent to rape.

Both simple and aggravated assault rates have been declining in the United States since 1994.[21]

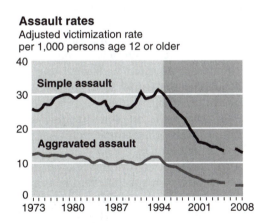

Assault rates
Adjusted victimization rate
per 1,000 persons age 12 or older

In many jurisdictions today, there are a large number of specialized assault statutes that seek to specially protect certain categories of victims. For example, as Professor Richard Singer points out, "[a]side from increased punishments for assaults on law enforcement officers, state codes now specially protect, among

---

[19]See Chapter 8 (Homicide).
[20]Model Penal Code §211(1).
[21]U.S. Dept. of Justice, Office of Justice Programs, Bureau of Justice Statistics, *Assault rates declined since 1994*, http://bjs.ojp.usdoj.gov/content/glance/aslt.cfm.

others, firefighters, school employees (variously described), judges, emergency medical personnel, jurors, public transportation workers, conservation officers, the 'young,' the 'old,' the disabled, and those officiating or coaching at athletic events."[22]

Illinois's aggravated battery statute is a good example of how complex and broad modern assault statues can be, punishing more severely than ordinary battery all of the following disparate acts. What follows is only a *part* of the statute, current as of 2010:

> (a) A person who, in committing a battery, intentionally or knowingly causes great bodily harm, or permanent disability or disfigurement commits aggravated battery.
>
> (b) In committing a battery, a person commits aggravated battery if he or she:
>
> (1) Uses a deadly weapon other than by the discharge of a firearm, or uses an air rifle . . . ;
>
> (2) Is hooded, robed or masked, in such manner as to conceal his identity;
>
> (3) Knows the individual harmed to be a teacher or other person employed in any school and such teacher or other employee is upon the grounds of a school or grounds adjacent thereto, or is in any part of a building used for school purposes; . . .
>
> (6) Knows the individual harmed to be a community policing volunteer while such volunteer is engaged in the execution of any official duties, or to prevent the volunteer from performing official duties, or in retaliation for the volunteer performing official duties, and the battery is committed other than by the discharge of a firearm;
>
> (7) Knows the individual harmed to be an emergency medical technician—ambulance, emergency medical technician—intermediate, emergency medical technician—paramedic, ambulance driver, other medical assistance, first aid personnel, or hospital personnel engaged in the performance of any of his or her official duties, or to prevent the emergency medical technician—ambulance, emergency medical technician—intermediate, emergency medical technician—paramedic, ambulance driver, other medical assistance, first aid personnel, or hospital personnel from performing official duties, or in retaliation for performing official duties;
>
> (8) Is, or the person battered is, on or about a public way, public property or public place of accommodation or amusement;
>
> (8.5) Is, or the person battered is, on a publicly or privately owned sports or entertainment arena, stadium, community or convention hall, special event center, amusement facility, or a special event center in a public park during any 24-hour period when a professional sporting event, National Collegiate Athletic Association (NCAA)-sanctioned sporting event, United States Olympic Committee-sanctioned sporting event, or International Olympic Committee-sanctioned sporting event is taking place in this venue;
>
> (9) Knows the individual harmed to be the driver, operator, employee or passenger of any transportation facility or system engaged in the business of transportation of the public for hire and the individual assaulted is then performing in such capacity or then using such public transportation as a

---

[22]Richard Singer, *The Model Penal Code and Three Two (and Possibly Only One) Ways Courts Avoid Mens Rea*, 4 Buff. Crim. L. Rev 139, 183-184 (2000) (footnotes omitted).

passenger or using any area of any description designated by the transportation facility or system as a vehicle boarding, departure, or transfer location;

(10) Knows the individual harmed to be an individual of 60 years of age or older;

(11) Knows the individual harmed is pregnant;

(12) Knows the individual harmed to be a judge whom the person intended to harm as a result of the judge's performance of his or her official duties as a judge; . . .

(14) Knows the individual harmed to be a person who is physically handicapped;

(15) Knowingly and without legal justification and by any means causes bodily harm to a merchant who detains the person for an alleged commission of retail theft . . . ;

(16) Is, or the person battered is, in any building or other structure used to provide shelter or other services to victims or to the dependent children of victims of domestic violence . . . , or the person battered is within 500 feet of such a building or other structure while going to or from such a building or other structure[;]

(18) Knows the individual harmed to be an officer or employee of the State of Illinois, a unit of local government, or school district engaged in the performance of his or her authorized duties as such officer or employee;

(19) Knows the individual harmed to be an emergency management worker engaged in the performance of any of his or her official duties, or to prevent the emergency management worker from performing official duties, or in retaliation for the emergency management worker performing official duties;

(20) Knows the individual harmed to be a private security officer engaged in the performance of any of his or her official duties, or to prevent the private security officer from performing official duties, or in retaliation for the private security officer performing official duties; or

(21) Knows the individual harmed to be a taxi driver and the battery is committed while the taxi driver is on duty; or

(22) Knows the individual harmed to be a utility worker, while the utility worker is engaged in the execution of his or her duties, or to prevent the utility worker from performing his or her duties, or in retaliation for the utility worker performing his or her duties. . . .[23]

It is hard to imagine a criminal statute more complicated than this one. But such complex and convoluted—flat-out "clunky"—aggravated assaultive conduct statutes, whether they are focused on assault or battery, are relatively common, although there are significant variations in coverage from state to state. Furthermore, such aggravated statutes *always* carry enhanced penalties in contrast to the basic assault offense.

Often such statutes include the element of use of a deadly weapon. While this term is usually defined specifically, it still can be difficult to determine when a deadly weapon is present. An unusual decision involving the question of what constitutes a deadly weapon, for example, was handed down by the Appeals Court of Massachusetts in *Commonwealth v. Shea.*[24] In *Shea*, defendant made sexual advances to

---

[23]720 Ill. Comp. Stat. 5/12-4.
[24]38 Mass. App. Ct. 7, 644 N.E.2d 244 (1995).

two women in a boat five miles off the coast of Boston. When they rebuffed his advances, he threw them overboard and left them. The question was whether he had committed the crime of "assault and battery by means of a dangerous weapon" where the weapon in question was *the ocean*! The court answered this question in the negative, concluding that the ocean in its natural state simply cannot be regarded as a weapon for these purposes. A "weapon," the court concluded, is something that the defendant controls "either through possession of or authority over it, for use of it in the intentional application of force. Because the ocean in its natural state cannot be possessed or controlled, it is not an object or instrumentality capable of use as a weapon. . . ."

Sidebar

WATERED-DOWN PUNISHMENT

Even though the *Shea* court found the ocean not to be a weapon (*but see* the *Sexton* decision discussed next), don't worry. . . . Shea didn't escape punishment for his actions. The *Shea* court nonetheless upheld his convictions for kidnapping and attempted murder, as well as indecent assault and battery, all arising out of the same set of events. It's always well to remember that even where an appellate court reverses a trial court decision, that does not necessarily mean that the accused will go free!

In contrast to *Shea*, however, consider *Commonwealth v. Sexton.*[25] Sexton became involved in a fight in a parking lot outside a bar. He pushed his opponent down and began banging his head on the concrete pavement. The Supreme Judicial Court of Massachusetts affirmed defendant's conviction for "battery by means of a dangerous weapon," concluding that a stationary object such as pavement could in fact be a dangerous weapon. The court noted that while some objects are designed to produce death or great bodily harm, others become dangerous simply because of the manner in which they are used. Rejecting in part the *Shea* court's ocean-is-not-a-deadly-weapon analysis, the court concluded that in fact the ocean *can* be a deadly weapon if, for example, it is used for the purpose of holding the victim's head underwater. The court rejected the notion that a dangerous weapon must be capable of being "possessed."

However, the *Sexton* court did not overrule *Shea* itself, agreeing that, where the danger caused was not due to bringing the victims "into contact with" the ocean, but rather due to deserting them five miles from shore, the ocean is *not* being used as a deadly weapon. The court regarded that situation as different than, say, dropping a victim into a vat of acid: "We contrast this to a situation in which a defendant might drop his victim into a vat of acid, in which the mere contact with the substance would directly pose the risk of serious bodily harm." Indeed, the court noted that banging the victim's head against the hard surface was no different than using a "broken slab of concrete to bludgeon" a victim.

The Model Penal Code contains an aggravated assault provision and does not, as mentioned previously, use the term "battery." That crime is committed when a person "(a) attempts to cause serious bodily injury to another, or causes such injury purposely, knowingly or recklessly under circumstances manifesting extreme indifference to the value of human life; or (b) attempts to cause or purposely or knowingly causes bodily injury to another with a deadly weapon."[26] The Code also provides for enhanced penalties for commission of this offense.[27]

[25]425 Mass. 146, 680 N.E.2d 23 (1997).
[26]Model Penal Code §211.1.
[27]*Id.*

The Model Penal Code differs from some more common aggravated assaultive conduct statutes in two significant ways. First, the Model Penal Code does not treat an assault on a law enforcement official as an aggravated assault.[28] In addition, the MPC does not treat assaults and batteries committed with the intent to commit other crimes as aggravated assaults.[29]

C. Consent Defense

Even though it is still a crime to assault another person, there are numerous circumstances in which the victim's consent to a physical injury or touching provides an accused person with a defense. For example, it is ordinarily an assaultive crime to intentionally inflict injury on another person, but one can consent to a surgical procedure, even though that procedure may cause physical pain.

The Model Penal Code also recognizes this defense. However, it provides that the defense only applies when the "consent [of the victim] negatives an element of the offense or precludes the infliction of the harm or evil sought to be prevented by the law defining the offense."[30] The defense extends even to the threat of bodily injury if the following conditions are met: "(a) the bodily injury consented to or threatened by the conduct consented to is not serious; or (b) the conduct and the injury are reasonably foreseeable hazards of joint participation in a lawful athletic contest or competitive sport or other concerted activity not forbidden by law; or (c) the consent establishes a justification for the conduct. . . ."[31] However, the MPC further provides—sensibly—that consent is ineffective if it is given by someone who is incompetent or who is forced or tricked into consenting.[32]

One situation in which consent is frequently used as a defense involves assaults occurring during the course of athletic events. In the rough and tumble of sports, individuals frequently bump into each other, to put it mildly, and sometimes cause pain and injuries as a result of the physical contact. However, if two athletes accidentally run into each other while playing basketball, for example, there is ordinarily no crime committed, even if one of them suffers a serious injury, such as a broken nose. In most instances, wholly aside from the issue of consent, it would be difficult or impossible to prove that an accused had the mens rea requisite to establish the commission of an assaultive offense. This is particularly true if the offense required proof of an intention to cause bodily injury. Even under the Model Penal Code, which allows recovery based on lesser mental states (e.g., knowledge or recklessness), it is difficult to show that a defendant exhibited criminal recklessness in a sports setting.

However, in some extreme and unusual situations, an athlete's conduct may be so sufficiently "over the top" that criminal sanctions are appropriate. For example, it probably should go without saying, but a basketball player may not use an automatic weapon to stop a member of the other team from scoring—or even a knife. But even physical contact without the use of such a deadly weapon may—in the right circumstances—rise to the level of criminal conduct.

---

[28]Model Penal Code §5.01. MPC §211.1, Comment (1)(c), at 182-183 (1980).
[29]*Id.*
[30]Model Penal Code §2.11(1).
[31]Model Penal Code §2.11(2).
[32]Model Penal Code §2.11(3).

In *State v. Shelley*,[33] for example, defendant Shelley was playing pickup basketball at a university intramural athletics facility. Gonzalez, who had a reputation for being "overly aggressive," fouled him several times, including one foul that scratched defendant's face and drew blood. Defendant suddenly struck Gonzalez when the latter put his hands up in defendant's line of vision as he was trying to catch the ball. Defendant said he "just reacted" because he was afraid of being hurt. Gonzalez required emergency surgery to repair his jaw from what his surgeon described as a "significant" blow. While recognizing that "consent must be an issue in sporting events because a person participates in a game knowing that it will involve potentially offensive contact," the court nonetheless indicated that it could not countenance "intentional excesses beyond those reasonably contemplated in the sport."

In the *Shelley* court's view, the question was whether defendant's conduct "constituted foreseeable behavior in the play of the game" so that the injury "occurred as a by-product of the game itself." Even accepting defendant's version of the facts, the court held that he exceeded the permissible scope of consent given the "magnitude and dangerousness" of what he did and upheld his assault conviction: "There is nothing in the game of basketball, or even rugby or hockey, that would permit consent as a defense to such conduct."

D. Modern Variations on Assault Crimes

In recent years, the crimes of assault and battery have been supplemented in most states by the enactment of a host of different but related crimes, related in the sense that they all involve assaultive conduct. Some of these crimes are designed to deal with special situations, such as stalking or domestic violence. Others deal with attempts to redefine, refine, or expand the scope of coverage of assaultive crimes.

As one example among many, Vermont has enacted a statute criminalizing criminal **stalking**, as have many other states. In Vermont, to "stalk" is defined as "engag[ing] in a course of conduct which consists of following, lying in wait for, or harassing, and: (A) serves no legitimate purpose; and (B) would cause a reasonable person to fear for his or her physical safety or would cause a reasonable person substantial emotional distress."[34]

---

[33]85 Wash. App. 24, 929 P.2d 489 (1997).
[34]Vt. Stat. Ann. tit. 13 §1061.

And, in Vermont, "[a]ny person who intentionally stalks another person shall be imprisoned not more than two years or fined not more than $5,000.00, or both."[35]

Similar to the common assault offense pattern of *simple* assault and *aggravated* assault, Vermont has also enacted a statute that criminalizes aggravated stalking. Aggravated stalking is defined as occurring when "[a] person . . . intentionally stalks another person, and (1) such conduct violates a court order that prohibits stalking and is in effect at the time of the offense; or (2) has been previously convicted of stalking or aggravated stalking; or (3) has been previously convicted of an offense an element of which involves an act of violence against the same person; or (4) the person being stalked is under the age of 16 years; or (5) had a deadly weapon, as defined in section 1021 of this title, in his or her possession while engaged in the act of stalking."[36] The penalties for aggravated stalking are higher than for ordinary stalking—imprisonment for up to five years and a fine of up to $25,000.00, or both—and the statute provides that the crime "aggravated stalking shall be considered a violent act for the purposes of determining bail."[37]

A number of modern statutes also deal with the problem of domestic assault and domestic violence. For example, another Vermont statute makes it a crime for "[a]ny person who attempts to cause or wilfully or recklessly causes bodily injury to a family or household member, or wilfully causes a family or household member to fear imminent serious bodily injury shall be imprisoned not more than one year or fined not more than $5,000.00, or both."[38]

Once again, Vermont has also enacted a more serious version of this "new" offense, this time, by dividing the offense into degrees. It is second-degree domestic assault, a more serious crime than mere domestic assault, in the following circumstances: "A person commits the crime of second degree aggravated domestic assault if the person: (1) commits the crime of domestic assault and causes bodily injury to another person and such conduct violates specific conditions of a criminal court order in effect at the time of the offense imposed to protect that other person; or (2) commits a second or subsequent offense of domestic assault, which causes bodily injury."[39] A person who commits the crime of second-degree aggravated domestic assault in Vermont "shall be imprisoned not more than five years or fined not more than $10,000.00, or both."[40]

Moreover, Vermont has also created the even more serious crime of first-degree aggravated domestic assault: "A person commits the crime of first degree aggravated domestic assault if the person: (1) attempts to cause or wilfully or recklessly causes serious bodily injury to a family or household member; or (2) uses, attempts to use or is armed with a deadly weapon and threatens to use the deadly weapon on a family or household member; or (3) commits the crime of domestic assault and has been previously convicted of aggravated domestic assault."[41] A person who commits the crime of first-degree aggravated domestic assault in Vermont "shall be imprisoned not more than 15 years or fined not more than $25,000.00, or both."[42]

[35]Vt. Stat. Ann. tit. 13 §1062.
[36]Vt. Stat. Ann. tit. 13 §1063.
[37]*Id.*
[38]Vt. Stat. Ann. tit. 13 §1042.
[39]Vt. Stat. Ann. tit. 13 §1044(a).
[40]Vt. Stat. Ann. tit. 13 §1044(b).
[41]Vt. Stat. Ann. tit. 13 §1043(a).
[42]Vt. Stat. Ann. tit. 13 §1043(b).

SUMMARY

- Assault and battery were separate crimes at common law. Today many jurisdictions have merged those crimes into the single offense of simple assault, but also criminalize separately more serious aggravated assaults.

- Simple assault exists when a person causes another person to fear that unlawful force is about to be used against him or her or when a person actually uses or attempts to use such force on another person.

- Aggravated forms of assault include more violent forms of assaultive conduct and/or assaultive conduct that has resulted in injury.

- Sometimes a victim's consent to otherwise assaultive conduct is deemed to be a valid defense.

CONNECTIONS

Relationship to Attempt

In many jurisdictions today, the crime of simple assault includes both the common law offenses of assault *and* battery, hence, in these states, an attempted battery is an assault, not a separate attempt offense. See Chapter 6.

Relationship to Homicide

Most homicides (see Chapter 8) result from assaultive conduct that is taken too far. In fact, it is often the case that an actor simply intends to engage in assaultive conduct but the unintended consequence of such acts is the death of the victim, resulting in charges of second-degree murder or involuntary manslaughter.

Relationship to Sex Crimes

Sex crimes (see Chapter 10) are simply assaultive crimes with additional elements added, related to the level of sexual contact or intrusion involved.

Relationship to Theft Offenses and Related Crimes

The crime of robbery is generally defined as the taking of property, including but not exclusively money, from another person by means of force, threat, or intimidation. See Chapter 11. Although the robbery offense includes some patently assaultive elements, for historical reasons it has been treated instead as a violent theft offense.

Rape and Sexual Assault

10

Rape has changed. Modern sexual assault statutes are often significantly different from the old, common law crime of rape. Some rape offenses today focus on the use of force by the accused and others on the absence of consent by the victim. The common law rape offense, in contrast, required the prosecutor to prove both. Indeed, virtually all modern rape offenses are less difficult to prove than common law rape. Many of the evidentiary impediments to successful rape prosecutions have also been eliminated and new provisions have been enacted in order to try and prevent irrelevant and humiliating intimidation of witnesses. Perhaps most significant, jurisdictions now possess a number of sexual offense crimes of varying gravity, in addition to the most serious sexual offense of rape itself.

OVERVIEW

A. ELEMENTS OF RAPE

1. Force Requirement
2. Consent
3. Mens Rea
4. Spousal Rape
5. Expanded Scope of Rape and Lesser Sexual Offenses

B. STATUTORY RAPE

C. EVIDENTIARY PROVISIONS

1. Rape Shield Laws
2. Defendant's Sexual Assault Record
3. Rape Trauma Syndrome

Persons convicted of the crime of rape at common law were subject to the death penalty. Perhaps because of the seriousness of the charge, the difficulties of proof, and the severe penalty that resulted from conviction, common law courts created various rules—procedural, evidentiary, and substantive—designed, theoretically, to ensure that innocent individuals were not wrongfully convicted of rape.

For example, the prosecution was traditionally required to prove that the victim resisted the rape "to the utmost." Moreover, a conviction could not be obtained based solely on the testimony of the victim. Corroborating evidence was required to make out the offense. In addition, evidence of the victim's prior sexual conduct was admissible in rape prosecutions on the theory that her "lack of chastity" reflected on her credibility, as well as on the question whether or not she actually consented to the sexual act in question.

Although such common law evidentiary rules arguably had the desirable effect of helping to ensure that innocent individuals were not wrongfully convicted, they also produced undesirable effects as well. In particular, the nature of rape prosecutions ended up discouraging victims from reporting sexual assaults. Many women did not report rapes because the prosecutorial process they subsequently had to endure was perceived to be and often was unnecessarily humiliating. Moreover, victims knew that—given the difficulties in proving rape at trial—the odds on a successful conviction were or at least appeared to be slim, particularly in cases of acquaintance rape, which did not fit the classic rape paradigm of sexual assault by a stranger. So why go through all the trauma of the prosecution if reporting the crime was not likely to lead to a conviction?

In addition, even when a rape was reported, victims often believed that it was unlikely that the rapist would be apprehended. In some instances, the police would reject the victim's report of a rape out of hand as unfounded. In other instances, because the alleged perpetrator was a stranger to the victim, the police encountered difficulties identifying, apprehending, and convicting the person the victim described. A number of other factors contributed to the difficulty the police and prosecution had in successfully prosecuting sexual offenders, including the often unwitting destruction of physical evidence by victims, the special evidentiary rules relating to proof of rape, and the difficulty of tying the offender to the crime by evidence other than the testimony of a victim who, because of the emotions surrounding the event and prevailing public attitudes, stereotypes, and misconceptions, often proved especially vulnerable to disbelief by the fact finder.

In recent decades, efforts have been made to reform the law relating to sexual assaults in virtually every jurisdiction. Whether or not these efforts have been a triggering cause, it is nonetheless true that the victimization rates for rape have fallen significantly since 1993, although the absolute number of sexual assaults in the United States each year continues to be extremely high.[1]

---

[1] *See, e.g.,* Callie Marie Rennison, *Rape and Sexual Assault: Reporting to Police and Medical Attention, 1992-2000*, U.S. Department of Justice, Office of Justice Programs, Bureau of Justice Statistics (August 2002): "Persons age 12 or older experienced an average annual 140,990 completed rapes, 109,230 attempted rapes, and 152,680 completed and attempted sexual assaults between 1992 and 2000, according to the National

Rape rates

Adjusted victimization rate
per 1,000 persons age 12 or older

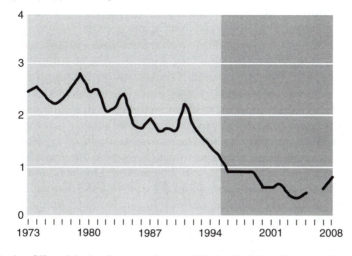

U.S. Dept. of Justice, Office of Justice Programs, Bureau of Justice Statistics, *Rape rates have been stable in recent years,* http://bjs.ojp.usdoj.gov/content/glance/rape.cfm.

A. Elements of Rape

(1) Force Requirement

At common law, in order to successfully convict an accused of **rape**, the prosecution was required to prove that the defendant engaged in sexual intercourse, including vaginal penetration, however slight, with a woman not his wife by the use of force or threat of force and without the victim's consent. Moreover, as previously mentioned, many courts supplemented these requisite elements of the crime with the further requirement that the victim "resist to the utmost."

This resistance requirement was imposed for a variety of reasons. To some extent, it probably reflected stereotypic concerns that, absent such a requirement, men who had successfully "seduced" women might later face accusations of rape when these women reconsidered the wisdom or propriety of their actions and *falsely,* out of embarrassment or for a host of other reasons, claimed lack of consent. Or, viewed more charitably, some judges and legislators may have believed at the time that if there was evidence of strong resistance on the victim's part, it made it clearer that the sexual act was truly forced and that the victim did not consent.

Over time, a host of commentators questioned whether it was fair—or even rational—to require proof that a rape victim had resisted to the utmost. This was

Crime Victimization Survey. Most rapes and sexual assaults were committed against females: Female victims accounted for 94% of all completed rapes, 91% of all attempted rapes, and 89% of all completed and attempted sexual assaults, 1992-2000. [Most] rapes and sexual assaults against females were not reported to the police. Thirty-six percent of rapes, 34% of attempted rapes, and 26% of sexual assaults were reported to police, 1992-2000."

not a requirement that was used for other serious crimes—no state required that a person resist to the utmost before surrendering his wallet to an armed robber in order for armed robbery to be established, for instance. It was not required for these crimes for any number of reasons, including the possibility that a victim's resistance might well result in additional—perhaps even worse—violence. Eventually, the point was made—and subsequently widely accepted—that victims who resisted sexual assaults, similarly, might well face a greater risk of suffering more serious injury, or even death, than they would if they submitted without resisting "to the utmost."

Today, no jurisdiction requires that a rape victim resist to the utmost. Some jurisdictions have reached this result by statute; others through changes in the prevailing case law. Pennsylvania law now provides expressly, for example, that "[t]he alleged victim need not resist the actor in prosecutions under this [sexual offenses] chapter: Provided, however, That nothing in this section shall be construed to prohibit a defendant from introducing evidence that the alleged victim consented to the conduct in question."[2]

However, it is nonetheless true that despite the formal elimination of the resistance requirement, some states continue to define the element of force or threat of force, at least in part, either expressly or implicitly, in terms of the defendant's actions overcoming the victim's resistance. For example, in Pennsylvania, which has expressly abrogated the resistance requirement by law, as set out above, the rape statute itself nonetheless still criminalizes, *inter alia*, "sexual intercourse with a complainant . . . [b]y threat of forcible compulsion *that would prevent resistance by a person of reasonable resolution*."[3]

Similarly, although the Model Penal Code eliminated the concepts of both non-consent and resistance from its rape formulation, the drafters nonetheless provided a cautionary warning: "This is not to say that consent by the victim is irrelevant or that inquiry into the level of resistance by the victim cannot or should not be made. Compulsion plainly implies non-consent, just as resistance is evidence of non-consent."[4]

Furthermore, unlike the common law, rape statutes in most jurisdictions today do *not* require proof of *both* the use of force *and* the absence of consent. Instead, they typically require proof of one of those elements or the other, not both.

Indeed, in some jurisdictions, one sexual assault statute might require proof of the use of force and yet another sexual assault statute—in the very same jurisdiction—might require proof of the absence of consent. Pennsylvania, for example, uses *both* elements . . . *but* in separate statutes. The most serious sexual assault statute in Pennsylvania, rape, is premised, *inter alia*, on the use of force or the threat of force by the accused: "A person commits a felony of the first degree when the person engages in sexual intercourse with a complainant: (1) *By forcible compulsion*[;] (2) By *threat of forcible compulsion* that would prevent resistance by a person of reasonable resolution."[5] But, a separate sexual assault statute, graded less seriously than the crime of rape, does not require the use of force; it is premised upon the victim's absence of consent: "[A] person commits a felony of the second degree when that person engages in sexual intercourse or deviate sexual intercourse with a complainant *without the complainant's consent*."[6]

---

[2]18 Pa. C.S.A. §3107.
[3]18 Pa. C.S.A. §3121(a)(2) (emphasis added).
[4]Model Penal Code §213.1, Comment (4)(a), at 306-307 (1980).
[5]18 Pa. C.S.A. §3121(a)(1) and (2) (emphasis added).
[6]18 Pa. C.S.A. §3124.1 (emphasis added).

Quite often, when a rape statute utilizes a "force" element, it also provides an alternative element focused upon the victim's "acquiescence" in the face of a "threat" of force or the "fear" of injury, or similar terminology. Consider, for example, the Supreme Court of California's decision in *People v. Iniguez*.[7] In *Iniguez*, the victim, Mercy, who weighed 105 pounds, spent the night before her wedding at the home of a family friend. Defendant, the friend's fiancé, who weighed 205 pounds, woke Mercy up in the middle of the night, pulled off her clothes, and put his penis in her vagina. Mercy didn't resist; instead, she "froze." When the defendant moved off her, she ran and hid and called a friend, who came and picked her up. Defendant was subsequently convicted of rape, which required that "the act of sexual intercourse was accomplished by means of force or fear of immediate and unlawful bodily injury." He argued that the element of force or fear of injury was absent.

The California Supreme Court affirmed his conviction, however, noting that the rape statute had been amended to eliminate both the resistance requirement and the requirement that the threat of immediate bodily harm be accompanied by an apparent power to inflict it. The amendments were motivated, the court added, by studies showing that, while some women actively resist sexual assaults, others are frozen with fear. With that in mind, the court concluded that the evidence clearly established that sexual intercourse was "accomplished against the victim's will by means of fear of immediate and unlawful bodily injury. . . . [T]here was substantial evidence that the victim genuinely feared immediate and unlawful bodily injury. . . . Any man or woman awakening to find himself or herself in this situation could reasonably react with fear of immediate and unlawful bodily injury."

Most of the sexual offenses set out in the Model Penal Code are now outdated. They are no longer representative of the law in most states, although they may well have been at one time. The Model Penal Code, for example, defines forcible rape as sexual penetration by a "male" who "compels [a female not his wife] to submit by force or by threat of imminent death, serious bodily injury, extreme pain or kidnapping, to be inflicted on anyone."[8] These gender references—both as to possible perpetrators and victims—are anachronistic today. Females may be rapists; males may be rape victims.

The Code also added the crime of Gross Sexual Imposition, which applies when a man compels a woman to submit to sexual penetration through use of "any threat that would prevent resistance by a woman of reasonable resolution."[9] Aside from the outdated gender references, some jurisdictions—a distinct minority at this point—still use language of this sort in their sexual assault statutes.

The MPC further provided that rape, unlike other crimes, could not be prosecuted unless it had been reported within three months.[10] Such a so-called prompt complaint or fresh complaint rule illustrates the extent to which suspicion and criticism of women who falsely complain of rape underlay much of our traditional rape and sexual assault law. Today, such rules are viewed as discriminatory and outdated, although similar provisions existed in many jurisdictions at one time and now have been largely abolished. Currently, three jurisdictions still retain a prompt complaint rule, but only in cases of spousal rape.[11]

---

[7] 7 Cal. 4th 847, 872 P.2d 1183, 30 Cal. Rptr. 2d 258 (1994).
[8] Model Penal Code §213.1(1)(a).
[9] Model Penal Code §213.1(2)(a).
[10] Model Penal Code §213.6(4).
[11] See Chapter 10(A)(4).

(2) Consent

At common law, in addition to the use of force, the absence of consent was a necessary prerequisite to a rape conviction, although consent was sometimes inappropriately inferred from the victim's lack of resistance. However, the consent requirement increasingly became the subject of a variety of criticisms. Most pointedly, it was claimed that the requirement—that rape be nonconsensual and against the victim's will—effectively placed the burden of proof on the victim to prove that she had not in fact consented to the sexual act.

As a result, rape cases frequently turned on questions of the victim's credibility and character, and courts often distrusted the testimony of rape victims, in the words of the framers of the Model Penal Code, "assuming that women lie about their lack of consent for various reasons: to blackmail men, to explain the discovery of a consensual affair, or because of psychological illness."[12] Once again, however wrong headedly, a woman's resistance was deemed to be a solution to this presumed credibility problem because "it was the 'outward manifestation of nonconsent,' [a] device for determining whether a woman actually gave consent."[13]

In an effort to shift and redefine the law of sexual assault, many criminal justice reformers sought—often successfully—to eliminate the consent requirement from the rape offense and replace it with a force element.

Reformers argued, among other things, that rape was a crime of violence, rather than a sexual crime, and it should be treated like other violent crimes. The original idea behind rape laws was to protect the supposed "property rights" of men in their wives and daughters. This idea influenced modern rape laws in the sense that rape was viewed as "a crime against the purity or chastity of a woman," and the "burden of protecting that chastity fell on the woman, with the state offering its protection only after the woman demonstrated that she had resisted sufficiently."[14] Reformers argued that, rather than focusing on the victim's conduct, the focus should be—strictly—on the conduct of the accused, more specifically on his use of force.

> **Common law rape: Force *and* no consent**
> **Modern rape statutes: *Either* force *or* no consent**

Even though a general consensus emerged that the rape offense needed to be modified—modernized—there were substantial differences of thought about the best and most appropriate way to actually redefine the crime. Some advocated that rape be defined simply as unconsented-to sexual intercourse (and that is what some jurisdictions did); some urged the elimination of any reference to consent from the definition of rape in favor of a strict focus on the use of force (and that is what some jurisdictions did); still others favored the adoption of both sorts of sexual assault statutes as complements to one another, as the examples from Pennsylvania, set out above, illustrate. Nonetheless, virtually all of the proponents of reform shared one central premise: that the burden of showing nonconsent should not fall on the victim of the crime.

---

[12]*Id.*
[13]*Id.*
[14]*Id.*

Although many modern rape statutes have simply eliminated the element of absence of consent, the issue still arises in rape prosecutions—almost inevitably—directly or indirectly. By definition, if sexual intercourse is consensual, there is no *forcible* rape. Because of this fact, even when the governing statute does not explicitly address the issue, many states allow defendants to raise the question of consent as a defense and also allow defendants to offer proof that the charged forcible sexual acts were in fact not forced at all, but were instead consensual.

For example, in *State of New Jersey in the Interest of M.T.S.*,[15] although the rape statute did not provide expressly for a consent defense, the court held that rape is committed only "in the absence of what a reasonable person would believe to be affirmative and freely-given permission to the act of sexual penetration." But, the court added, "that permission may be inferred either from acts or statements reasonably viewed in light of the surrounding circumstances. . . . Permission to engage in an act of sexual penetration can be and indeed often is indicated through physical actions rather than words. Permission is demonstrated when the evidence, in whatever form, is sufficient to demonstrate that a reasonable person would have believed that the alleged victim had affirmatively and freely given authorization to the act."

The holding of the Wisconsin Court of Appeals in *State v. Lederer* illustrates the modern approach to consent issues.[16] In *Lederer*, defendant arranged for the victim to inspect a rental property. When he began to take her clothes off, she objected vociferously. However, because defendant told her

"CONSENT" TO SEX REDEFINED

Some jurisdictions retain the absence-of-consent element, but essentially redefine it. For example, California's statute provides that "'consent' shall be defined to mean positive cooperation in act or attitude pursuant to an exercise of free will. The person must act freely and voluntarily and have knowledge of the nature of the act or transaction involved." Calif. Penal Code §261.6.

Other state statutes redefine consent in a manner that expressly rejects outdated stereotypes about when consent did or did not exist. For example, Illinois provides that: "'Consent' means a freely given agreement to the act of sexual penetration or sexual conduct in question. Lack of verbal or physical resistance or submission by the victim resulting from the use of force or threat of force by the accused shall not constitute consent. The manner of dress of the victim at the time of the offense shall not constitute consent." Ill. Cons. Stat. Ch. 720, §5/12-17(a).

that it would be worse for her if she fought him, she ultimately permitted him to engage in sex acts with her, despite her continuing protests. Under the applicable sexual assault statute, consent was defined as "words or overt actions by a person who is competent to give informed consent indicating a freely given agreement to have sexual intercourse or sexual contact." The Wisconsin court held that failure to resist is not consent, and that "two parties may [not] enter into consensual sexual relations without manifesting freely given consent through words or acts." On the facts presented, the court found a clear lack of consent since the victim objected from the very beginning of the encounter.

(3) Mens Rea

Traditionally, no mens rea was required for the absence-of-consent element of the crime of rape; it was not necessary, accordingly, for the prosecution to prove that the defendant knew or should have known that the victim did not consent. However, in

---

[15]129 N.J. 422, 609 A.2d 1266 (1992).
[16]99 Wis. 2d 430, 299 N.W.2d 457 (App. 1980).

some (but by no means all) jurisdictions, a mens rea requirement did exist for the use of force element. In these jurisdictions, as the "resistance to the utmost" standard was slowly abandoned or modified, courts began to permit a defense of mistake— that is, a defendant could defend successfully against rape charges by establishing that he honestly believed that his victim was consenting to sexual intercourse.

F   A   Q

Q: What is the relationship between the absence of mens rea with respect to consent and the common law resistance requirement?

A: Despite the fact that knowledge of lack of consent was not an element of the crime of rape, in order to ensure that the sexual act was nonconsensual, as previously discussed, courts often in the past required the prosecution to prove that the victim "resisted to the utmost."

In most jurisdictions today, however, mistake is *not* a viable mens rea defense to a rape charge. In *State v. Koperski*,[17] for example, the Nebraska Supreme Court concluded cogently that "[a] mistake of fact as to the victim's consent is . . . not a defense to first degree sexual assault." This result followed from the fact that the court found that "[w]hile [this statute] does not expressly state any requisite level of criminal intent with regard to any of the elements of the crime and first degree sexual assault is clearly not a specific intent crime, we conclude that [it] is, nevertheless, a general intent crime [and] criminal intent is inferred from the commission of the acts constituting the elements of the crime of first degree sexual assault. Therefore, the only burden on the prosecution in order to prove general criminal intent . . . is to prove beyond a reasonable doubt that the accused subjected another person to sexual penetration and overcame the victim by force, threat of force, coercion, or deception."[18]

Despite the holding in *Koperski*, reflecting the majority rule, some courts (a minority) nonetheless have interpreted their rape statutes as providing a defense for a "reasonable" and "good faith" mistake. In some instances, the defense is qualified by a requirement that the defendant cannot be reckless, although he can act negligently in good faith.

For example, in *People v. Mayberry*,[19] the California Supreme Court held that when a defendant argues that the victim's claimed lack of consent was ambiguously stated, he is entitled to an instruction regarding the impact of a reasonable mistake of fact. The *Mayberry* court noted that "the legislature has substantially enhanced the risk of conviction in ambiguous circumstances by eliminating the requirement that the state prove 'resistance' and by substantially broadening the definitions of 'force' and 'physical injury . . . ,'" but the legislature also counterbalanced these changes by "shifting the focus of the jury's attention from the victim's resistance or actions to the defendant's understanding of the totality of the circumstances. The state must prove that defendant acted recklessly with regard to consent."

[17]254 Neb. 624, 578 N.W.2d 837, 845 (1998).
[18]See discussion of general and specific intent in Chapter 3 (Mens Rea).
[19]15 Cal. 3d 143, 125 Cal. Rptr. 745, 542 P.2d 1337 (Cal. 1975).

(4) Spousal Rape

At common law, there was a spousal rape exemption that precluded a man from being convicted for raping his wife. In large part, this exemption reflected the outdated belief that a woman lost the right *not* to consent to sexual activity with her husband after she was married. Chief Justice Hale of England infamously commented in the seventeenth century that a husband could not be guilty of rape of his wife "for by their mutual matrimonial consent and contract the wife hath given up herself in this kind unto the husband which she cannot retract."

Even as late as the 1960s, the drafters of the Model Penal Code continued to rationalize this exclusion by arguing that "[t]he gravity of the crime of forcible rape derives not merely from its violent character but also from its achievement of a particularly degrading kind of unwanted intimacy. Where the attacker stands in an ongoing relation of sexual intimacy, that evil, as distinct from the force used to compel submission, may well be thought qualitatively different."[20] As a result, the Model Penal Code proposed that the spousal rape exemption should be retained, and even that it be extended to unmarried persons living together as spouses, but not married individuals living apart from each other under judicial decree of separation.

In recent decades, attitudes toward spousal rape have changed significantly. The overwhelming majority of courts and legislatures have come to recognize that a spousal rape exemption is inappropriate, unfair, and unwarranted. Indeed, recent research has established quite clearly that victims of spousal or partner rape suffer even longer-lasting trauma than do victims of stranger rape. The failure of states to protect spouses, usually women, from such marital rape is viewed by many as a human rights violation.

Since the late 1970s, most states have eliminated the spousal rape exemption altogether. Some other states have responded by eliminating the exemption, treating spousal rape as a sexual assault *but* treating it as a less serious sexual assault than the rape of a non-spouse, usually with different and additional statutory elements— for example, using a force element rather than a consent element and/or retaining a prompt complaint requirement. In these jurisdictions, while spousal rape is now a crime, prosecutors still have to overcome additional legal hurdles not present for other victims of rape in order to secure a conviction.

Sidebar

THE RIGHT NOT TO BE SUBJECTED TO MARITAL RAPE IS A HUMAN RIGHT

Article 2 of the U.N. Declaration on the Elimination of Violence Against Women provides:

Violence against women shall be understood to encompass, but not be limited to, the following:

(a) Physical, sexual and psychological violence occurring in the family, including battering, sexual abuse of female children in the household, dowry-related violence, *marital rape*, female genital mutilation and other traditional practices harmful to women, non-spousal violence and violence related to exploitation;

(b) Physical, sexual and psychological violence occurring within the general community, including rape, sexual abuse, sexual harassment and intimidation at work, in educational institutions and elsewhere, trafficking in women and forced prostitution;

(c) Physical, sexual and psychological violence perpetrated or condoned by the State, wherever it occurs.

Article 4 provides further that "states should condemn violence against women and should not invoke any custom, tradition or religious consideration to avoid their obligations with respect to its elimination. States should pursue by all appropriate means and without delay a policy of eliminating violence against women."

U.N. General Assembly Resolution 48/104 of 20 December 1993.

---

[20]Model Penal Code §213.1, Comment (8)(c), at 345-346 (1980).

(5) Expanded Scope of Rape and Lesser Sexual Offenses

The common law definition of rape has been amended in every jurisdiction, as has been discussed, although somewhat differently in every state. In addition to the modernizing changes in the rape offense already noted, newer variations on the basic offense have been enacted as well. These include provisions relating, for example, to sexual activity with unconscious or incompetent victims; with minor clients, patients, students, or other individuals in an actor's care; or by means of fraud or the unsuspecting administration of drugs to overcome a victim's resistance.

As a result, the rape offense in some jurisdictions contains a long "laundry list" of separate offenses, each with its own elements, each of which amounts to commission of rape. In Oklahoma, for example, non-spousal, non-statutory rape includes the following acts: "Rape is an act of sexual intercourse involving vaginal or anal penetration accomplished with a male or female who is not the spouse of the perpetrator and who may be of the same or the opposite sex as the perpetrator under any of the following circumstances: . . . 2. Where the victim is incapable through mental illness or any other unsoundness of mind, whether temporary or permanent, of giving legal consent; 3. Where force or violence is used or threatened, accompanied by apparent power of execution to the victim or to another person; 4. Where the victim is intoxicated by a narcotic or anesthetic agent, administered by or with the privity of the accused as a means of forcing the victim to submit; 5. Where the victim is at the time unconscious of the nature of the act and this fact is known to the accused; 6. Where the victim submits to sexual intercourse under the belief that the person committing the act is a spouse, and this belief is induced by artifice, pretense, or concealment practiced by the accused or by the accused in collusion with the spouse with intent to induce that belief . . . ; 7. Where the victim is under the legal custody or supervision of a state agency, a federal agency, a county, a municipality or a political subdivision and engages in sexual intercourse with a state, federal, county, municipal or political subdivision employee or an employee of a contractor of the state, the federal government, a county, a municipality or a political subdivision that exercises authority over the victim; or 8. Where the victim is at least sixteen (16) years of age and is less than twenty (20) years of age and is a student, or under the legal custody or supervision of any public or private elementary or secondary school, junior high or high school, or public vocational school, and engages in sexual intercourse with a person who is eighteen (18) years of age or older and is an employee of the same school system."[21]

Moreover, in addition to the most serious sexual offense in a jurisdiction's crimes code—often still called "rape" or "forcible rape"—every jurisdiction has enacted a host of other, less serious—less serious as determined by the legislature, at least—sexual offenses as well. Sometimes these offenses are "lesser included" offenses of rape; sometimes, they are simply different offenses altogether, such as incest. Spousal rape is sometimes treated as a separate offense from stranger rape, as previously discussed. Statutory rape, a different type of sexual offense, is discussed separately below.

---

[21]Okla. St. Ann. §1111(A).

Q: What is incest and why is it a crime?

A: Incest is sexual intercourse between parents and children, siblings, and other defined categories of family members, and it is criminalized in most jurisdictions. The traditional rationale for this criminal prohibition is based on genetics, preventing the deleterious health consequences of inbreeding. However, in the modern view, incest is also criminalized in the interests of preserving family unity and preventing sexual predation.

Furthermore, many jurisdictions separately punish forcible or nonconsensual anal and/or oral sexual activity differently than vaginal sexual assaults. And most jurisdictions, in addition to rape, also criminalize assaultive sexual offenses that do *not* include the actual penetration of the victim's genitals as is traditionally required to establish rape. Such additional offenses sometimes are broken down by degrees— like homicide offenses often are—and sometimes they simply include separate crimes styled something like indecent exposure, bestiality, indecent assault, aggravated indecent assault, indecent contact, aggravated indecent contact, seduction, institutional sexual assault, and sexual imposition.

B. Statutory Rape

At common law, the crime of **statutory rape** punished sexual intercourse by a male with a female under the age of ten years old. What makes statutory rape different from the crime of rape itself is that the consent of the minor is *not* a defense. The rationale for this position has traditionally been that a victim of statutory rape is so young that she—and today, *he*, as well—is incapable as a matter of law of consenting to sexual activity. Today, statutory rape remains a crime in every jurisdiction, although the so-called age of consent—no longer ten, as it was at the common law—varies state by state, ranging from 14 to 18 years of age.

AGE OF CONSENT BY STATE

Where two ages are separated by a slash, the lower age applies when the age gap between partners is small or when the older partner is below a certain age.

Alabama 16	Connecticut 16
Alaska 16	D.C. 16
Arizona 18	Delaware 16/18
Arkansas 16	Florida 16/18
California 18	Georgia 16
Colorado 15/17	Hawaii 16

Idaho 16/18	New York 17
Illinois 17	North Carolina 16
Indiana 16	North Dakota 18
Iowa 14/16	Ohio 16
Kansas 16	Oklahoma 16
Kentucky 16	Oregon 18
Louisiana 17	Pennsylvania 16
Maine 16	Rhode Island 16
Maryland 16	South Carolina 14
Massachusetts 16	South Dakota 16
Michigan 16	Tennessee 18
Minnesota 16	Texas 17
Mississippi 16	Utah 16/18
Missouri 14/17	Vermont 16
Montana 16/18	Virginia 18
Nebraska 17	Washington 16/18
Nevada 16	West Virginia 16
New Hampshire 16	Wisconsin 18
New Jersey 16	Wyoming 16/18
New Mexico 17	

Avert, *Worldwide ages of consent,* http://www.avert.org/aofconsent.htm.

Since the crime of statutory rape is often enacted as a strict liability offense, the defendant's alleged mistake as to the victim's age, even a reasonable mistake, is often deemed *not* to be a defense to the crime of statutory rape because there is no mens rea and mistake of fact should not apply ordinarily. However, as the crime of statutory rape was gradually extended to teenage but still minor victims—and to consensual sexual activity between teenagers themselves—some courts and legislatures began to rethink their handling of the mistake defense and, to some limited degree, changed their minds on this score.

Some jurisdictions, accordingly, by statute or court ruling, have created or recognized the defense of reasonable mistake as to the victim's age, at least where the victim is at or above a specified minimum age.[22] Many jurisdictions, however, continue to hold to the traditional rule, namely that there is no mistake defense at all in statutory rape prosecutions.

Another common change from the common law in statutory rape statutes is that many jurisdictions have adopted gender neutral language or otherwise interpreted their statutes as applying to both genders, recognizing expressly that male defendants can be prosecuted for having sexual intercourse with underage males or females and that female defendants can be prosecuted for having sexual intercourse with underage males or females.

Yet another common change from the common law that some jurisdictions have made is to require a significant age gap between the defendant and victim for a rape prosecution. The Model Penal Code provided that, for victims between the ages of 10 years old and 16 years old, a four-year age gap between the defendant and the victim must exist before a conviction could be obtained. This age differential requirement was designed "to reflect the prevailing pattern of secondary education," so that "a school age romancer" should not be subjected to "felony sanctions for mutually consensual behavior with a person whom society regards as a fit associate."[23]

While no jurisdiction today has followed the MPC approach of pegging the age of consent at only ten years old, a few jurisdictions have adopted an age-gap requirement, usually four years, and some other jurisdictions have simply established a minimum age, usually 18 or 21, for a person to be subject to prosecution for statutory rape.

C. Evidentiary Provisions

Common law courts, as previously discussed, utilized various rules—procedural, evidentiary, and substantive—that had the effect if not the intent of making it more difficult to prosecute and convict accused rapists. In recent decades, not only have many of the outdated evidentiary requirements been largely eliminated—for instance, the corroboration requirement—but a number of new evidentiary provisions have been enacted in an attempt to eliminate some of the perceived unfairness and unnecessary humiliation of the victim that prevailed in too many instances in the past. Some of these changes are briefly noted here.

(1) Rape Shield Laws

Rape shield laws are rules of evidence designed to limit irrelevant inquiry into a sexual assault victim's prior sexual behavior. Such laws were adopted in response to trial courts that commonly permitted broad inquiry into a victim's sexual history, including the victim's lack of chastity, reputation, and prior sexual relations with people other than the accused.

As the Tennessee Supreme Court made the point, often what defense counsel was seeking to accomplish by using prejudicial and embarrassing evidence of this

---

[22]*See, e.g., State v. Yanez*, 716 A.2d 759 (R.I. 1998) (noting that a substantial minority of states provide for a reasonable-mistake-of-age defense when the victim is at least ten years of age); 18 Pa. Cons. Stat. Ann. §3102 ("Except as otherwise provided, whenever in this chapter the criminality of conduct depends on a child being below the age of 14 years, it is no defense that the defendant did not know the age of the child or reasonably believed the child to be the age of 14 years or older. When criminality depends on the child's being below a critical age older than 14 years, it is a defense for the defendant to prove by a preponderance of the evidence that he or she reasonably believed the child to be above the critical age.").

[23]Model Penal Code §213.3(1)(a), Comment (2), at 386 (1980).

sort was to demonstrate—directly or indirectly—that the victim, usually female, was "a woman who had sexual relations in the past [and] was[, accordingly,] more likely to have consented to sexual relations with a specific criminal defendant. Those attitudes," the court continued, "resulted in two rape trials at the same time—the trial of the defendant and the trial of the rape victim based on her past sexual conduct. It has been said that the victim of a sexual assault is assaulted twice—once by the criminal justice system." Rape shield laws were enacted in an attempt to minimize the likelihood that evidence of the alleged victim's sexual history might cause the jury to be unfairly prejudiced against the victim.

The concern with rape shield laws, however, is that they may sometimes unduly limit a defendant's right to defend himself, impinging both on his rights to a fair trial and to confront the witnesses against him. Because of these concerns, legislatures and courts have constructed and construed their rape shield laws in a fashion intended to insure that the effect of these provisions is not to keep the defendant from introducing evidence—whether or not it relates to the victim's past sexual conduct—that has some legitimate relevancy to the defendant's actual defense in the case at bar. Accordingly, these laws are often applied in such a way that trial judges must exercise discretion whether to admit specific evidence of prior sexual conduct, after weighing its likely probative value against its possible prejudicial effect.

F   A   Q

Q: When might a trial judge permit evidence of a victim's sexual history to be used at a rape trial?

A: Typically, the defense in a rape case will be allowed to offer proof of a prior sexual relationship between the defendant and the victim and also to establish that the victim had sexual relations with someone else around the same time as the sexual assault in question in an effort to prove that the defendant was not the person who inflicted whatever physical signs of sexual activity that may have existed.

(2) Defendant's Sexual Assault Record

Historically, evidence of a defendant's prior conduct or "bad acts" was held inadmissible as a general rule for the purpose of proving guilt because it was regarded as unduly prejudicial. However, exceptions to this general rule did exist that allowed such evidence to be used to prove motive, identity, a common plan, or absence of mistake. Today, because of changes in some evidentiary rules in some jurisdictions, more liberal use of prior conduct evidence is often permitted in sexual offense cases.

(3) Rape Trauma Syndrome

In 1974, "rape trauma syndrome" (RTS) was first identified[24] as a syndrome that consists of a variety of post-sexual assault physical and emotional traits that many

---

[24]*See* Ann Wolbert Burgess & Lynda Lytle Holmstrom, *Rape Trauma Syndrome*, 131 Am. J. Psychiatry, Sept. 1974, at 981.

rape victims apparently share. It also focuses on the often counterintuitive behaviors that many rape victims display, behaviors that are different from the way many lay people would expect a rape victim to act. Since these behaviors are contrary to common intuition, their presence may lead a fact finder to disbelieve the victim. Hence, the prosecution in a sexual assault trial might well want to introduce expert testimony about RTS in order to explain a victim's behavior that appears to be, but may not actually be, inconsistent with the fact that a sexual assault took place.

One significant difficulty with the use of expert evidence of this sort in criminal trials is that rape trauma syndrome is not a valid diagnostic tool for determining whether a rape actually occurred; rather it is simply a description of the emotional and psychological reactions that a woman who has been raped may have after the sexual assault. Since it doesn't legitimately go to the question whether a rape occurred, a number of questions arise, including, first, is such evidence reliable? And, second, is it relevant? Or, instead, might it be overly prejudicial to the defendant as tending to demonstrate to a jury "indirectly" and inappropriately that a supposed victim who is exhibiting many of the characteristics of this syndrome actually was in fact raped?

Considering these issues, while many courts have permitted the introduction of rape trauma syndrome expert evidence in the appropriate circumstances in a sexual assault prosecution, some have not. As the Minnesota Supreme Court has explained, "At best, the syndrome describes only symptoms that occur with some frequency, but makes no pretense of describing every single case. The jury must not decide this case on the basis of how most people react to rape or on whether [this alleged victim's] reactions were the typical reactions of a person who has been a victim of rape. Rather, the jury must decide what happened in this case, and whether the elements of the alleged crime have been proved beyond a reasonable doubt. The scientific evaluation of rape trauma syndrome has not reached a level of reliability that surpasses the quality of common sense evaluation present in jury deliberations."[25]

---

[25]*State v. Saldana*, 324 N.W.2d 227, 229-230 (Minn. 1982).

Sidebar

THE PHASES OF RTS

"[In] the acute phase, the victim goes through three types of reactions: (1) impact reactions, (2) emotional reactions, and (3) somatic reactions. Impact reactions are those that occur immediately after the rape[. The] emotional reactions [can] vary but [these] reactions fit into two general categories. In the first[,] the woman can exhibit her emotional status with an expressed style 'in which feelings of fear, anger, and anxiety [are] shown through such behavior as crying, sobbing, smiling, restlessness and tenseness.' In the second[,] a woman can exhibit her emotional status in a controlled style 'in which feelings [are] masked or hidden and a calm, composed, or subdued affect [is] seen.' The significance of this observation is its contrast to the stereotypical perceptions of what a rape victim 'should' be acting like.

"In the somatic reaction phase, physical manifestations [occur]. A woman may have physical trauma such as general soreness or bruising, tension headaches, fatigue, sleep disturbances, stomach pains, experience vaginal discharge, itching, a burning sensation when urinating, chronic vaginal infections and in cases of forced anal sex, rectal bleeding and pain.

"In the emotional reaction phase, a woman can feel a wide range of emotions. Feelings such as fear, anger, shame, and embarrassment are not uncommon.

"[In] the reorganization phase, which is the long-term phase, a woman attempts to cope with the trauma she has suffered and put some order back into her life.

"[The] last symptom [is] traumatophobia which is a phobic reaction to a traumatic situation. 'The phobia develops as a defensive reaction to the circumstances of the rape.' For example, a woman who is raped in her home might develop a fear of indoors [and] a woman who is raped outside of the home might develop a fear of the outdoors."

Arthur H. Garrison, *Rape Trauma Syndrome: A Review of a Behavioral Science Theory and Its Admissibility in Criminal Trials*, 23 Am. J. Trial Advoc. 591, 594-598 (2000) (footnotes omitted).

SUMMARY

■ Unlike the common law, a rape victim need not "resist to the utmost," although some states still define the force element in their rape statutes in terms of the defendant's acts that overcame the victim's resistance.

■ Unlike the common law, most rape statutes do not require proof of both the use of force and the absence of consent, typically requiring proof of only one of those elements or the other.

■ Most rape statutes utilizing a force element also provide an alternative element focused on the defendant's threat of force or the victim's fear of injury.

■ In most jurisdictions, a mistaken belief that the victim consented is not a viable defense to a rape charge.

■ The common law spousal exemption from rape prosecution has mostly been eliminated, although some states still treat spousal rape as a less serious sexual assault than rape of a non-spouse, with additional statutory elements.

■ Many jurisdictions punish forcible or nonconsensual anal and/or oral sexual activity differently than vaginal sexual assaults, and most jurisdictions also criminalize lesser sexual offenses that do not include the penetration of the victim's genitals.

■ Statutory rape occurs when an actor engages in sexual relations with a victim under a specified age (age of consent), whether or not there was actual consent to the contact. Mistake about the victim's age is often not a defense.

■ Rape shield laws are evidentiary rules designed to limit irrelevant inquiry into a rape victim's prior sexual behavior.

CONNECTIONS

Relationship to Actus Reus

Significantly, unlike the common law, modern rape statutes in most jurisdictions do *not* require proof of *both* the actus reus elements (see Chapter 2), the use of force *and* the absence of consent. Instead, they typically require proof of one of those elements or the other, not both.

Relationship to Assault and Battery

Sexual offenses are assaultive crimes (see Chapter 9) with additional elements added, related to the level of sexual contact or intrusion involved.

Relationship to Mens Rea

Sexual offenses are unusual in that many of the most serious offenses, such as forcible rape, often are deemed to be strict liability offenses. As discussed in Chapter 3, most strict liability offenses are less serious offenses, often involving so-called public welfare, regulatory offenses.

Relationship to Purposes of the Criminal Law

Much of the history of the evolving definition of sexual offenses reflects legislative enactments and judicial decisions that arguably resulted less from the legitimate purposes of the criminal law, at least as viewed by modern eyes (see Chapter 1), than from gender stereotyping and outdated notions of women as property and as witnesses lacking in credibility.

Theft Offenses and Related Crimes

11

OVERVIEW

At common law, a number of different theft offenses existed that were distinguished from one another by the existence (or lack) of different factual elements. These distinctions existed for historical reasons but, frankly, eventually they did not reflect sound common sense. In fact, because of the complexity and illogical nature of some of these elements, it was often difficult to determine whether a defendant had committed one theft crime as opposed to another or whether he had committed any crime at all. The current law of theft in the United States both reflects *and* is a reaction to the curious and often illogical evolution of theft offenses at the common law. Today, a number of jurisdictions have consolidated many of the common law theft crimes into a single criminal offense that is simply called "theft."

A. TRADITIONAL THEFT OFFENSES

1. Larceny
2. Larceny by Trick

B. LEGISLATIVE EXPANSION OF THEFT CRIMES

1. Embezzlement
2. False Pretenses

C. MODERN CONSOLIDATED AND EXPANDED THEFT CRIMES

D. ROBBERY

E. BURGLARY

F. RECEIVING STOLEN PROPERTY

G. CARJACKING

"History has its own logic."[1] The common law included a vast array of separate and distinct theft offenses, each with its own separate and idiosyncratic elements. This crazy quilt of crimes—particularly larceny, larceny by trick, larceny by false pretenses, and embezzlement—created serious problems for prosecutors and judges due to the array of often confusing, arbitrary, and arcane distinctions involved in these seemingly similar theft offenses.

The Model Penal Code sought to resolve these problems by consolidating most of these separate crimes into a single generic theft offense. This consolidated theft offense is used today to apply to larcenous activity in the majority of (but not all) states.

A. Traditional Theft Offenses

The earliest theft crime, **larceny**, was one of only nine common law felonies: murder, manslaughter, rape, arson, burglary, robbery, larceny, mayhem, and prison breach. Larceny was defined at common law as the wrongful taking and carrying away of personal property that is in the possession of another with the intent to convert it or permanently deprive the owner thereof. Over time, a distinction developed at the common law between simple larceny and **larceny by trick**.

(1) Larceny

Larceny was originally designed simply to prevent breaches of the peace occurring when property was forcibly taken from its rightful possessor. Over time, theft offenses expanded to cover other takings—"by stealth or by trick," for example—but the essence of larceny remained the same: the wrongful taking of tangible property from someone else who possessed it. It would be many years before additional theft crimes were created, such as embezzlement, larceny by trick, false pretenses, robbery, extortion, and receiving stolen property.

In the meantime, common law courts gradually extended the larcenous concept of "possession" to allow for convictions of defendants who might otherwise have been assumed *not* to be in possession of property. When this expansion of larceny eventually stopped, the law was left with some exceedingly narrow and often technical distinctions between such crimes as larceny and embezzlement.

Unfortunately, all of these fine distinctions created a potential trap for prosecutors. If a prosecutor charged a defendant with one crime, such as, larceny, but ended up proving instead the elements of another, closely related theft crime, such as

---

[1]Model Penal Code §223.1, comment b, at 130.

embezzlement, the accused was not guilty. Or, if the trial court found him guilty, his conviction would be reversed. In addition, since the early common law definition of larceny was so narrow and particular, instead of creating new theft offenses at that time, courts just bent over backwards to reinterpret the existing elements of larceny in "creative" ways. Those creative interpretations of various elements persisted long after new theft offenses were in fact created.

(a) Custody Versus Possession

The distinctions between custody and possession were—and sometimes continue to be—complex. For example, if a third party gave property to a servant or employee for delivery to his master, as opposed to the property being given by the employer to the employee, the employee was regarded as gaining possession and not custody. As a result, the employee could not be convicted of larceny if he stole the property. For example, in the old classic, *Bazeley's Case,*[2] a bank teller received a large bank note from a customer, but took it instead of placing it in the cash drawer. The court concluded that, since the employer had never officially received the property, the employee had possession of it, and the employee could not commit larceny since he had not trespassed against his employer's right of possession.

By contrast, if the employee received property and delivered it to his employer before taking it, the employee could be found guilty of larceny because the property had shifted to the possession of the employer. For example, in *Nolan v. State,*[3] a bank manager received payments on behalf of his employer and placed them in a cash drawer. At the end of the day, he returned and took the money from the drawer. The Maryland Court of Appeals concluded that this employee had committed larceny because he had put the cash in the drawer before taking it.

Similarly, under common law property rules, when an employer entrusted her employee with a piece of property—for example, a horse—you might have thought that the employee would be considered to be in temporary possession of the horse. That was not the case. If that view of possession had been adopted, then if the employee stole the horse, he would not be guilty of larceny because there was no trespass, as was required to prove larceny. So instead, common law courts ruled—avoiding this result—that when an employee received property from his employer,

---

[2][1799] 168 Eng. Rep. 517.
[3]213 Md. 298, 131 A.2d 851 (Md. App. 1957).

he was only gaining custody, not possession. As a result, if an employee stole such property, he was guilty of larceny.[4]

In some more recent decisions this distinction has persisted. For example, consider the Ninth Circuit's decision in *United States v. Mafnas*.[5] In that case, defendant Mafnas, an armored car employee, was charged with stealing money from banks that used him to transport money. He argued that he could not be convicted of larceny, however, because he had lawful possession of the money. The Ninth Circuit disagreed, holding, *inter alia*, that Mafnas only had custody of the bags, not possession, because he had been given the money only for a limited purpose and the owners, the banks, retained "constructive possession until the custodian's task was completed." *You see?* The more things change, the more they stay the same.

(b) Bailments

Common law judges also created fine distinctions between larcenous and non-larcenous bailees based upon their conduct. If a bailee received bales of goods, for example, and converted them, he was regarded as only having custody, not possession, so that the crime was larceny. On the other hand, in the classic, old *Carrier's Case*,[6] a defendant was hired to transport bales to a nearby city, but he broke the bales open and made off with the contents. By "breaking bulk," the bailee lost possession of the bales, the court held, and therefore trespassed against possession and committed the crime of larceny.

(c) Lost and Mislaid Property

Similar distinctions were made at common law regarding lost property. One might have naturally assumed that lost or mislaid property was not really in the possession of anyone. As a result, if someone picked it up and carried it away, intending to take it and keep it, that shouldn't be larceny ... *should it?* Finders keepers, right? No. Common law courts thought differently. The common law included the fiction that someone who mislaid property nonetheless retained possession of it. As a result, the person who picked the item up, intending to keep it, was indeed guilty of larceny.

However, the law placed great emphasis on the individual's intent at the time of the taking. If the finder picked up lost or mislaid property intending to return it to its rightful owner, but *later* decided to steal it, there was no larceny. The reason for that odd result was that when the finder picked the property up *not* intending to take it for her own, she gained possession of the property, and the owner's constructive possession ended.

(d) Owner's Presence

Problems also arose with regard to transactions to be completed in the owner's presence. For example, in the nineteenth-century case of *Hildebrand v. People*,[7] a customer handed a bartender a $50 bill to pay for a ten cent glass of soda. When defendant gave the customer only a "few coppers" (less than $1) in exchange, and the customer demanded the rest of his change, the bartender had the customer thrown

---

[4]*See, e.g., Nolan v. State*, 213 Md. 298, 131 A.2d 851 (Md. App. 1957).
[5]701 F.2d 83 (9th Cir. 1983).
[6][1473] 13 Edw. IV, f. 9, pl. 5.
[7]56 N.Y. 394 (1874).

out of the bar. In a situation like this, you might have thought that there could be no crime against possession. After all, the customer had given the $50 bill to the bartender with no expectation of ever seeing the particular bill again.

But if you thought that (sensibly enough), you would have been wrong. When the bartender refused to give the customer the proper change, there was a crime against possession, the court held, reasoning as follows: "It was an incomplete transaction, to be consummated in the presence and under the personal control of the prosecutor. There was no trust or confidence reposed in the [defendant], and none intended to be. The delivery of the bill and the giving change were to be simultaneous acts, and until the latter was paid, the delivery was not complete."

(e) Mistaken Delivery

Larceny could also be committed when property was delivered to someone by mistake and that person, realizing the mistake, took the property anyway. For example, over a century ago, in *Cooper v. Commonwealth*,[8] defendant took $2 to a bank and asked for change. The teller gave him two half-dollars along with a roll of coins that she described as containing twenty nickels. In fact, the roll contained twenty $5 gold coins, and defendant was charged with larceny when he kept them. Logically, again, you could certainly argue that defendant did not commit larceny because the teller willingly conveyed possession to him, hence, there was no trespass. But—as we keep seeing time after time—logic is not a reliable predictor in many of these old cases. The court in *Cooper* concluded instead that larceny was committed if defendant realized the mistake at the time of the transfer and took the gold pieces anyway, intending to keep them from the bank.

(f) Consent

At common law, there was also considerable litigation on the subject whether an owner of property had consented to a taking. Issues of consent commonly arose in situations where an employer pretended to cooperate with would-be thieves in order to catch them in the act.

For example, in the Wisconsin Supreme Court's century-old decision in *Topolewski v. State*,[9] defendant arranged for a meat-packing plant employee to place three barrels of meat on the company's loading platform so that he could steal them. The employee informed the employer, who then told the employee to feign cooperation so that defendant could be caught and prosecuted. In his defense, defendant claimed that because the employer was playing along, he had essentially consented to the taking. The Wisconsin court agreed: "[T]here can be no larceny without a trespass. So if one procures his property to be taken by another intending to commit larceny, or delivers his property to such other, the latter purposing to commit such crime, the element of trespass is wanting and the crime not fully consummated however plain may be the guilty purpose of the one possessing himself of such property." Subsequently and sensibly, however, a number of courts disagreed with this arguably contorted analysis.

---

[8]110 Ky. 123, 60 S.W. 938 (1901).
[9]130 Wis. 244, 109 N.W. 1037 (1906).

(g) Carrying Away

Another point needs to be taken into consideration. At common law, in order for the crime of larceny to be committed, not only did there have to be a trespassory taking of personal property, but the property also had to be "carried away," sometimes called the "asportation requirement." Common law courts and modern courts in jurisdictions retaining this element required very little actual movement, however, to find a carrying away.

Indeed, many courts subsequently dispensed with this asportation requirement altogether, in favor of a more sensible "dominion and control" test. Consider, for example, the holding of the New York Court of Appeals in *People v. Alamo*,[10] a case in which defendant broke into another person's car, turned on the lights and started the engine, but never moved it before he was caught. The court found that defendant had exercised sufficient dominion and control over the vehicle to be convicted: "To require that the vehicle be moved by the operator is to slavishly adhere to the auxiliary common-law element of asportation which is simply not necessary to the finding of the primary elements of dominion and control where an activated automobile is concerned."

(h) Personal Property

The crime of larceny also required that the accused take personal property. Larceny could not be committed when there was a taking only of *real* property; nor could it be committed when only intangible personal property was taken.

Moreover, the common law crime excluded domestic animals, real estate fixtures, and growing but not severed crops. For example, in *State v. Collins*,[11] defendant cut timber on another person's land and took it away. The court concluded that things "constituting a part of the land [are] not, at common law, the subjects of larceny, until they have become severed from the realty of which they are constructively a part." Since the defendant had severed and taken the timber as part of one continuous act, the court concluded that no larceny was committed.

(i) Wild Animals

Traditionally, wild animals—and wild things—could not be the subject of larceny either. For example, in *People v. Hutchinson*,[12] defendant was charged with larceny for taking honey produced by wild bees from another person's land. The court concluded, however, that larceny could not be established on these facts, absent proof that the bees were the property of the owner of the land. Since the bees were wild rather than domesticated, there was no larceny.

(j) New Forms of Property

As new forms of property were created over time—particularly intellectual property—some courts have been reluctant to expand the traditional definition of property for purposes of the crime of larceny. In *Commonwealth v. Yourawski*,[13] for example, the question arose whether a video cassette tape of a motion picture constituted property within the meaning of a larceny statute. The statute defined

---

[10] 34 N.Y.2d 453, 358 N.Y.S.2d 375 (1974).
[11] 188 S.C. 338, 199 S.E. 303 (1938).
[12] 169 Misc. 724, 9 N.Y.S.2d 656 (N.Y. Co. Ct. 1938).
[13] 384 Mass. 386, 425 N.E.2d 298 (1981).

property as including the following: "[M]oney, personal chattels, a bank note, bond, promissory note, bill of exchange or other bill, order or certificate, a book of accounts for or concerning money or goods due or to become due or to be delivered, a deed or writing containing a conveyance of land, any valuable contract in force, a receipt, release or defeasance, a writ, process, certificate of title or duplicate certificate issued under chapter one hundred and eighty-five, a public record, anything which is of the realty or is annexed thereto, a security deposit . . . and any domesticated animal, other than a dog, or a beast or bird which is ordinarily kept in confinement and is not the subject of larceny at common law."

Q: Is intellectual property outside the reach of larceny laws?

A: No. Numerous statutes have been enacted in the past few decades dealing *expressly* with the theft of intellectual property. Moreover, some modern courts have extended by interpretation more traditional larceny statutes to cover newer forms of property.

The Supreme Judicial Court of Massachusetts concluded that this language did not include a videotape: "We do not read the definition of 'property' . . . as reaching the property interest that is alleged to have been stolen in this case. Certainly, the images and sounds captured on the cassette tapes are not within any of the items specified in [this statute]."

(k) Intent to Steal

The common law crime of larceny also required a showing that the accused took property with the intent to steal it. At common law, the term "steal" meant that defendant intended to deprive the owner of it permanently or for an unreasonable length of time. As a result, a person who took property intending to return it and having the capacity to do so, was not guilty of larceny. However, if a person stole property intending to use it recklessly before returning it—for example, she took money intending to gamble with it at a casino—the requisite intent to steal might well exist.

Moreover, if a person held an honest claim of right to the property in question—that is, she believed that the property belonged to her or that she had a lawful claim to it—then she could not be convicted of larceny because she also lacked the intent to steal.

For example, consider the decision of the Maryland Court of Appeals in *Binnie v. State*.[14] In *Binnie*, a state statute provided a defense for one who "acted in the honest belief that he had the right to obtain or exert control over the property as he did." Binnie claimed that he found a dirty hat without a price tag on the floor of a department store. Since it did not look like the other hats for sale, Binnie claimed that he asked a sales clerk about it and she laughed and said, "Well, I guess it is yours." However, when Binnie left the store, he concealed it inside his jacket. The court

---

[14]321 Md. 572, 583 A.2d 1037 (1991).

concluded that Binnie had produced sufficient evidence of his claim of right to justify its submission to the jury: "If the jury believed Binnie, the honest belief defense was generated by his testimony and operated as a total defense to the charge."

(I) Degrees of Larceny

Although the common law did not distinguish between more serious and less serious forms of larceny, many modern statutes do make this distinction. Often, they distinguish between "grand larceny" and "petit larceny," using the French words for "large" and "small." (Sometimes "petit larceny" is Anglicized to "petty larceny.") Typically, the distinction is based on the value of the property taken. In other words, if defendant steals property worth more than a certain, fixed amount—for example, $2,000—the crime is "grand larceny." On the other hand, if the value of the property is below that amount, the crime is "petit larceny."

(2) Larceny by Trick

In 1779, a common law court in *Pear's Case*[15] created the separate crime of **larceny by trick**. In *Pear's Case*, Pear rented a horse from Finch. He said he was going to ride it to Surrey, but instead he rode it to Smithfield and sold it there. In Pear's trial for larceny, the barrier to conviction was that he had acquired the horse by delivery from Finch and thus he had presumably acquired possession. So the problem posed was the traditional one: If Pear had fraudulently intended to steal the horse from the beginning, was that intent to steal sufficient to override the fact that he had presumably acquired possession of the horse? The traditional answer to this question, as previously discussed, was negative.

However, in this case, the English judges decided to call Pear's conduct larceny in any event by holding that the false promise to return the horse was a trick that could be treated as a trespass, thus making the defendant's conduct a taking from possession. As the owner's act of parting with possession was based on fraud, it was nonconsensual and therefore did not create lawful possession in the taker.

But the emergence of the crime of larceny by trick did not put an end to difficult and arcane distinctions in theft law. To the contrary. If a renter received property—a horse, for example—intending to return it, but *subsequently* decided to sell it, the renter *did* receive possession of the horse and therefore he would *not* be guilty of larceny.

Modern crimes codes typically avoid the necessity for engaging in this sort of convoluted analysis by expressly criminalizing a renter's failure to return rental property. Indeed, many applicable statutes extend far beyond the scope of the common law larceny by trick offense. For example, today in Missouri, "[a] person commits the crime of failing to return leased or rented property if, with the intent to deprive the owner thereof, he purposefully fails to return leased or rented personal property to the place and within the time specified in an agreement in writing providing for the leasing or renting of such personal property. In addition, any person who has leased or rented personal property of another who conceals the property from the owner, or who otherwise sells, pawns, loans, abandons or gives away the leased or rented property is guilty of the crime of failing to return leased or rented property. . . ."[16]

---

[15][1779] 1 Leach 211, 168 Eng. Rep. 208.
[16]Rev. Stat. Mo. §578.150.1.

B. Legislative Expansion of Theft Crimes

For some time, as previously discussed, common law judges went to great lengths to find the existence of a trespass—often using largely fictional distinctions between custody and possession—which allowed them to convict defendants of the crime of larceny. By the end of the eighteenth century, however, they refused to expand the crime of larceny itself any further. About this same time, there was a "general advance in prestige and power of Parliament" along with a shift in how judges were viewed.[17] No longer were judges seen as legitimate framers of legal policy.[18]

Moreover, at this same time, there was a general public "revulsion against capital punishment, which was the penalty for all theft offenses except petty larceny during much of the 18th century. The severity of this penalty [made] the judges reluctant to enlarge felonious [larceny]."[19] The significance of these events was that as the courts declined to expand the crime of theft, further expansions were undertaken instead by Parliament. More specifically, Parliament enacted the new crimes of embezzlement and false pretenses.

(1) Embezzlement

The crime of **embezzlement**, broadly defined, was committed when a person fraudulently converted the property of another while he was already in possession of that property. Early embezzlement statutes provided that only certain, limited categories of individuals, such as bailees and bankers, were subject to prosecution. Over time, these categories were expanded to include many different categories of individuals, including directors, agents, clerks, servants, or officers of companies, trustees, factors, carriers, bailees, clerks, agents, and servants. As new situations arose where someone not already covered by existing statutory language was found to have converted property, the statutory language was expanded. Conversion, unlike stealing, required a serious interference with the property.

Even after the crime of embezzlement was enacted and subsequently expanded, the crime of larceny continued to exist as a separate and distinct crime. Sometimes, it became difficult to distinguish precisely between these two crimes. This blurring often created significant difficulties. If a defendant was charged and convicted of one crime—larceny, for example—but was found instead to have committed the other crime, embezzlement, or vice-versa, the conviction would be reversed.

For example, in *State v. Taylor*,[20] defendant Taylor was employed to pick up scrap meat and bones from butcher shops and cafes. One customer required payment in cash, so defendant would cash a company check and make the payment directly to that customer. However, in order to steal some of the cash for himself, he issued shorted receipts to other customers. When he was found out, he was tried and convicted of embezzlement. In his appeal, he claimed that the evidence actually proved larceny, not embezzlement. The Utah Supreme Court agreed, holding that "[w]here the intent to take the property of another is formed before the taking, and is coupled with some deception or trick to acquire possession of the property, the crime is not embezzlement." As a result, his conviction was reversed.

---

[17]Model Penal Code §223.2, Comment (1)(a), at 128-129 (1980).
[18]*Id.*
[19]*Id.*
[20]14 Utah 2d 107, 378 P.2d 352 (1963).

(2) False Pretenses

English common law judges applied the crime of larceny by trick to situations where an individual obtained possession, but not title, by trick. To fill this gap, Parliament enacted the crime of **false pretenses**. That crime was committed when a person made a representation of present or past facts that that person knew to be false and used that misrepresentation to defraud a victim into conveying title to property.

C. Modern Consolidated and Expanded Theft Crimes

Because of the complexity and, sometimes, the illogical nature of the different elements of the common law theft crimes, it was often difficult to determine whether a defendant had committed one theft crime as opposed to another or whether he had committed any crime at all.

Q: What happens when a defendant is convicted of one theft crime but the facts proved at trial demonstrate that he was actually guilty of a *different* theft crime?

A: In states with no consolidated theft statutes, if a defendant is convicted of larceny, for example, but can prove on appeal that the facts adduced at trial established that his offense was actually a different theft crime, such as embezzlement, he can have his conviction reversed on that ground. In other words, the facts established that he had committed a crime, but—as it turned out—given the vagaries of the different theft crime elements involved, he had been prosecuted for and convicted of the wrong offense.

The Model Penal Code addressed this problem by urging consolidation of many of the common law theft crimes into a single criminal offense that it simply calls "theft."[21] This MPC theft offense consolidates in one offense what had been eight separate and distinct ways to commit that crime:

1. theft by unlawful taking or disposition
2. theft by deception
3. theft by extortion
4. theft of property lost, mislaid, or delivered by mistake
5. receiving stolen property
6. theft of services
7. theft by failure to make required disposition of funds received
8. unauthorized use of automobiles and other vehicles.[22]

Today, a majority of jurisdictions in the United States use this consolidated approach, although they do not all use the MPC's suggested language in doing so.

---

[21]Model Penal Code §223.1(1).
[22]Model Penal Code §223.

However, the most important innovation introduced by the MPC with respect to theft is that once a prosecutor charges a defendant with a consolidated theft offense, she need not prove that specific type of theft was committed in order to successfully convict the defendant. If, for example, the prosecutor charges a defendant with theft by unlawful taking or disposition, but the evidence actually adduced at trial establishes instead that the defendant committed theft of property lost, mislaid, or delivered by mistake, unlike the common law, the conviction would still be valid. As the MPC commentary makes clear, an "accusation of theft may be supported by evidence that it was committed in any manner that would be theft under [the consolidated approach], notwithstanding the specification of a different manner in the indictment or information, subject only to the power of the Court to ensure fair trial by granting a continuance or other appropriate relief where the conduct of the defense would be prejudiced by lack of fair notice or by surprise."[23] This approach is now used in a majority of American jurisdictions.

Despite consolidation, the Model Penal Code does distinguish, as most jurisdictions do, between the various forms of theft for purposes of punishment—although not, as discussed, for conviction. For example, the Model Penal Code treats theft as a felony of the first degree "if the amount involved exceeds $500, or if the property stolen is a firearm, automobile, airplane, motorcycle, motor boat, or other motor-propelled vehicle, or in the case of theft by receiving stolen property, if the receiver is in the business of buying or selling stolen property."[24] Otherwise, theft is generally treated as a misdemeanor.[25] In determining the amount of a theft, the MPC provides that it "shall be deemed to be the highest value, by any reasonable standard, of the property or services which the actor stole or attempted to steal. . . ."[26]

Moreover, despite the widespread acceptance of consolidation of theft offenses, the common law definitions of larceny, embezzlement, larceny by trick, and false pretenses are not completely irrelevant in modern theft formulations. On the contrary, those definitions still help inform courts as they interpret each of the consolidated theft provisions. For example, the MPC's crime of theft by unlawful taking or disposition was purposefully drafted broadly enough to include the common law crimes of larceny and embezzlement. However, the Model Penal Code theft crime eliminates the common law embezzlement requirements of entrustment and the intent to convert.[27] In addition, as to the mens rea of theft, the Code requires the purpose to deprive (for movable property), and the intent to benefit (for non-movable property).[28] And the Code defines the actus reus of theft as nothing more than a simple "taking."[29]

The Model Penal Code also differs from the common law in that it defines the term "property" more expansively, thereby eliminating some of the vagaries of the common law definitions. The MPC definition includes both movable and immovable property, as well as "anything of value, including real estate, tangible and intangible property, contract rights, choses-in-action and other interests in or claims to wealth, admission or transportation tickets, captured or domestic animals, food and drink, electric or other power."[30]

---

[23]Id.
[24]Model Penal Code §223.1(2)(a).
[25]Model Penal Code §223.1(2)(b).
[26]Model Penal Code §223.1(2)(c).
[27]Model Penal Code §223.2(1) and (2).
[28]Id.
[29]Id.
[30]Model Penal Code §223.0.

The crime of **theft by deception** was also designed broadly enough to sweep in both the common law crimes of larceny by trick and false pretenses. The MPC drafters chose the term "deception" as a way of replacing the terms "false pretense or representation."[31] However, the Code drafters included an exception for situations when there is "falsity as to matters having no pecuniary significance, or puffing by statements unlikely to deceive ordinary persons in the group addressed."[32] The Code Commentary explains this exception as follows: "[This] excluded category is falsification as to matters having no pecuniary significance, *e.g.*, where a salesman misrepresents his political, religious, or social affiliations. Such misrepresentations may succeed in securing the buyer's patronage and in that sense it could be said that whatever is paid for the purchase is money obtained by deception. But the injury done to the buyer is not a property deprivation of the sort that should be condemned and punished as theft, since the deceived person secures exactly what he bargained for in the way of property."[33]

The no pecuniary significance exception was discussed by the Iowa Supreme Court in *State v. Miller*.[34] In *Miller*, a female prisoner had extensive correspondence and phone calls with three men that she met through singles advertisements. She made expressions of affection, long-term commitments, and promises of explicit sexual gratification. The court concluded that all three men believed that Miller planned to move in with them after her release from prison. Miller also asked and received from the men cash and personal items. Each man believed Miller needed financial assistance and each one regarded his help as an investment in his and Miller's future together. Miller was eventually charged with theft, defined as "obtaining possession, control, or ownership of the property of another, or the beneficial use of property of another, by deception," and defended on the basis that "criminal culpability cannot rest on deceit regarding 'romantic intentions.'" Noting that the governing statute in Iowa was patterned after the MPC, which includes theft by deception, the Iowa court upheld defendant's conviction: "The record plainly reveals that Miller has not been prosecuted for merely breaking promises of romantic intention, but for deliberately using her false promises as a vehicle for parting her victims from their money. . . . [T]he record is replete with proof of her deliberate intent to mislead the men from the outset."

The Model Penal Code does, notably, contain a defense for someone who obtains property under a claim of right that "he had a right to acquire or dispose of it as he did."[35] It is also a defense that a defendant "took property exposed for sale, intending to purchase and pay for it promptly, or reasonably believing that the owner, if present, would have consented."[36]

The Model Penal Code's theft formulation also refers to **theft of services** as another form of theft. The term "services" is defined as including "labor, professional services, transportation, telephone or other public service, accommodation in hotels, restaurants or elsewhere, admission to exhibitions, use of vehicles or other movable property."[37]

D. Robbery

At common law, **robbery** was "larceny plus." More precisely, the crime of robbery encompassed all of the elements of larceny, a trespassory taking and carrying away of

[31]*See* Model Penal Code §223.3, Comment (1), at 181 (1980).
[32]Model Penal Code §223.3.
[33]Model Penal Code §223.3, Comment (3)(d), at 194-195 (1980).
[34]590 N.W.2d 45 (Iowa 1999).
[35]Model Penal Code §223.1(3)(b).
[36]Model Penal Code §223.1(3)(c).
[37]Model Penal Code §223.7(1).

the personal property of another with the intent to steal, but it also included the additional elements of a taking "from the person or in the presence of the victim" that was "accomplished by violence or a threat of violence." Because it was committed violently or with the threat of violence, robbery was and still is regarded as a more serious crime than simple larceny.

Even though the Model Penal Code consolidated most of the common law theft crimes, it continued to treat robbery as a separate and distinct crime. That is the case in the consolidated theft offense jurisdictions, too—robbery is a separate and generally more serious offense.

The MPC, however, unlike the common law, does not require that the taking at issue be from the person or in the presence of the victim. The Commentary to the robbery section explained this omission as follows: "It is enough that there be actual force or the threat of immediate force. The [person or presence] requirement [excludes] some cases that should be covered and adds little by way of narrowing the scope of the offense in any appropriate manner."[38] Instead, the Model Penal Code provided that robbery is committed when, while committing a theft, defendant "(a) inflicts serious bodily injury upon another; or (b) threatens another with or purposely puts him in fear of immediate serious bodily injury; or (c) commits or threatens immediately to commit any felony of the first or second degree."[39]

The Model Penal Code further provides that an "act shall be deemed 'in the course of committing a theft' if it occurs in an attempt to commit theft or in flight after the attempt or commission."[40]

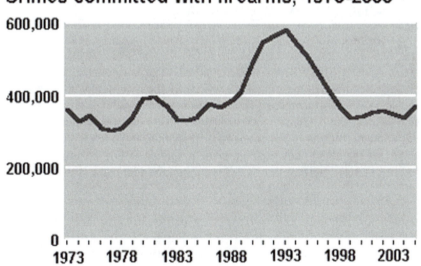

Crimes committed with firearms, 1973-2005

U.S. Dept. of Justice, Office of Justice Programs, Bureau of Justice Statistics, *After peaking in 1993, the number of gun crimes reported to police declined and then stabilized at levels last seen in 1988,* http://www.ojp.usdoj.gov/bjs/glance/guncrime.htm.[41]

---

[38]Model Penal Code §222.1, Comment (3)(d), at 112 (1980).
[39]Model Penal Code §222.1(1).
[40]*Id.*
[41]*See also* U.S. Dept. of Justice, Office of Justice Programs, Bureau of Justice Statistics, National Crime Victimization Survey 2008, http://bjs.ojp.usdoj.gov/index.cfm?ty=tp&tid=43 ("In 2008—[a]n offender was armed with a gun, knife, or other object used as a weapon in an estimated 20% of all incidents of violent crime[; o]ffenders used firearms to commit 7% of violent crime incidents in 2008[; r]obberies (40%) were the most likely crime to involve an armed offender.").

In general, robbery is still defined today in most jurisdictions as the taking of property, including but not exclusively money, from another person by means of force, threat, or intimidation. Many jurisdictions also possess a more serious grade of robbery often called "armed robbery," which is robbery undertaken with a deadly weapon, like a firearm.

E. Burglary

Common law **burglary** was committed when a person broke and entered into a dwelling belonging to another person at night with the intent to commit a felony therein. The crime was designed to deal with the special dangers posed by a criminal who decides to enter a home at night, when the occupants are more likely to be asleep and are less able to defend themselves. In addition to the general intent to break and enter, along with the attendant circumstances of a "dwelling, of another, at night," defendant must possess the specific intent to commit a felony inside.

Because burglary required a breaking and entering, the crime could not be committed if the actor entered through an open door or window. Burglary could also not be committed by someone who entered with the permission of the owner.

Most modern burglary statutes have largely retained the common law elements of burglary, *except* that they have expanded the crime to include daytime entries into houses and, sometimes, other structures as well.

F   A   Q

Q: What happens if someone enters someone else's home, but it is not clear that he or she intends to commit a felony on the premises?

A: Most jurisdictions use the crime of criminal trespass to deal with less serious invasions of real property interests than are criminalized by the offense of burglary. The Model Penal Code, for example, provides that trespass is committed when a person, "knowing that he is not licensed or privileged to do so, . . . enters or surreptitiously remains in any building or occupied structure, or separately secured or occupied portion thereof." Model Penal Code §222.2(1).

In many jurisdictions, however, the crime of burglary is broken into degrees, with different levels of severity of punishment depending on the perceived gravity and danger of the actor's conduct. For example, in South Dakota, first-degree burglary is defined as: "Any person who enters or remains in an occupied structure, with intent to commit any crime, unless the premises are, at the time, open to the public or the person is licensed or privileged to enter or remain, is guilty of first degree burglary if: (1) The offender inflicts, or attempts or threatens to inflict, physical harm on another; (2) The offender is armed with a dangerous weapon; or (3) The offense is committed in the nighttime."[42] Second-degree burglary is defined as: "Any person who enters or remains in an occupied structure with intent to commit any crime, unless the

---

[42]S.D.C.L. §22-32-1.

premises are, at the time, open to the public or the person is licensed or privileged to enter or remain, under circumstances not amounting to first degree burglary, is guilty of second degree burglary."[43] And third-degree burglary is defined as: "Any person who enters or remains in an unoccupied structure, other than a motor vehicle, with intent to commit any crime, unless the premises are, at the time, open to the public or the person is licensed or privileged to enter or remain, is guilty of third degree burglary."[44]

The Model Penal Code extended the crime of burglary beyond the common law requirements, but not as far as some other modern statutes. The Code does provide that burglary can be committed either at day or at night, and it does provide that the crime extends to the entry of any "building or occupied structure, or separately secured or occupied portion thereof, with purpose to commit a crime therein."[45]

But the Commentary to the Model Penal Code argued that "a greatly expanded burglary statute authorizes the prosecutor and the courts to treat as burglary behavior that is distinguishable from theft [only] on purely artificial grounds."[46] As a result, the MPC drafters sought to use the crime of burglary to deal with "the distinctive situation for which it was originally devised," in particular, situations involving the "invasion of premises under circumstances that are likely to terrorize occupants."[47] As a result, the Code's burglary provision does not extend to abandoned buildings.[48]

F. Receiving Stolen Property

The crime of **receiving stolen property** (often shorthanded as RSP in many states, and sometimes referred to, slangily, as "fencing") is usually defined as a person gaining control over an item, knowing that it was obtained in a criminal manner, intending to permanently deprive the rightful owner of his or her interest in that property.

Traditionally, the RSP crime was defined broadly enough to include an individual who received either actual possession or constructive possession of an item. However, this possessory element—actual or constructive—must still be established clearly.

For example, in *State v. McCoy*,[49] defendant McCoy was charged with receiving a stolen car. McCoy claimed that a friend had called him over to his car and that the moment he placed his hands on it, a police officer told him to "freeze." Since McCoy had not yet even entered the car, the question was whether he had actually received it. The New Jersey Supreme Court first observed that "constructive possession exists when a person intentionally obtains a measure of control or dominion over the stolen goods although they are under the physical control of another." However, on these facts, the court concluded that there was no such constructive possession: "The facts reveal nothing more than that he had placed his hands on the automobile with the

---

[43]S.D.C.L. §22-32-3.
[44]S.D.C.L. §22-32-8.
[45]Model Penal Code §222.1(1).
[46]Model Penal Code §222.1, Comment (1), at 63 (1980).
[47]*Id.*, Comment (2), at 67 (1980).
[48]Model Penal Code §222.1.
[49]116 N.J. 293, 561 A.2d 582 (1989).

S i d e b a r

CARJACKING: THE NUMBERS

"On average, during the decade from 1993-2002, about 38,000 carjacking victimizations occurred each year. [Additionally]:

- Men were more often victimized than women; blacks more than whites; and Hispanics more than non-Hispanics.
- Households with annual incomes of $50,000 or more had lower rates than those making below $50,000.
- Carjacking victimization rates were highest in urban areas, followed by suburban and rural areas. Ninety-three percent of carjackings occurred in cities or suburbs.
- A weapon was used in 74% of carjacking victimizations. Firearms were used in 45% of carjackings, knives in 11%, and other weapons in 18%.
- About 32% of victims of completed carjackings and about 17% of victims of attempted carjackings were injured. Serious injuries, such as gunshot or knife wounds, broken bones, or internal injuries occurred in about 9%. More minor injuries, such as bruises and chipped teeth, occurred in about 15%. . . .
- Males committed 93% of carjacking incidents, while groups involving both males and females committed 3%. Women committed about 3% of carjackings.
- 68% of carjacking incidents occurred at night (6 p.m. - 6 a.m.). Forty-two percent of carjackings at night and 50% of those in the day were completed.
- About 63% of carjacking incidents occurred within 5 miles of the victim's home, including the 17% that occurred at or near the home. Four percent occurred more than 50 miles from the victim's home."

U.S. Dept. of Justice, Office of Justice Programs, Bureau of Justice Statistics, *Carjacking, 1993-2002 (July 2004)*, http://www.ojp.usdoj .gov/bjs/pub/pdf/c02.pdf.

intent 'to ride around in it,' knowing the driver, and knowing that the automobile was stolen."

At common law, courts struggled with the requirement that the property must be stolen. In some instances, such as when property was conveyed pursuant to a sting operation so that it had not actually been "stolen," prosecutors were simply unable to convict.[50] In response, the Model Penal Code reversed the common law rule and provided that defendants could be convicted of RSP if they believed that the property at issue had probably been stolen.[51]

Not all states follow the position taken in this Code provision, however. As the Pennsylvania Superior Court stated, proceeding without the actually stolen requirement "would, in fact, shift the burden of proof to the defendant to show that his possession of an item was legitimate before the [prosecutor] has established that the defendant's possession was even suspect, much less criminal. That would be directly contrary to the most basic principle of criminal jurisprudence—the presumption of innocence."[52] In jurisdictions that retain the actually stolen requirement, a person who believes—incorrectly—that he is receiving stolen property might well be convicted nonetheless of the separate offense of attempting to receive stolen property.[53]

The Model Penal Code definition of the term "receiving" expands the common law definition by including "acquiring possession, control or title," and includes "lending on security" so as to include pawnbrokers who purchase stolen property. The MPC also covers defendants who retain stolen property, so as to punish those who receive property innocently and then later learn the property is stolen and choose to keep it.[54]

Finally, the Model Penal Code presumes that a defendant knows or believes that property is stolen when he: "(a) is found in possession or control of property stolen from two or more persons on separate occasions; or (b) has received stolen property in another transaction within the year preceding the transaction charged; or

---

[50]*See* Model Penal Code §223.6, Comment 4(b), at 239-240 (1980).
[51]Model Penal Code §222.2 (1).
[52]*Commonwealth v. Stafford*, 424 Pa. Super. 591, 623 A.2d 838 (1993), *aff'd*, 539 Pa. 278, 652 A.2d 297 (1995).
[53]See Chapter 6.
[54]Model Penal Code §223.6, Comment 2, at 235 (1980).

(c) being a dealer in property of the sort received, acquires it for a consideration which he knows is far below its reasonable value."[55]

A number of jurisdictions use a similar presumption. However, even without such a presumption, prosecutors can use circumstantial evidence to demonstrate a person's knowledge or belief that property he or she has received was stolen.

G. Carjacking

Most jurisdictions today also supplement their array of theft crimes, particularly robbery, with the newer crime of carjacking, which imposes more severe penalties than ordinary robbery, where a person's car is taken from him or her by force.

The specific elements of the crime of carjacking are different jurisdiction by jurisdiction. As one example, in *Harris v. State*,[56] the Maryland Court of Appeals construed Maryland's carjacking statute as applying when an "individual obtains unauthorized possession or control of a motor vehicle from another individual in actual possession by force or violence, or by putting that individual in fear through intimidation or threat of force or violence." The court construed the statute, however, as *not* requiring that the defendant intend to "permanently deprive the owner of the motor vehicle."

As another example, in *United States v. Lake*,[57] the Third Circuit discussed a prosecution raising issues under the federal carjacking statute.[58] In that case, Lake grabbed a woman's keys with the intention of taking her car. A scuffle ensued, but the woman gave up the keys when Lake pulled a gun on her. Lake then drove off. When he was captured, he was charged under the federal carjacking statute. Even though Lake claimed he had used a toy gun rather than a real one, Judge (now United States Supreme Court Justice) Alito, writing for the court, dismissed this argument, noting that his victim "perceived the gun as real, and Lake put it to her head and threatened death or serious bodily injury."

Moreover, Lake's claim that he did not take the car "from the person or presence" of his victim was found not to be meritorious even though the car was up a hill at the time that Lake took his victim's keys and he had to go some distance to get it. As Judge Alito concluded, "Under these statutes, 'property is in the presence of a person if it is "so within his reach, observation or control, that he could if not overcome by violence or prevented by fear, retain his possession of it."'"

SUMMARY

■ Common law theft offenses, particularly larceny, larceny by trick, larceny by false pretenses, and embezzlement, contained confusing, arbitrary, and arcane distinctions for seemingly similar crimes.

---

[55]Model Penal Code §223.6(2).
[56]353 Md. 596, 728 A.2d 180 (1999).
[57]150 F.3d 269 (3d Cir. 1998).
[58]18 U.S.C.A. §2119 ("Whoever, with the intent to cause death or serious bodily harm takes a motor vehicle that has been transported, shipped, or received in interstate or foreign commerce from the person or presence of another by force and violence or by intimidation, or attempts to do so, shall—(1) be fined under this title or imprisoned not more than 15 years, or both, (2) if serious bodily injury . . . results, be fined under this title or imprisoned not more than 25 years, or both, and (3) if death results, be fined under this title or imprisoned for any number of years up to life, or both, or sentenced to death.").

- The MPC consolidated most common law theft offenses into a single, generic theft offense, and that consolidated approach is used in a majority of states.

- Despite consolidation, most jurisdictions still distinguish between various forms of theft for purposes of punishment.

- Robbery is the taking of property, including but not exclusively money, from another person by means of force, threat, or intimidation.

- Burglary is the crime of breaking and entering into another person's dwelling or other specified place with the intent to commit a felony therein.

- The crime of receiving stolen property criminalizes the act of gaining control over an item, knowing that it was obtained in a criminal manner, intending to permanently deprive the rightful owner of his or her interest in that property.

CONNECTIONS

Relationship to Actus Reus

The prosecution of theft crimes traditionally relied heavily on the clear proof of specified actus reus elements (see Chapter 2). If a prosecutor at trial established the actus reus element of a theft offense that had not been charged, the prosecution failed. Today, with the consolidation of many theft offenses in most jurisdictions, this is far less of a problem.

Relationship to Assault and Battery

The crime of robbery is generally defined as the taking of property, including but not exclusively money, from another person by means of force, threat, or intimidation. Although the robbery offense includes some patently assaultive elements (see Chapter 9), for historical reasons it has been treated instead as a violent theft offense.

Relationship to Complicity

Like the separate concepts of principals and accomplices at the common law, which have largely merged in modern crimes codes (see Chapter 5), the various, separate common law theft offenses have largely been consolidated into a single, general theft offense in most modern crimes codes.

Justification Defenses

12

Sometimes, it is perfectly lawful to commit a crime. The commission of a criminal offense is deemed *not* to be culpable and punishable—for example, when a person's conduct fits within the terms of a specific—usually statutory—"justification" defense. Justification defenses typically focus on the act, not the actor; they exculpate otherwise criminal conduct because it is deemed beneficial to society or because the conduct is in some other way judged to be socially useful or desirable, as is the case with lawful self-defense, for example. In these cases, the defendant is deemed to be *not* guilty of the charged offense, even though all of the elements of the offense may have otherwise been proven.

OVERVIEW

A. SELF-DEFENSE

1. Imminency
2. Honest and Reasonable Belief
3. Deadly Force
4. Aggressors
5. Retreat

B. IMPERFECT DEFENSE

C. DEFENSE OF OTHERS

D. DEFENSE OF PROPERTY

E. LAW ENFORCEMENT DEFENSE

F. NECESSITY

G. OTHER JUSTIFICATION DEFENSES

To this point, we have focused primarily on the fundamental requirements for the imposition of criminal punishment, including the basic elements of most criminal offenses, such as mens rea and actus reus. We have, in addition, reviewed the nature and scope of many of the most common substantive criminal offenses themselves. This chapter goes in a different direction. Instead of considering offenses, we consider one important category of defenses.

Traditionally, **justification defenses** are defenses that are recognized as being necessary to respond to forces outside of the actor, as opposed to excuses.[1] Put another way, justification defenses typically focus on the act, not the actor; they exculpate otherwise criminal conduct because such conduct is deemed beneficial to society, or because the conduct is in some other way judged to be socially useful or desirable. **Excuse defenses**, in contrast, traditionally focus on the actor, not the act; they exculpate even though an actor's conduct may have harmed society because the actor is deemed not to be blameworthy. What are the accepted justification defenses? Why do we have them? And how do they work? This chapter answers these questions.

We deal with the last question first. *How do they work?* Justification defenses are usually **affirmative defenses**. Unlike traditional failure-of-proof defenses, defenses that succeed when defense counsel manages to negate one or more of the elements of the crime charged, affirmative defenses operate without regard to the elements of the offense. Even though the accused may have committed all of the elements of the offense, he is nonetheless still deemed to be *not* guilty where his conduct is found to have been justified pursuant to one of these defenses.

To succeed in this fashion, however, the accused—not the prosecution as is the case with elements of a crime—must establish affirmatively all of the elements of an applicable justification defense recognized in that jurisdiction.

F   A   Q

Q: What happened to the prosecutor's obligation to prove the commission of a crime beyond a reasonable doubt?

A: Typically, to be entitled to a jury instruction on an affirmative, justification defense, the defendant must produce enough evidence supporting each of the elements of that defense that a reasonable jury could rule in her favor. The burden of proof most often used to establish an affirmative defense is a preponderance of the evidence. Once the defendant has met this burden, however, *then* the burden of proof shifts back to the prosecution, which must disprove the affirmative defense at issue beyond a reasonable doubt.

---

[1]See Chapter 13 (Excuses).

A. Self-Defense

The law has always recognized **self-defense**, the right of an individual within certain limits to defend herself from attack. As the Supreme Court has recently recognized, "Self-defense is a basic right, recognized by many legal systems from ancient times to the present day . . . ."[2] At common law, an individual could use force to protect herself against an attack by another person when she was threatened with the immediate or imminent use of unlawful force and the use of responsive force was necessary to repel that attack.

Not much has changed. Today, in most jurisdictions, an individual can still use otherwise unlawful but not deadly force to protect herself against an attack by another person when she believes she is being threatened with the imminent use of unlawful force and the use of responsive force is necessary to repel the attack. This defense is available, however, *only*—significantly—when her belief in these elements is objectively *reasonable*.

For example, suppose that A is leaving work at the end of the day when B comes rushing at him, screaming, brandishing a knife, and threatening to kill him. Under these circumstances, A is entitled to use force in self-defense as necessary to repel the attack as he is threatened with the imminent use of unlawful force, the use of force in response was immediately necessary to repel the attack, and a reasonable person would have believed as much.

The right to self-defense is fully consistent with the justifications for punishment.[3] When an individual is faced with an attack, particularly one involving the possibility of death or serious bodily injury, it is difficult to justify retribution against that person if he or she responds to this eventuality with force. An ordinary and reasonable person would presumably respond with force under such circumstances. There is no need to express the community's strong feelings about the moral wrongfulness of behavior like this. Moreover, it is also difficult to argue that the State can hope to—or should—deter individuals by the threat of punishment from acting in self-defense. It is a natural human instinct for people to act to defend themselves when and if it is necessary. In addition, it is difficult to argue that one who uses force only in self-defense needs either to be restrained or rehabilitated.

(1) Imminency

(a) Limited Use of Force

As previously noted, before an individual can exercise the right to self-defense, she must be threatened with the imminent use of unlawful physical force against her person. For example, suppose that X threatens Y, and tells her that she "is a goner. I'm going to return with my gun and kill you." Y, in response, pulls out a gun and shoots X, killing her. Because the threat to Y was not imminent, Y cannot establish successfully that she acted in self-defense.

In *State v. Daniels*,[4] for example, there was evidence suggesting that Nolan began a fight, but eventually pushed Daniels away from him, saying that he had "had enough." When Daniels advanced toward Nolan with a knife, Nolan grabbed a

---

[2]*McDonald v. City of Chicago, Ill.,* ____ U.S. ____, 130 S. Ct. 3020, 3036 (2010).
[3]See Chapter 1 (Purposes of the Criminal Law).
[4]210 Mont. 1, 682 P.2d 173 (1984).

pair of horseshoe nippers and struck Daniels on the skull. At that point, Daniels got his pistol from his car and started shooting. A man who was with Nolan was shot to death. The Montana Supreme Court held that an individual threatened with the use of "imminent force" against him is entitled to use force against that person "when and to the extent that he reasonably believes that such conduct is necessary." But, the court added, that person must act "instantly," he must respond "*when* and to the extent that he reasonably believes that such conduct is necessary."

The law imposes the requirement of imminency on the theory that a citizen should only resort to the use of force when it is truly necessary. If a person is not subject to an *immediate* threat, then he might be able to protect himself by other means, and he should make that attempt. For example, he might be able to contact the police, or take other evasive action, and still protect himself adequately from a threatened use of force against him. The Model Penal Code reinforces this idea by requiring that to be entitled to a defense of self-defense, the use of force must be necessary "on the present occasion."[5]

Despite the requirement of imminency, an actor is not required to wait until the last possible moment before using force in self-defense. In *Commonwealth v. Lindsey*,[6] for example, defendant exchanged angry words at work with Michel. A day or so later, Michel challenged defendant to a fight and pursued him with a knife. Defendant managed to escape and then filed a police complaint. Michel responded by claiming he would "get" defendant. Fearing that he might be attacked again, defendant carried a gun to work with him. On the way to work, he was again confronted by Michel, who pulled a knife and advanced toward him. Defendant fired and shot Michel when he was still six feet away. The Supreme Judicial Court of Massachusetts ruled in *obiter dictum* that "[t]he evidence in this case warranted the conclusion that, once Michel made his armed attack, there was no way the defendant could have avoided the confrontation and that the defendant used his weapon in reasonable apprehension of death or serious bodily injury."

(b) Battered Spouses

Some commentators have argued that the imminency requirement should be relaxed when force is used to prevent instances of domestic violence. When one spouse has repeatedly physically abused and injured the other spouse, the victimized spouse may lash out and attack the abusing spouse, but—sometimes—at a moment when it is possible to respond in that fashion without being abused—for example, when the abusing spouse is asleep. Under a strict application of the imminency requirement, however, self-defense is unavailable in such situations, as force was used at a moment when no attack was imminent and imminence, as discussed, is an element of self-defense.

Some (but not all) jurisdictions have permitted introduction—ordinarily through expert testimony—of evidence relating to the existence of the Battered Woman (or Wife or Spouse) Syndrome, sometimes called BWS, the view that there is a cycle of violence in many abusive spousal relationships that affects the abused spouse's ability to react to violence at the time it occurs, and that also produces a greater

---

[5]Model Penal Code §3.04 ("Subject to the provisions of this Section and of Section 3.09, the use of force upon or toward another person is justifiable when the actor believes that such force is immediately necessary for the purpose of protecting himself against the use of unlawful force by such other person on the present occasion.").
[6]396 Mass. 840, 489 N.E.2d 666 (1986).

sensitivity to danger at points where the imminent use of violence might appear less likely—not imminent—to outsiders.

For example, the Oklahoma Court of Criminal Appeals concluded in *Bechtel v. State*[7] that battered woman syndrome testimony *is* admissible on the question of whether a battered woman acted in self-defense in killing her husband as it goes to the reasonableness of her belief that she was in imminent danger: "It is during the tension-building period that the battered woman develops a heightened sensitivity to any kinds of cues of distress. Thus, because of her intimate knowledge of her batterer, the battered woman perceives danger faster and more accurately as she is more acutely aware that a new or escalated violent episode is about to occur."

In many jurisdictions, a defendant is held *not* to be entitled to a self-defense charge in battered woman type cases where there was no imminent threat to her safety. Additionally, such charges are generally not permitted because courts have also held in such situations that no reasonable person would respond to a non-imminent threat with deadly force.

(2) Honest and Reasonable Belief

The general rule is that, before an individual can act in self-defense, he must establish that he honestly (subjective test) believed that he needed to use force to protect himself against the imminent use of unlawful physical force against him, *and* that this belief was "reasonable" (objective test) under the circumstances. If the actor's belief is unreasonable, the defense is not available.[8]

For example, consider the case of *People v. Wesley*.[9] In *Wesley*, defendant Wesley was being insulted and called names by a group of teenagers. One of the them, Stone, brandished a stick or a pipe and struck him. Wesley responded by stabbing Stone in the chest and killing him. The New York Court of Appeals held that Wesley's right to act in self-defense was determined by reference to "the circumstances actually confronting him at the time of the incident, and what a reasonable person in those circumstances and having defendant's background and experiences would conclude." This evaluation needed to be made based on the totality of the circumstances, and "[e]vidence of a defendant's 'circumstances' includes relevant knowledge that the defendant may have had about the victim, the physical attributes of all those involved in the incident, and any prior experiences that the defendant may have had 'which could provide a reasonable basis for a belief that another

> ## Sidebar
>
> **BATTERED SPOUSES: PROVOCATION DEFENSE?**
>
> "Currently, when a battered woman kills her abuser in the United States, she will generally either be found guilty of an intentional killing or acquitted on the basis of self-defense. If a battered defendant advances a self-defense argument, the use of BWS evidence may place excessive blame on the deceased abuser and focus attention on the woman's so-called psychological dysfunction. . . .
>
> "Under the law of provocation, countries like England have recognized that a woman may react to battering and abuse out of fear as well as anger, and the killing of her abuser can be seen as reasonable in this light. . . . The United States should use a reformed version of provocation law to accommodate battered women who kill their sleeping abusers, as this . . . will more readily yield substantive justice for women who kill out of legitimate fear in a nonconfrontational circumstance."
>
> Christine M. Belew, *Killing One's Abuser: Premeditation, Pathology, or Provocation?*, 59 Emory L.J. 769, 806-807 (2010).

---

[7]840 P.2d 1 (Okla. Crim. App. 1992).
[8]But see imperfect defenses, discussion below.
[9]76 N.Y.2d 555, 561 N.Y.S.2d 707, 563 N.E.2d 21 (Ct. App. 1990).

person's intentions were to injure or rob him or that the use of deadly force was necessary.'"

In most jurisdictions today, the defendant's particular physical characteristics may be considered by the fact finder in determining whether the defendant has acted reasonably under the circumstances.

Moreover, a person can be mistaken about the seriousness of the threat that she faces, but still act reasonably in defending herself by using force. *Acting mistakenly is not the same thing as acting unreasonably.* A person can be mistaken about whether an attacker has a gun in his hand, for example, but if the mistake is reasonable, she is still entitled to use the force necessary to protect herself from what reasonably appears to her to be an unlawful attack.

Under the Model Penal Code, "the use of force upon or toward another person is justifiable when the actor believes that such force is immediately necessary for the purpose of protecting himself against the use of unlawful force by such other person on the present occasion."[10]

This MPC provision does not require expressly that the actor's belief be objectively reasonable, focusing instead only on the actor's subjective belief. But it is nonetheless qualified by the further proscription in the Code that self-defense is not available as a defense "[w]hen the actor believes that the use of force upon or toward the person of another is necessary . . . but the actor is reckless or negligent in having such belief or in acquiring or failing to acquire any knowledge or belief that is material to the justifiability of his use of force. . . ."[11] Such a qualification adds some measure of the requisite reasonableness to the MPC self-defense calculus since reasonableness is a part of the determination of recklessness and negligence.[12]

(3) Deadly Force

The amount of force that can be used in self-defense depends entirely on the circumstances. In general, a defender's response must be proportional to the amount of force with which she is threatened. As a result, if the defender is threatened only with non-deadly force, force *not* readily capable under the circumstances of causing death or serious bodily injury (e.g., X tries to shove defendant around), she can respond lawfully *only* with non-deadly force.

More to the point, she *cannot* lawfully pull out a .357 Magnum and shoot X or use any other form of deadly force—that is, force that *is* readily capable under the circumstances of causing death or serious bodily injury. As the Model Penal Code provides, for example, the "use of deadly force is not justifiable . . . unless the actor believes that such force is necessary to protect himself against death, serious bodily harm, kidnapping or sexual intercourse compelled by force or threat."[13]

When a person is in fact threatened with deadly force—instead of shoving defendant, for instance, X advances toward defendant, brandishing a hunting knife—defendant is permitted to use deadly force in response against the attacker, assuming that all of the other elements of self-defense are also met. In other words, a

---

[10]Model Penal Code §3.04(1). *See also* Model Penal Code §3.04(2)(b) ("The use of deadly force is not justifiable . . . unless the actor believes that such force is necessary to protect himself against death, serious bodily injury, kidnaping or sexual intercourse compelled by force or threat. . . .").
[11]Model Penal Code §3.09(2).
[12]See Chapter 3 (Mens Rea).
[13]Model Penal Code §3.04(2)(b).

defendant in this situation is justified by law in committing an act that might otherwise be regarded as an assault or an intentional homicide.

FACING UNLAWFUL FORCE	☞	**CAN RESPOND WITH UNLAWFUL FORCE**
FACING DEADLY FORCE	☞	**CAN RESPOND WITH DEADLY FORCE**

The basic force-equivalency principles at play here are not new. They reflect a longstanding desire to try to limit as much as is reasonably possible the level of violence used, even when a defender is entitled by law to use some defensive force.

Consider in this regard the nineteenth-century case of *Shorter v. People*.[14] In that case, Shorter was involved in a fight with another man, Brush, who used his fists. Although Brush struck the first blow, Shorter readily entered into the fight and eventually took the fight a step further. He pulled out a knife and stabbed Brush nine times, killing him. The New York Court of Appeals held that Shorter was not entitled to resort to deadly force: "When a man is struck with the naked hand, and has no reason to apprehend a design to do him any great bodily harm, he must not return the blow with a dangerous weapon."

Had Brush begun the attack by using deadly force, such as rushing at Shorter with a large piece of jagged glass, then Shorter's use of the knife in response might well have been permissible. Moreover, if Brush had escalated the attack from an initial fist fight by using deadly force after the fight was ongoing, then Shorter would have been free to respond with deadly force. But neither of those possibilities actually occurred.

(4) Aggressors

In general, the initial aggressor in a physical confrontation is *not* entitled to justify his use of force as a matter of self-defense. The Model Penal Code, for example, provides that self-defense is unavailable where "the actor, with the purpose of causing death or serious bodily harm, provoked the use of force against himself in the same encounter."[15]

However, an initial aggressor can regain his right to use force in self-defense if he withdraws—other than temporarily or strategically—from the attack and makes it clear to his victim that he has withdrawn. Under such circumstances, an initial aggressor can have his self-defense rights restored. They are restored in the sense that if the former victim now initiates an attack against him, that former victim now becomes the aggressor and loses the right to use self-defense, while the former aggressor now becomes the victim and regains the right to use self-defense.

For example, consider *Connell v. Commonwealth*.[16] In that case, defendant Connell provoked a violent response from his victim, Lord, by following him in a

---

[14]2 N.Y. 193 (1849).
[15]Model Penal Code §3.04(2)(b)(i).
[16]34 Va. App. 429, 542 S.E.2d 49 (2001).

threatening manner. When Lord attacked Connell, Connell fired warning shots over Lord's head and warned him to stay back. When Lord continued to advance, however, Connell ran away but Lord caught him. Connell then fired a fatal shot into Lord's side with his pistol. The Virginia Court of Appeals concluded that Connell, the initial aggressor, had abandoned the fight sufficiently to be entitled to a jury instruction on self-defense and that he had "killed [Lord] out of a reasonably apparent necessity to preserve his own life."

An initial aggressor is also permitted to use self-defense when the person he has initially attacked responds with excessive force. For example, suppose that defendant shoves X, thereby giving X the right to protect himself by using unlawful force. However, instead of responding with unlawful, non-deadly force, X responds instead by pulling out a pistol and firing at defendant. Under these circumstances, defendant would now be permitted to respond with deadly force in order to protect himself, assuming that all of the other elements of deadly force had been met.

Finally, there has been considerable controversy about whether an individual should be allowed to exercise the right of self-defense against law enforcement officials. At common law, an individual did have the right to use force to resist an *unlawful* arrest. Today, however, many jurisdictions hold that an individual has the right to use non-deadly force, but not deadly force, to resist an unlawful arrest. The Model Penal Code provides that the "use of force is not justifiable . . . to resist an arrest which the actor knows is being made by a peace officer, although the arrest is unlawful."[17]

For example, in *United States v. Branch*,[18] when federal agents raided the compound of a religious sect in Waco, Texas, the occupants of the compound responded to the officers with deadly force. In rejecting one of the occupants' claim of entitlement to respond in that manner as a matter of self-defense, the Fifth Circuit Court of Appeals held that he was not justified in his use of deadly force in these circumstances: "Surely, a citizen may not initiate a firefight solely on the ground that the police sent too many well-armed officers to arrest him. The suggestion that a defendant would be entitled to claim self-defense simply by pointing to the police's tactical decision to send twenty heavily-armed officers instead of two lightly-armed ones is untenable."

(5) Retreat

At common law, an individual who was attacked by another person was not required to **retreat** before otherwise being entitled to use responsive force in his own defense, whether it was deadly or non-deadly force. It was, quite simply, a different time. To retreat from a physical confrontation seemed to many people then, and to some people now, to be a weak and timid—even humiliating—response, and so a victim who was under attack then was allowed to act in self-defense without having made any effort to avoid the use of violence.

In contrast, the Model Penal Code, and the crimes codes in many jurisdictions today, *do* impose a retreat obligation on a person who is otherwise entitled to use deadly force in self-defense. As the MPC provides, the right to use deadly force in self-defense is unavailable if "the actor knows that he can avoid the necessity of using such force with complete safety by retreating or by surrendering possession of a thing

---

[17]Model Penal Code §3.04(2)(i).
[18]91 F.3d 699 (5th Cir. 1996).

to a person asserting a claim of right thereto or by complying with a demand that he abstain from any action which he has no duty to take."[19]

The justification for the retreat doctrine is the notion that someone should not be allowed to take the life of another when it is possible to safely retreat. Jurisdictions that impose a retreat obligation, however, generally require that the defendant be able to retreat in complete safety before the retreat obligation applies.

There is an exception to the retreat doctrine, however: the so-called castle doctrine. The castle doctrine is taken from the old adage that "a man's home is his castle." Most jurisdictions with a retreat obligation do *not* require actors who are otherwise entitled to use deadly force to retreat from their own homes (their castles) or their workplaces. The Model Penal Code provision on point provides, for example, that an "actor is not obliged to retreat from his dwelling or place of work, unless he was the initial aggressor or is assailed in his place of work by another person whose place of work the actor knows it to be."[20]

In *Weiand v. State*,[21] for example, defendant Weiand was charged with murdering her husband in their apartment. She claimed self-defense and offered evidence of battered spouse syndrome. She sought to prove that her husband had beaten and choked her repeatedly during their marriage and had threatened further violence if she attempted to leave him. The Florida Supreme Court held that Weiand was not required to retreat from her residence before using deadly force, recognizing the rhetorical question asked by other courts: "[I]f the duty to retreat from the home is applied to a defendant attacked by a co-occupant in the home, whither shall he flee, and how far, and when may he be permitted to return?" The court also noted that "attacks are often repeated over time, and escape from the home is rarely possible without the threat of great personal violence or death." Although the court's decision was premised upon the impact of the retreat rule on cases of domestic violence, the court fashioned a broad rule that imposed a limited duty to retreat "within the residence to the extent reasonably possible, but no duty to flee the residence."

As previously noted, before a duty to retreat applies, where it is applicable, the actor must be able to retreat in complete safety. For example, assume that defendant has just gotten out of her car and is walking down the street when she is approached by a person who asks her for money. The person holds a broken bottle that he points

---

[19]Model Penal Code §3.04(b)(ii).
[20]Model Penal Code §3.04(b)(ii)(1).
[21]732 So. 2d 1044 (Fla. 1999).

menacingly toward her and his entire demeanor is threatening. Defendant thinks about retreating into a nearby building, but she is worried that her attacker might follow her there. Defendant also thinks about jumping back into her car and attempting to drive away. However, her assailant is simply too close to allow her to re-enter her car safely. Under these circumstances, defendant might well be justified in resorting to force, including deadly force, in self-defense, without any obligation to retreat first.

B. Imperfect Defense

As previously discussed elsewhere,[22] many (but not all) jurisdictions mitigate intentional murders to voluntary manslaughter by means of a so-called **imperfect defense**. An imperfect defense is a traditional justification defense—like self-defense—where the actor's belief in the need to take protective action is honest but unreasonable. In short, in those jurisdictions that recognize this defense, when a complete defense is imperfectly established—that is, every element is met except the reasonableness of the actor's belief—the crime is mitigated from murder to voluntary manslaughter.

F   A   Q

Q: Can an accused raise the defenses of self-defense and imperfect self-defense at the same time?

A: Absolutely. Defendants can and often do argue that a killing was justified as legitimate self-defense, but if the jury doesn't believe that the reasonableness element of that defense was made out successfully, then the defendant hopes to mitigate the homicide from murder to voluntary manslaughter.

The Model Penal Code does not recognize imperfect self-defense. However, it does provide criminal defendants with a limited defense if they act mistakenly. The MPC provides that "[w]hen the actor believes that the use of force upon or toward the person of another is necessary for any of the purposes for which such belief would establish a justification under [applicable law] but the actor is reckless or negligent in having such belief or in acquiring or failing to acquire any knowledge or belief which is material to the justifiability of his use of force, the justification afforded by [such law] is unavailable in a prosecution for an offense for which recklessness or negligence, as the case may be, suffices to establish culpability."[23] In other words, in essence, the defense *is* available with respect to a crime that requires purpose or knowledge as the mens rea for its commission, but is not available if the crime involves a mens rea of recklessness or negligence.

Consistent with the Model Penal Code, some courts refuse to apply the concept of imperfect self-defense to crimes involving recklessness or negligence. For example, in *Duran v. State*,[24] Duran began to argue with her boyfriend-roommate

---

[22]See Chapter 8 (Homicide).
[23]Model Penal Code §3.09(2).
[24]990 P.2d 1005 (Wyo. 1999).

at a bar. She left the bar and went to her car. When her boyfriend followed and caught up to her, he pushed her into the car and caused her to bump her head, and Duran locked the door. The boyfriend then tried to get into the car through a partially opened window. Fearful, Duran drove off with her boyfriend on the hood, and swerved in an attempt to dislodge him. The boyfriend fell, hit his head on the pavement, and later died from his injuries. Duran was convicted of aggravated vehicular homicide. The trial court refused to give a self-defense instruction because it found that she did not intend to inflict personal injury on him, but was instead trying to avoid a further confrontation with him and "accidentally" caused his injury. The court held that self-defense could *not* be a defense to a crime involving recklessness.

C. Defense of Others

The common law recognized not only the right to act in self-defense, but also the right to act in **defense of others**, at least where there was a defined familial relationship between the defender and the other, such as parent-child. Today, however, most jurisdictions no longer impose a familial relationship limitation. One can come to the defense of persons other than close relatives.

Nonetheless, the defense of others can be problematic in situations where the person providing aid comes to the defense of someone who does not actually have the right to act in his or her own defense. For example, suppose that A is walking down the street when she sees B attacking C, her spouse, with a knife, apparently intending to kill him. At common law, an individual had the right to come to the defense of another in such a situation. Moreover, the common law essentially gave the individual providing aid the right to respond with the level of force that the person being aided could have used in his own defense under the circumstances. Since C was threatened with deadly force, A could use deadly force against B on C's behalf.

Less certainty about A's right to defend C exists where A *thought* that C was under attack, but was wrong. Suppose that B and C were simply rehearsing their roles in a play and the knife was a prop. C was facing no real threat whatsoever and had no right to use self-defense himself. The critical question in a case like this is whether A's right to defend C should be determined by the situation as it reasonably appeared to A (a threat), or by the actual truth of the circumstances at issue (no threat).

Many common law jurisdictions originally applied what was sometimes called the alter ego rule. That rule provided that an individual's right to come to the defense of another person must be determined by, and is only co-extensive with, the other person's right to defend himself. In other words, in asserting the defense, the defender (A) "steps into the shoes" of the person she is trying to defend (C). Since C had no right to defend himself against B, and certainly did not have the right to use deadly force, A would not have the right to defend him or to use deadly force either. Sometimes, this rule is also likened to standing in the shoes of the person who is being attacked, in that the person using force in defense of another can only use the amount of force he would be entitled to use if he was in exactly the same position as the person he saw being attacked.

The Wyoming Supreme Court's decision in *Leeper v. State*[25] illustrates this alter ego rule. In that case, Leeper killed a man who was fighting with her husband. At the time of the shooting, her husband was on the ground with the victim standing over him, but not attacking. Leeper testified that she thought her husband was dead.

---

[25]589 P.2d 379 (Wyo. 1979).

Applying the alter ego rule, the court stated that as "the rights of [a] defender are coterminous with the right of the defense of self, and as one who initiated a battle had no right to self-defense absent abandonment, withdrawal or retreat available or communicated, one who defends an aggressor does so at his or her peril." The court held that the husband had no right to self-defense because he had engaged in mutual combat of a non-deadly nature, and therefore was not entitled to respond with deadly force. As a result, as an alter ego, his wife, the defendant, did not have a right to use deadly force in his defense.

Largely due to questions about the fairness of the rule, the alter ego rule is now the minority position in American jurisdictions. In *State v. Beeley*,[26] for example, Beeley was convicted of simple assault when he intervened in a fight between two men. One of the men called to Beeley for assistance and he came over and hit the other man. Beeley claimed that he believed that the other man was an intruder who had raped his friend's wife. In fact, there had been no rape, and it was doubtful whether the husband had the right to assault the other man or to defend himself. Nonetheless, the Rhode Island Supreme Court rejected the alter ego rule, concluding instead that it would judge "a defendant upon his or her own reasonable perceptions as he or she comes to the aid of the apparent victim." As the court concluded, "only as a matter of justice should one 'not be convicted of a crime if he selflessly attempts to protect the victim of an apparently unjustified assault, but how else can we encourage bystanders to go to the aid of another who is being subjected to assault?'" The requirements imposed by the Rhode Island court for invocation of the right to defend others is that the actor "reasonably believes that the other is being unlawfully attacked."

Similarly, the Model Penal Code rejected the alter ego rule in favor of a rule that provides that an individual's right to defend another should not be determined by the other's actual right to defend himself, but should instead be determined by the defender's reasonable belief regarding the other person's need for assistance. The Model Penal Code provides that "the use of force upon or toward the person of another is justifiable to protect a third person when: (a) the actor would be justified . . . in using such force to protect himself against the injury he believes to be threatened to the person whom he seeks to protect; and (b) under the circumstances as the actor believes them to be the person whom he seeks to protect would be justified in using such protective force; and (c) the actor believes that his intervention is necessary for the protection of such other person."[27]

In the example discussed above, involving A's attack on B in defense of her husband, C, the Model Penal Code approach would provide A with a defense because A believed that B was trying to kill C, had no reason to believe that C did not have the right to exercise force in his self-defense, and A believed that it was necessary to intervene to protect C against a threat of death.

In some defense of others cases, questions have also arisen about whether the defender was obligated to retreat before resorting to the use of deadly force. The general rule is that the defender's obligation to retreat is tied to the person being defended. Unless both can retreat in complete safety, the defender is not obligated to retreat.

The Model Penal Code's provision on defense of others is consistent with this approach, providing that "(a) when the actor would be obliged . . . to retreat, to surrender the possession of a thing or to comply with a demand before using force in self-protection, he is not obliged to do so before using force for the protection

---

[26]653 A.2d 722 (R.I. 1995).
[27]Model Penal Code §3.05(1).

of another person, unless he knows that he can thereby secure the complete safety of such other person."[28] If the person being defended has an obligation to retreat, furthermore, the defender must encourage him to retreat if it can be accomplished in complete safety.[29]

D. Defense of Property

The common law allowed an individual to use reasonable force to defend his property, especially against crimes such as burglary, criminal mischief, or theft. However, because the law placed a higher value on saving lives than on saving property, an individual's right to defend his property was never co-extensive with his right to defend himself. It still isn't.

At common law, **defense of property** was permitted insofar as an individual could use *non-deadly force* to protect his property if he reasonably believed that the use of such force was immediately necessary. *Deadly force* was generally prohibited, except in the most limited of situations, such as when a person attempting to protect his property was met with force against his person, and in turn lawfully responded in self-defense. In short, although the common law might have regarded your home as your castle, you nonetheless did not always have the right to use deadly force to defend your castle.

Q: Could a person using force in his home also claim *self-defense* rights?

A: Yes, where self-defense is permitted by law. A person could use deadly force to defend her home, for example, when there was a corresponding threat of death or serious bodily injury to her or to other occupants of the house. In addition, the common law also allowed a person to use deadly force to resist dispossession from her home.

In many states, legislatures have altered the common law rule by statute to give homeowners far greater rights to defend their dwellings with force, even deadly force. For example, *State v. Anderson*[30] involved Oklahoma's Make My Day Law. (The phrase "make my day" was taken from a well-known line uttered by Clint Eastwood in the movie *Dirty Harry*.) The law provided that "[a]ny occupant of a dwelling is justified in using any degree of physical force, including but not limited to deadly force, against another person who has made an unlawful entry into that dwelling, and when the occupant has a reasonable belief that such other person might use any physical force, no matter how slight, against any occupant of the dwelling."

In *Anderson*, the victims tried to break into a home in which defendant was a guest, and he shot and killed them. The Oklahoma Court of Criminal Appeals construed the

---

[28]Model Penal Code §3.05(2)(a).
[29]Model Penal Code §3.05(2)(b) ("when the person whom the actor seeks to protect would be obliged under Section 3.04 to retreat, to surrender the possession of a thing or to comply with a demand if he knew that he could obtain complete safety by so doing, the actor is obliged to try to cause him to do so before using force in his protection if the actor knows that he can obtain complete safety in that way").
[30]972 P.2d 32 (Okla. Crim. App. 1998).

Sidebar

THE RIGHT TO "STAND YOUR GROUND"

Some jurisdictions have considered taking principles applicable to protection of property and applying them in other places. For example, consider this analysis of a new Florida law:

> Sixty-four years ago, Professor Prosser summarized the common law rule of self-defense applicable to both civil and criminal claims: "[S]ince the law has always placed a higher value upon human safety than upon mere rights in property, it is the accepted rule that there is no privilege to use any force calculated to cause death or serious bodily injury to repel the threat to land or chattels, unless there is also such a threat to the defendant's personal safety as to justify self-defense."
>
> Earlier this year, the Florida House and Senate departed from this universally accepted principle. Florida's Protection of Persons Bill[*] allows a person outside of his home to stand his ground in the face of an attack and inside of his home or vehicle against an intruder, even if there is no threat of harm.
>
> The first significant change that the bill makes is that it eliminates the duty to retreat before using deadly force if the person acting in self-defense is in a place where he has a right to be. . . . Although jurisdictions that adhere to the common law duty to retreat recognize the costs of requiring a person assailed to "seek dishonor in flight," the supreme value of life serves as the justification for this duty. However, since the late nineteenth century, the duty to retreat has eroded as most jurisdictions have begun to view it as an unreasonable burden on societal notions of courage and dignity. Florida joins these jurisdictions and now allows a person to stand his ground when attacked and to meet force with force, even if an avenue of safe retreat is within reach.

Recent Developments, *Florida's Protection of Persons Bill,* 43 Harv. J. Legis. 199, 199-201 (2006).

---

*H.B. 249, creating Fla. Stat. Ann. §776.013(3) (West 2005) ("[A] person, not engaged in an unlawful activity, who is attacked in any other place where he has a right to be has no duty to retreat and has the right to stand his or her ground and meet force with force, including deadly force if he or she reasonably believes it is necessary to do so, to prevent death or great bodily harm to himself, herself, or another or to prevent the commission of a forcible felony.").

---

statute broadly, authorizing the use of deadly force against intruders even by a guest. The court regarded as "groundless" the State's argument that inclusion of mere occupants under the law would invite "carnage": "When one intrudes into the dwelling of another, the harm is the violation of the sanctity of the dwelling itself, not merely to a particular person's property interest. An invited guest in a dwelling has just a much right to expect safety therein as the owner."

Although, as noted, many jurisdictions go further than this, the Model Penal Code generally prohibits the use of deadly force by an individual to protect his or her property.[31] As with the common law, the Model Penal Codes assumes that life should be preserved over property. However, the MPC does recognize some exceptional situations where the use of deadly force *is* permissible. For example, like the common law, the Model Penal Code allows an individual to use deadly force to prevent dispossession from his home, unless the dispossessor is acting under a claim of right.[32]

And an individual may also use deadly force to prevent the commission or consummation of arson, burglary, robbery, or other felonious theft or property destruction, provided that the perpetrator "(1) has employed or threatened deadly force against or in the presence of the actor; or (2) the use of force other than deadly force to prevent the commission or the consummation of the crime would expose the actor or another in his presence to substantial danger of serious bodily harm."[33]

The criminal law has also struggled with the question whether individuals may use mechanical or other devices to protect their property. The Model Penal Code generally answers that question in the negative. It permits the use of mechanical devices to protect property *only* when "(a) the device is not designed to cause or known to create a substantial risk of causing death or serious bodily harm; and (b) the use of the particular device to protect the property from entry or trespass is reasonable under the circumstances, as the actor believes them to be; and (c) the device is one customarily used for such a purpose or reasonable care is taken to make known to probable intruders the fact that it is used."[34]

---

[31]Model Penal Code §3.06(3)(d).
[32]Model Penal Code §3.06(3)(d)(i).
[33]Model Penal Code §3.06(3)(d)(ii).
[34]Model Penal Code §3.06(5).

The Code generally prohibits the use of trap-guns, because they create a "substantial risk of causing death or serious bodily injury." The MPC does not, however, prohibit the use of mechanical devices that do not pose a risk of causing death or serious bodily harm.

E. Law Enforcement Defense

The common law recognized a defense for police officers who used force to accomplish legitimate law enforcement ends. Under this common law privilege, a law enforcement officer could use any force reasonably necessary to make a felony arrest and could use any necessary non-deadly force to effect a misdemeanor arrest.

At common law, this law enforcement defense also extended to private citizens who were asked by law enforcement officers to assist them. Under such circumstances, private individuals were treated like law enforcement officials. However, when private individuals acted strictly on their own, they generally had less authority, and they took considerably more personal risk in using force to accomplish law enforcement ends.

Today, more justifiable homicides are committed by police officers than by ordinary citizens, although overall, the number of total justifiable homicides in the United States has decreased by 13% in the period from 1976 to 2005.[35]

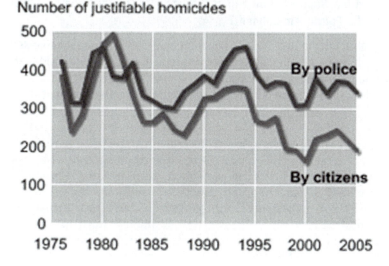

In *People v. Pena*,[36] for example, defendant's store was robbed by masked gunmen, and defendant store owner ran after the robbers with a gun. Seeing two men who he thought were the perpetrators, he fired, killing one of them. Unfortunately,

[35]U.S. Dept. of Justice, Office of Justice Programs, Bureau of Justice Statistics, *The number of justifiable homicides has been declining,* http://www.ojp.usdoj.gov/bjs/homicide/justify.htm.
[36]169 Misc. 2d 75, 641 N.Y.S.2d 794 (1996).

the person he killed was not one of the robbers. Under the applicable New York statute, a police officer could use deadly force to arrest a person who was fleeing after commission of a felony, and he did not need to be correct in who he tried to apprehend, provided that his belief that he had the right person was reasonable. In contrast, however, before using deadly physical force, a private citizen *must be correct* in his belief that the person he is seeking to arrest actually committed a felony, and that such person was in immediate flight. As the New York Supreme Court observed, the distinction between law enforcement officers (who have greater rights to use force) and private citizens (who have less right to use force) is based on the fact that police officers are specially trained "in the responsible use of firearms under trying circumstances."

There are constitutional limits as well on a police officer's right to use deadly force. In *Tennessee v. Garner*,[37] the Supreme Court held that a police officer could use deadly force to apprehend a fleeing felon *only* when it was "necessary to prevent the [felon's] escape and the officer has probable cause to believe that the suspect poses a significant threat of death or serious physical injury to the officer or others." In the Court's view, it is simply "not better that all felony suspects die than that they escape," at least when that "suspect poses no immediate threat to the officer and no threat to others." In that event, "the harm resulting from failing to apprehend him does not justify the use of deadly force to do so." Given its constitutional dimension under the Fourth Amendment, the *Garner* decision applies to the actions of both federal and state officials.

F   A   Q

Q: How could the Supreme Court limit the use of a law enforcement defense pursuant to the Fourth Amendment?

A: The Fourth Amendment to the U.S. Constitution prohibits unreasonable searches and seizures by governmental actors. The Supreme Court in *Garner* held that "there can be no question that apprehension by the use of deadly force is a seizure subject to the reasonableness requirement of the Fourth Amendment."

The Model Penal Code also limits the use of deadly force for law enforcement purposes. In general, the MPC allows the use of force to make or assist in making an arrest when the "actor believes that such force is immediately necessary to effect a lawful arrest."[38] However, the Code nonetheless prohibits the use of force except when "(i) the actor makes known the purpose of the arrest or believes that it is otherwise known by or cannot reasonably be made known to the person to be arrested; and (ii) when the arrest is made under a warrant, the warrant is valid or believed by the actor to be valid."[39]

In addition, the Code allows private individuals to use force to effect an arrest when summoned by a peace officer to assist with the arrest. In that situation, a

---

[37]471 U.S. 1 (1985). See also *Scott v. Harris*, 550 U.S. 372, 127 S. Ct. 1769, 167 L. Ed. 2d 686 (2007) (police officer's actions in making seizure must be "reasonable" and use of technique to stop fleeing vehicle in car chase was held reasonable).
[38]Model Penal Code §3.07(1).
[39]Model Penal Code §3.07(2)(a).

private person "is justified in using any force which he would be justified in using if the arrest were lawful, provided that he does not believe the arrest is unlawful."[40] However, the Code places several conditions on the use of force by a private individual; such use of force by a private person is lawful if "(i) he believes the arrest is lawful, and (ii) the arrest would be lawful if the facts were as he believes them to be."[41]

Even though the Model Penal Code permits the use of force to make an arrest, it does limit the use of *deadly* force, prohibiting it except when "(i) the arrest is for a felony; and (ii) the person effecting the arrest is authorized to act as a peace officer or is assisting a person whom he believes to be authorized to act as a peace officer; and (iii) the actor believes that the force employed creates no substantial risk of injury to innocent persons; and (iv) the actor believes that: (1) the crime for which the arrest is made involved conduct including the use or threatened use of deadly force; or (2) there is a substantial risk that the person to be arrested will cause death or serious bodily harm if his apprehension is delayed."[42]

In other words, the Code generally limits the use of deadly force to police officers, except when private individuals are assisting them. But even peace officers may not use deadly force except when the person being arrested committed a crime involving the "use or threatened use of deadly force," and a "substantial risk that the person to be arrested will cause death or serious bodily harm if his apprehension is delayed"[43] must also exist.

The MPC also includes a specific provision relating to the use of force against those who seek to escape from custody. In general, this provision allows the use of force in these circumstances "when the force could justifiably have been employed to effect the arrest under which the person is in custody."[44] However, the Code also specifically allows "a guard or other person authorized to act as a peace officer" to use "any force, including deadly force," that he "believes to be immediately necessary to prevent the escape of a person from a jail, prison, or other institution for the detention of persons charged with or convicted of a crime."[45]

F. Necessity

The defense of **necessity**, sometimes referred to as "choice of evils," raises difficult philosophical questions related to the justifications for punishment.[46] The defense is usually raised when a defendant has engaged in conduct that would constitute a crime, but she argues that her conduct was justified by the need to avoid a greater evil by engaging in a lesser, but nonetheless prohibited, one. In some (but not all) circumstances, society agrees that a violation of the criminal law is justified in these circumstances and therefore that defendant should not be held responsible.

For example, suppose that two hikers, trapped by a severe and unexpected snowstorm in a remote area, are suffering from extreme cold and lack of shelter. In dire

---

[40]Model Penal Code §3.07(4).
[41]*Id.*
[42]Model Penal Code §3.07(2)(b).
[43]Model Penal Code §3.07(2)(b).
[44]Model Penal Code §3.07(3).
[45]*Id.*
[46]See Chapter 1 (Purposes of the Criminal Law).

straits, near death, they happen upon a cabin that has a fireplace and is stocked with wood and food. From a societal perspective, it is preferable for these campers to break into the cabin, keep warm, and eat, rather than die from starvation or freezing. As a result, the necessity or choice of evils defense could be used as a defense to the crimes of trespass (breaking into the cabin) and theft (of the wood and the food).

Traditionally, the necessity defense has been treated as a justification for undertaking criminal conduct, usually in response to threats from natural sources (e.g., tornadoes and hurricanes). The related defense of duress has, in contrast, typically been treated as an excuse rather than a justification, usually involving a response to human threats (e.g., actions ordered with a gun to the head).[47] A minority of courts have, however, treated duress as a form of the necessity defense and as a justification for engaging in criminal conduct rather than as an excuse, since the actor is forced to choose between two evils in acting, in the same way as under the necessity defense.

The common law allowed defendants to invoke the defense of necessity only when they were faced with a threat of imminent injury and had no viable alternative other than violation of the law. These requirements are satisfied in the case of the hikers. They were trapped in the wilderness due to a snowstorm and were faced with the possibility of starvation or of freezing to death. Under the circumstances, breaking into the cabin, eating the food, and building a fire clearly were a "lesser evil."

Suppose that A is a homeless person who is frequently hungry. From time to time, he obtains food at soup kitchens or is given food by strangers, and therefore he is in no danger of death by starvation. Under these circumstances, A would not be justified in stealing food from a supermarket. Although one might question whether he was in fact engaging in a lesser evil (theft) to avoid a greater one (starvation), A has other options available to him for obtaining food, such as continuing to go shelters to obtain food or, perhaps, working to obtain money to buy food.

Before they can invoke the necessity defense, defendants must also have made a conscious decision to choose the lesser evil over the greater one. As in the prior discussion, suppose that two hikers decide to break into an isolated cabin, build a fire, and eat the food. At the time of the break-in, however, they are in no imminent danger. They break in simply because they want to be more comfortable. During the night, a heavy snowfall traps them so that, had they not already done so, they would have needed to break into the cabin to avoid freezing to death or starvation. Although the hikers would have been able to claim the defense of necessity had they broken in *after* the snowfall when they were starving, the defense is not available to them at this point because they were not starving or freezing when they actually broke into the cabin. Moreover, the harm that they were seeking to avoid (discomfort) when they broke into the cabin was not greater than the harm that they caused (breaking and entering and theft).

The need to use the necessity defense can arise in an almost infinite variety of situations. Suppose, for example, that defendant is driving on a city street when one of his tires suddenly blows out due to no fault of his own. His car is heading straight for a group of schoolchildren. Defendant can avoid the children, but only by swerving, which would cause him to ram into another person's car. Defendant chooses to steer into the car, totaling it. Although defendant caused an evil (damaging an

---

[47]See Chapter 13.

automobile), he did so to avoid a greater evil (killing or seriously injuring the children), and therefore the defense would certainly apply.

However, significantly, in applying the necessity defense, a defendant's subjective perception of what is "necessary" does not control over a societal determination. Put another way, necessity is judged objectively, not subjectively. For example, suppose that an actor believes that abortion is murder and, as a result, trespasses at an abortion clinic and destroys property there in an attempt to prevent abortions from taking place. Defendant argues that he committed a lesser evil (trespass and destruction of property) in order to avoid a greater evil (what he believes to be murder). Nevertheless, given that the right to have an abortion is constitutionally protected and is not deemed to be murder, defendant's claim of necessity would be and has been rejected.[48] Defendant's subjective balancing of evils does not control over society's objective evaluation.

Most jurisdictions also reject the defense of necessity altogether in cases of intentional homicide. In *Regina v. Dudley and Stephens*,[49] the "lifeboat case,"[50] three stranded sailors were adrift in a lifeboat with little hope of rescue. Starving and near death, they killed and ate the remains of a cabin boy. Although the circumstances of that case were extreme, defendants nonetheless were not permitted to avail themselves of the necessity defense because the criminal action involved an intentional homicide.

The Model Penal Code version of a choice of evils defense is somewhat broader than the traditional common law view. The MPC provides that "[c]onduct which the actor believes to be necessary to avoid a harm or evil to himself or to another is justifiable, provided that: (a) the harm or evil sought to be avoided by such conduct is greater than that sought to be prevented by the law defining the offense charged; and (b) neither the Code nor other law defining the offense provides exceptions or defenses dealing with the specific situation involved; and (c) a legislative purpose to exclude the justification claimed does not otherwise plainly appear."[51]

---

[48]*See, e.g., McMillan v. City of Jackson*, 701 So. 2d 1105 (Miss. 1997).
[49][1884] 14 Q.B.D. 273.
[50]See discussion in Chapter 1.
[51]Model Penal Code §3.02(1).

The Model Penal Code also differs from the common law and the law today in most jurisdictions in that it allows a defendant to assert the choice of evils defense to a crime of intentional homicide.

However, one cannot easily make a comparative harm argument when one kills one person (X) merely to save another (himself). In such situations, defendant is not avoiding a greater harm by committing a lesser harm. However, if defendant acts to save multiple people by killing a single person, the MPC defense might be available. Suppose, for example, that defendant is driving down a city street when his car suddenly has a blow-out due to no fault of his own. The car veers off the road, heading straight for a group of ten small children. If defendant veers to the left, or for that matter to the right, defendant will hit and probably kill a pedestrian, but only one. Under the Code, unlike the common law and the law in most jurisdictions, defendant can elect to save the ten children by taking the life of the solo pedestrian, either the one to the left or to the right.

Notably, the Model Penal Code also qualifies the choice of evil defense by providing that "[w]hen the actor was reckless or negligent in bringing about the situation requiring a choice of harms or evils or in appraising the necessity for his conduct, the justification afforded by this Section is unavailable in a prosecution for any offense for which recklessness or negligence, as the case may be, suffices to establish culpability."[52]

Suppose, for example, that the motorist in the prior example was driving at an extremely high rate of speed (70 mph). Had he been traveling at the speed limit (25 mph), he would have been able to safely stop and would not have been presented with a choice between killing the children or killing a pedestrian. Under the circumstances, the motorist acted recklessly or negligently in bringing about the situation requiring a choice of evils; therefore he would be denied the defense under the MPC in a prosecution for any offense based on recklessness or negligence.

Whether an individual can use the defense of necessity to justify an escape from prison or jail has been a source of much controversy. In *State v. Culp*,[53] for example, defendant, who had just been convicted for sale of a controlled substance, walked away from the custody of a deputy who was escorting him to jail. In response to a charge of felony-escape, defendant claimed necessity, contending that he feared for his life in the jail and that he had escaped in order to protect himself.

The Tennessee Court of Criminal Appeals ruled that an escape from custody could be justified on the grounds of necessity if and only if four conditions were met: "(1) The person reasonably believes the conduct is immediately necessary to avoid imminent harm; (2) The desirability and urgency of avoiding the harm clearly outweigh, according to ordinary standards of reasonableness, the harm sought to be prevented by the law proscribing the conduct; (3) There is no time for a complaint to the authorities or there exists a history of futile complaints which make any result from such compliance illusory; and (4) The prisoner immediately reports to the proper authorities when he has attained a position of safety from the immediate threat."[54] The court remanded the case for consideration of defendant's contentions pursuant to these standards. In other jurisdictions that accept the use of a necessity defense to charges of prison escape, similar requirements have been imposed.

---

[52]Model Penal Code §3.02(2).
[53]900 S.W.2d 707 (Tenn. Crim. App. 1994).
[54]*Id.*

G. Other Justification Defenses

There are also provisions in the Model Penal Code allowing parents or guardians to use force against minors or incompetents under their general care and supervision, provided that the force does not cause death, serious bodily harm, disfigurement, extreme pain, mental distress, or gross degradation, and also allowing teachers or other persons charged with the care or supervision for a special purpose of a minor to use force in order to maintain reasonable discipline in a school environment.[55] A defense is also provided to doctors or other therapists for recognized forms of treatment administered with a patient's consent or in an emergency.[56]

Similar defenses are provided to individuals responsible for the safety of a vessel or an aircraft,[57] or on any other "vehicle, train or other carrier or in a place where others are assembled."[58] Various specific statutes of this sort can be found in every jurisdiction.

SUMMARY

- Justification defenses are defenses that permit otherwise criminal conduct that is viewed as necessary to respond to outside forces where such a response is deemed beneficial to society, as opposed to excuses that focus upon the actor, not the act.

- An actor may use otherwise unlawful but not deadly force in self-defense to protect herself against an attack by another person when she reasonably believes she is being threatened with the imminent use of unlawful force and the use of responsive force is necessary to repel the attack.

- The amount of force that can be used in self-defense depends on the amount of force that is threatened; hence, unless an actor is threatened with force that she reasonably believes might cause death or serious bodily injury, she cannot respond by using deadly force.

- An aggressor is not entitled to justify his use of force as a matter of self-defense unless he has clearly withdrawn from the confrontation.

- In many jurisdictions, unless he is in his home, a person who is otherwise entitled to use deadly force in self-defense may not do so if he can avoid it by safely retreating to another place.

- An imperfect defense mitigates murder to voluntary manslaughter where the actor's belief in the need to take protective action is honest but unreasonable (e.g., imperfect self-defense).

- In most jurisdictions, a person may use force in defense of others where he would be justified in using it to protect himself against the injury he believes to be threatened, under the circumstances as the actor believes them to be where the person whom he seeks to protect would be justified in using such force, and when the actor believes that intervention is necessary for the protection of the other person.

[55]Model Penal Code §3.05(3).
[56]Model Penal Code §3.05(4).
[57]Model Penal Code §3.05(6).
[58]Model Penal Code §3.05(7).

■ Use of force in defense of property is usually permitted where an actor reasonably believes it is immediately necessary, but use of deadly force is generally prohibited, although some states give homeowners greater rights to defend their dwellings with deadly force.

■ A necessity defense is often available where an actor commits a criminal act reasonably believing it to be necessary to do so to avoid the occurrence of a greater harm, although, in most jurisdictions, this defense is inapplicable to an act of homicide.

CONNECTIONS

Relationship to Actus Reus and Mens Rea
The actus reus (see Chapter 2) and mens rea (see Chapter 3) of a crime are elements of the criminal offense. The classic defense to a criminal charge is to establish the prosecution's failure of proof of one of those or any other elements of the crime. In contrast, justification defenses are usually affirmative defenses that need to be proven by the accused without regard to proof of the elements of the offense.

Relationship to Excuses
Justification defenses typically focus on the act, not the actor; they exculpate otherwise criminal conduct because such conduct is deemed beneficial to society, or because the conduct is in some other way judged to be socially useful or desirable. Excuse defenses (see Chapter 13), in contrast, traditionally focus on the actor, not the act; they exculpate even though an actor's conduct may have harmed society because the actor's conduct is deemed not to be blameworthy.

Relationship to Homicide
In most jurisdictions, an imperfect justification defense (e.g., an honest but unreasonable belief that the actor who killed another person was acting in self-defense) may mitigate the offense of intentional murder to voluntary manslaughter (see Chapter 8).

Relationship to Purposes of the Criminal Law
The commission of some criminal acts is deemed to be justified because the conduct at issue is deemed beneficial to society or because the conduct is in some other way judged to be socially useful or desirable (see Chapter 1).

Excuses

OVERVIEW

Some criminal conduct, while not justifiable in the sense that it is *not* beneficial, *not* useful, and *not* desirable to society, is nonetheless viewed by the criminal justice system as understandable. As a result, it is excused and the offender is not held culpable or otherwise punished. In order to be excused in this way, such conduct must fit within the terms of a specific—usually statutory—excuse defense. Such excuse defenses traditionally focus on the actor, not on the act; they exculpate even though an actor's conduct may have harmed society because the actor's conduct is deemed nonetheless not to be blameworthy. In these cases, and the defense of insanity is a good example, the defendant is found to be *not* guilty of the charged offense, despite the fact that all of the elements of the offense may have otherwise been proven.

A. DURESS

B. INSANITY AND RELATED MENTAL DEFENSES

1. Insanity Tests
2. Compulsive Gambling Disorder
3. Diminished Capacity
4. Guilty but Mentally Ill
5. Burden of Proof
6. Competency

C. INFANCY

Traditionally, in contrast to justification defenses,[1] **excuse defenses** focus on the actor, not the act; excuse defenses exculpate even though an actor's conduct may have harmed society because the actor is deemed not to be blameworthy. In contrast, **justification defenses** traditionally focus on the act, not the actor; they exculpate otherwise criminal conduct because such conduct is deemed beneficial to society or because the conduct is in some other way judged to be socially useful or desirable.

What are the accepted excuses?[2] Why do we have them? How do they work? This chapter answers those questions.

A. Duress

The **duress** defense applies when an individual reasonably believes that he is being subjected to an unlawful threat of death or serious injury if he does not commit a criminal act, and he responds to that coercion by committing the act. The law does not usually find actions undertaken under such circumstances to be justifiable as such conduct is not deemed to be beneficial to society,[3] *but* we nonetheless excuse this conduct even though it may harm others because the actor's conduct is deemed to be understandable and, hence, not blameworthy.

An example should best illustrate. Suppose that A holds a pistol on B and orders him to steal money from a store. B, unwilling to risk the possibility that A will actually shoot him, complies and steals the money. Because B acted under the threat of duress, the criminal law provides him with an excuse defense. B's conduct was not beneficial to society, hence, it was not justified, but we nonetheless excuse it because it is understandable why he acted in this way—to save his life. Accordingly, we do not find his actions to be blameworthy.

F   A   Q

Q: Does the duress defense mean that a crime may be committed and no one can be held responsible for its commission?

A: No. The person who forces another person to commit a criminal act is as guilty of that act as if she had committed it herself.

When an individual commits a crime under duress, there is little reason for imposing punishment, at least on *that* person. In the example referred to in the prior paragraph, it is not clear that B deserves retribution. Sure, B committed what would otherwise be regarded as theft, a criminal act. However, faced with comparable coercion, most people would respond in a similar fashion and some of those who would not, would be shot. Moreover, it is unlikely that the threat of punishment would deter B from committing the crime again, assuming that he is faced with a comparable situation, or that it would deter others from engaging in similar conduct

---

[1]See Chapter 12 (Justification Defenses).
[2]See also discussion of the intoxication defense in Chapter 3 (Mens Rea). This defense, when and where it is accepted, is sometimes treated as an excuse defense as well. More commonly, however, it is viewed simply as a way to negate the requisite mens rea for a criminal offense.
[3]See Chapter 12 (Justification Defenses).

in the future when faced with similar coercive threats. While there is a possibility of criminal punishment if B commits the crime, there is a higher likelihood that he will suffer death or serious bodily injury if he does not. Under circumstances such as these, there is no indication that B needs to be restrained or needs rehabilitation or that the community's strong feelings about the moral wrongfulness of such behavior should be reinforced.

In order for the defense of duress to apply, it must be shown that defendant was subjected to a threat that a reasonable person could not be expected to resist. Consider, for example, the case of *Anguish v. State*,[4] where defendant stole a van, drove it to the drive-in window at a bank, and threatened to blow it up unless he was given money. Defendant claimed that he acted under duress because two men told him to rob a bank or his family would be harmed. The Texas Court of Appeals ruled that the defense of duress applies when a defendant "engaged in the proscribed conduct because he was compelled to do so by threat of imminent death or serious bodily injury to himself or another." In *Anguish*, the court *rejected* the application of the defense, however, because the threat was made four days before defendant robbed the bank, and therefore the threat of injury was not "imminent."

Traditionally, the duress defense has been treated by courts as an excuse, usually involving threats from human sources, while the necessity defense, discussed previously,[5] has been treated as a justification. Typically, duress has been viewed as a response to human threats (e.g., a gun to the head) while necessity is viewed as a response to threats from natural sources (e.g., tornadoes and hurricanes). A minority of courts have, however, treated duress as a form of the necessity defense and a justification for engaging in criminal conduct rather than an excuse, since the actor is forced to choose between two evils in acting, as under the necessity defense.

DURESS (EXCUSE) VS. NECESSITY (JUSTIFICATION)

Duress:	Typically, threats from human sources
Necessity:	Typically, threats from natural sources

Many jurisdictions refuse to recognize duress as a defense to a crime involving intentional murder. While it is not clear that the law can hope to deter someone from committing an intentional murder when faced with sufficient coercion—for example, A puts a gun to B's head and orders him to kill C on pain of death—the law nonetheless makes a value judgment not to exonerate someone who commits an intentional homicide. Who is to say that B's life is more valuable than C's? However, duress can and does serve as a defense to many other crimes, including burglary, robbery, trespass, and theft.

The Model Penal Code provides for "an affirmative defense that the actor engaged in the conduct charged to constitute an offense because he was coerced to do so by the use of, or a threat to use, unlawful force against his person or the person of another, which a person of reasonable firmness in his situation would have

---

[4]991 S.W.2d 883 (Tex. App. 1999).
[5]See Chapter 12 (Justification Defenses).

been unable to resist."[6] Unlike *Anguish*, however, the Model Penal Code does not impose an "imminence" requirement.[7] It also does not preclude using the defense against a charge of intentional homicide.

The Model Penal Code does impose several other qualifications, however. First, as with the necessity defense,[8] the Code provides that the duress defense "is unavailable if the actor recklessly placed himself in a situation in which it was probable that he would be subjected to duress."[9] "The defense is also unavailable if he was negligent in placing himself in such a situation, whenever negligence suffices to establish culpability for the offense charged."[10] Finally, unlike the early common law, the Code provides that it "is not a defense that a woman acted on the command of her husband, unless she acted under such coercion as would establish a [duress] defense. . . ."[11]

In general, in applying the duress defense, courts use an objective standard in gauging the actual level of coercion, rather than a subjective standard that simply looks to what the actor being coerced believed. For example, in *State v. VanNatta*,[12] defendant attempted to introduce evidence that he had a "submissive personality," which made him particularly susceptible to a "forceful or coercive significant other." Defendant claimed that another person's pressure coerced him into committing a bank robbery by threatening to shoot him if he refused. The Oregon Court of Appeals rejected this argument, concluding that an objective standard applies: "The trial court was correct that whether defendant was a timid individual easily coerced is not relevant to whether, at the time of the robbery, defendant was subjected to a physical force of such a degree as to overcome earnest resistance." The Model Penal Code is in accord, providing that the focus should be on whether a "person of reasonable firmness," rather than the actual actor, would not have been able to resist.

B. Insanity and Related Mental Defenses

One of the excuses most commonly raised by criminal defendants—although usually unsuccessfully—is insanity. When an individual is found to be not guilty by reason of insanity (often shorthanded as NGRI), he or she is relieved entirely of criminal responsibility for his or her actions at issue. In both application and form, the insanity defense is, perhaps, the most controversial of the excuse defenses.

Many people (but not everyone) argue that there is little justification for punishing individuals who commit crimes while they are mentally ill. As the Second Circuit Court of Appeals concluded in *United States v. Freeman*,[13] "Those who are substantially unable to restrain their conduct are, by definition, undeterrable and their 'punishment' is no example for others; those who are unaware of or do not appreciate the nature and quality of their actions can hardly be expected rationally to weigh the consequences of their conduct." "Finally," the court continued, "what

---

[6]Model Penal Code §2.09(1).
[7]*See* Model Penal Code §2.09.
[8]See Chapter 12 (Justification Defenses).
[9]Model Penal Code §2.09(2).
[10]*Id.*
[11]*Id.*
[12]149 Or. App. 587, 945 P.2d 1062 (1997).
[13]357 F.2d 606, 615 (2d Cir. 1966).

segment of society can feel its desire for retribution satisfied when it wreaks vengeance upon the incompetent? Although an understandable emotion, a need for retribution can never be permitted in a civilized society to degenerate into a sadistic form of revenge."

One could well argue that society is justified in punishing the criminally insane in order to restrain them or to try to rehabilitate them. Nonetheless, many—but again, by no means all—people believe that the objectives of restraint and rehabilitation can and should be more effectively and justly achieved through involuntary *civil* commitment to a mental institution, rather than by imprisonment after conviction in a *criminal* trial.

As a result of these sorts of differences of opinion about precisely how we should treat individuals who are mentally ill and who have committed crimes, jurisdictions in the United States have taken significantly different approaches to the use of the insanity defense. Indeed, some jurisdictions have abolished the defense outright.

Moreover, the particular form of insanity defense used in many jurisdictions has changed significantly over time, making it even more difficult to find some form of uniform approach to the subject. One of the most potent spurs to change was the NGRI verdict in the trial of John Hinckley, the attempted assassin of former President Ronald Reagan in March of 1981. Many people felt that Hinckley should have been held criminally responsible for his conduct, or that he "got off easy" when he was confined to a mental institution. As a result, many jurisdictions amended their insanity statutes in an attempt to make insanity more difficult to establish.

Sidebar

INSANITY DEFENSE CRAZINESS

Professor Michael Perlin has argued that debate over the appropriate focus of the insanity defense is made more difficult by some common myths that surround its use:

> The empirical research [about the insanity defense] revealed that at least half a dozen myths had arisen and been perpetuated, but that all were "unequivocally disproven by the facts." The research showed that the insanity defense opens only a "small window of nonculpability," defendants found NGRI "do not beat the rap," and, perhaps most importantly, the "tenacity of these misbeliefs in the face of contrary data" is profound.
>
> Myth #1: The insanity defense is overused.
> Myth #2: The use of the insanity defense is limited to murder cases.
> Myth #3: There is no risk to the defendant who pleads insanity.
> Myth #4: NGRI acquittees are quickly released from custody.
> Myth #5: NGRI acquittees spend much less time in custody than do defendants convicted of the same offenses.
> Myth #6: Criminal defendants who plead insanity are usually faking.
> Myth #7: Criminal defense attorneys employ the insanity defense plea solely to 'beat the rap.'

Michael L. Perlin, *Unpacking the Myths: The Symbolism Mythology of Insanity Defense Jurisprudence,* 40 Case W. Res. L. Rev. 599, 648-654 (1989/90).

(1) Insanity Tests

In *Clark v. Arizona*, decided in 2006, the Supreme Court described four different approaches to the insanity defense currently existing in the various jurisdictions: cognitive incapacity, moral incapacity, volitional incapacity, and product-of-mental-illness tests.[14] The Court concluded that "[t]he first two emanate from the alternatives stated in the *M'Naghten* rule. The volitional incapacity or irresistible-impulse test . . . asks whether a person was so lacking in volition due to a mental defect or illness that he could not have controlled his actions. And the product-of-mental-illness test . . . simply asks whether a person's action was a product of a mental disease or defect."[15]

---

[14]*Clark v. Arizona*, 126 S. Ct. 2709, 2720 (2006).
[15]*Id.* (footnotes omitted).

S i d e b a r

OBSESSED WITH JODIE FOSTER

John Hinckley, after repeatedly watching the 1976 film *Taxi Driver*, in which the actress Jodie Foster played a child prostitute, became obsessed with her, stalked her, and ultimately attempted to assassinate President Reagan in a deluded attempt to impress her. After his NGRI verdict in the criminal trial, Hinckley was civilly committed to St. Elizabeth's Hospital in Washington, D.C., where he remains confined today.

The Supreme Court has found further that "[s]eventeen States and the Federal Government have adopted a recognizable version of the *M'Naghten* test with both its cognitive incapacity and moral incapacity components. One State has adopted only *M'Naghten*'s cognitive incapacity test, and 10 . . . have adopted the moral incapacity test alone. Fourteen jurisdictions, inspired by the Model Penal Code, have in place an amalgam of the volitional incapacity test and some variant of the moral incapacity test. . . . Three States combine a full *M'Naghten* test with a volitional incapacity formula. And New Hampshire alone stands by the product-of-mental-illness test."[16]

The variety of approaches to insanity "are multiplied further," the Supreme Court has added, "by variations in the prescribed insanity verdict: a significant number of these jurisdictions supplement the traditional 'not guilty by reason of insanity' verdict with an alternative of 'guilty but mentally ill.' Finally, four States have no affirmative insanity defense, though one provides for a 'guilty and mentally ill' verdict. These four, like a number of others that recognize an affirmative insanity defense, allow consideration of evidence of mental illness directly on the element of mens rea defining the offense."[17]

BASIC INSANITY TESTS

M'Naghten *Test:*	A person is not responsible for criminal conduct if at the time of such conduct he was suffering from such a mental disease or defect as not to know the nature and quality of the act or, if he did know, that he did not know that what he was doing was wrong.
Durham *"Product" Test:*	A person is not criminally responsible if his unlawful act was the product of mental disease or mental defect.
ALI Model Penal Code Test:	A person is not responsible for criminal conduct if at the time of such conduct as a result of mental disease or defect he lacks substantial capacity either to appreciate the wrongfulness of his conduct or to conform his conduct to the requirements of law.

---

[16]*Id.* at 2720-2721 (footnotes omitted).
[17]*Id.* at 2721-2722 (footnotes omitted).

(a) *M'Naghten* and Irresistible Impulse

The earliest insanity test was articulated in *Daniel M'Naghten's Case* (sometimes spelled *McNaughten's Case*).[18] The case arose when Daniel M'Naghten shot at British Prime Minister Sir Robert Peel's carriage, intending to kill him. As it turned out, M'Naghten actually shot and killed Edward Drummond, Peel's private secretary, who was inside the carriage. At his trial, M'Naghten claimed that he acted under the influence of insane delusions, and the jury found him NGRI. The House of Lords concluded that, in order to prove insanity, "it must be clearly proved that, at the time of the committing of the act, the party accused was labouring under such a defect of reason, from disease of the mind, as not to know the nature and quality of the act he was doing; or, if he did know it, that he did not know he was doing what was wrong." This is the **M'Naghten test**.

As the Supreme Court explained in its 2006 *Clark* decision, the *M'Naghten* test has two separate parts: "The first part asks about cognitive capacity: whether a mental defect leaves a defendant unable to understand what he is doing. The second part presents an ostensibly alternative basis for recognizing a defense of insanity understood as a lack of moral capacity: whether a mental disease or defect leaves a defendant unable to understand that his action is wrong."[19]

As previously noted, a significant number of jurisdictions use the *M'Naghten* test as the basis for their insanity defense, although some of those jurisdictions use only one of the two parts of the traditional test.

The Supreme Court made clear in its *Clark* decision that every jurisdiction has the constitutional right to determine what if any insanity defense it chooses to use: "[I]t is clear that no particular formulation has evolved into a baseline for due process, and that the insanity rule, like the conceptualization of criminal offenses, is substantially open to state choice. Indeed, the legitimacy of such choice is the more obvious when one considers the interplay of legal concepts of mental illness or deficiency required for an insanity defense, with the medical concepts of mental abnormality that influence the expert opinion testimony by psychologists and psychiatrists commonly introduced to support or contest insanity claims. For medical definitions devised to justify treatment, like legal ones devised to excuse from conventional criminal responsibility, are subject to flux and disagreement. There being such fodder for reasonable debate about what the cognate legal and medical tests should be, due process imposes no single canonical formulation of legal insanity."[20]

A few jurisdictions also supplement the *M'Naghten* test with use of the so-called **irresistible impulse** test. This test provides that even if a defendant knew the difference between right and wrong and knew that his actions were wrong, he is still insane if he acted pursuant to an irresistible impulse. As the Alabama Supreme Court explained in the leading case from the nineteenth century, *Parsons v. State*,[21] an irresistible impulse exists "if the insane delusion [so] subverts his will as to destroy his free agency by rendering him powerless to resist by reason of the duress of the disease."

How does the M'Naghten *test apply?* Consider, for example, a defendant who killed another person by strangling him. Assume that this actor was so mentally ill that she did not even realize that she was squeezing another person's neck; rather,

---

[18]10 Cl. & F. 200, 8 Eng. Rep. 718 (House of Lords 1843).
[19]126 S. Ct. at 2719.
[20]126 S. Ct. at 2722.
[21]81 Ala. 577, 2 So. 854 (1887).

she honestly thought that she was squeezing a grapefruit instead. Under *M'Naghten*, such a person is clearly insane because she neither understood nor appreciated the nature and quality of her act, nor did she know that what she was doing was wrong, as it is perfectly okay to squeeze a grapefruit.

In applying the *M'Naghten* question about whether the accused "knew the difference between right and wrong," there has been some disagreement about whether the reference is to a "legal wrong" or a "moral wrong." Most courts conclude that the latter approach is correct. In *State v. Cameron*,[22] for example, the Washington Supreme Court concluded that, even though defendant realized that it was a criminal act to kill others, because he "believed he was responding to God's directive and thus had an obligation to rid the world of this 'demon,' 'sorceress' or 'evil spirit,' " when he killed his stepmother, he was still insane. As the court stressed, "one who believes that he is acting under the direct command of God is no less insane because he nevertheless knows murder is prohibited by the laws of man. Indeed, it may actually emphasize his insanity."

(b) *Durham* "Product" Test

Because of dissatisfaction with the *M'Naghten* and irresistible impulse tests, courts in the 1950s and 1960s searched for alternate ways to formulate a test for insanity. In *Durham v. United States*,[23] the District of Columbia Court of Appeals found that the *M'Naghten* right-wrong test was " 'based on an entirely obsolete and misleading conception of the nature of insanity.' The science of psychiatry now recognizes that a man is an integrated personality and that reason, which is only one element in that personality, is not the sole determinant of his conduct. The right-wrong test, which considers knowledge or reason alone, is therefore an inadequate guide to mental responsibility for criminal behavior." Accordingly, fashioning its rule after a longstanding New Hampshire test, the court articulated what came to be called the **product test**, namely that a defendant should not be held criminally responsible "if his unlawful act was the product of mental disease or mental defect."

The product test, recognizing the "modern" science of psychiatry, was intended to give psychiatric and psychological experts more influence in deciding whether an accused person was insane. But, largely because the test lacked any real standards for determining when a person was insane and because—in essence—it turned over the legal decision when insanity existed to these experts, rather than leaving it to the fact finder, the product test has been abandoned and only continues to be used in New Hampshire, the jurisdiction from which the test was originally taken.

(c) ALI Model Penal Code Test

In the Model Penal Code, the American Law Institute (ALI) rejected the *M'Naghten* test in favor of an insanity test that focuses instead on whether the defendant lacks "substantial capacity." The **ALI insanity test** provides that "[a] person is not responsible for criminal conduct if at the time of such conduct as a result of mental disease or defect he lacks substantial capacity either to appreciate the wrongfulness of his conduct or to conform his conduct to the requirements of law."[24]

---

[22]100 Wash. 2d 520, 674 P.2d 650 (en banc, 1983).
[23]94 U.S. App. D.C. 228, 214 F.2d 862 (1954).
[24]Model Penal Code §4.01(1).

The goal of the Model Penal Code formulation was to view "the mind as a unified entity" and to recognize that mental disease or defect might impair its functioning in various ways. By choosing the term "substantial capacity," the ALI test requires that a defendant have a significant but not a total impairment of capacity. In addition, by using the term "appreciate," the ALI test suggests that a defendant's awareness that his or her conduct is wrong is not a sufficient basis, in and of itself, for imposing criminal responsibility. Defendant must have had an "appreciation or understanding of the moral or legal import of behavior."

The ALI test permits the use of psychiatric testimony, but experts are advised to use "sufficiently precise terms to provide the jury with a workable standard that is comprehensible to laymen." As the Supreme Court's *Clark* decision points out, a number of jurisdictions (but a distinct minority) still use some version of this ALI test.

Under the ALI test, "the terms 'mental disease or defect' do not include an abnormality manifested only by repeated criminal or otherwise anti-social conduct."[25] In other words, the mere fact that a defendant claiming to be insane is a recidivist or suffers from an addiction to narcotics does not provide a sufficient basis, in and of itself, to justify an NGRI acquittal.

In *United States v. Lyons*,[26] for example, defendant Lyons was charged with obtaining controlled narcotics by fraud, and he claimed insanity on the ground that he was a drug addict and therefore lacked substantial capacity to conform his conduct to the requirements of law. The Fifth Circuit rejected this contention, noting that "the great weight of legal authority clearly supports the view that evidence of mere narcotics addiction, standing alone and without other physiological or psychological involvement, raises no issue of such a mental defect or disease as can serve as a basis for the insanity defense." However, the court added that, to the extent Lyons claimed that his drug use had damaged his brain, he should be allowed to offer proof on that point.

Sidebar

HINCKLEY VERDICT CHANGED THE LAW

"In the wake of dissatisfaction with John Hinckley's NGRI verdict in the shooting of President Reagan, the federal government and a majority of states set about to review their procedures for treatment and retention of individuals who were acquitted by reason of insanity so as to make it more difficult for insanity defenses to succeed. Twenty-five states changed their insanity defense from July 1982 through September 1985. By 1990, twenty-five states and the District of Columbia had adopted a version of the *McNaughton* test; twenty states implemented the ALI test; and twelve states allowed 'the guilty but mentally ill' verdict. Many states dropped the ALI concept of a defendant's ability 'to conform his conduct to the requirements of law' and simply re-adopted the old *McNaughton* knowledge-based standard of responsibility. Other changes included shifting the prosecutor's burden of proving sanity to the defendant, adopting knowledge-based standards of proof, and preventing experts from testifying on the ultimate issue of sanity or insanity."

Jennifer S. Bard, *Re-Arranging Deck Chairs on the Titanic: Why the Incarceration of Individuals with Serious Mental Illness Violates Public Health, Ethical, and Constitutional Principles and Therefore Cannot Be Made Right by Piecemeal Changes to the Insanity Defense*, 5 Hous. J. Health L. & Pol'y 1, 35-36 (Spring 2005).

(2) Compulsive Gambling Disorder

Courts have rejected arguments that a tenable excuse defense exists where defendant's compulsive gambling disorder causes him to violate various criminal laws in

---

[25]Model Penal Code §4.01(2).
[26]731 F.2d 243 (5th Cir. 1984).

order to obtain money to gamble. The American Psychiatric Association's Diagnostic and Statistical Manual of Mental Disorders does suggest that "pathological gambling" is a psychiatric disorder, involving a chronic and progressive failure to resist impulses to gamble and gambling behavior that compromises, disrupts, or damages personal, family, or vocational pursuits. As a result, some defendants have claimed that they were "insane" on this basis when they committed various criminal acts.

This has not proven to be a very good argument. In *United States v. Gould*,[27] for example, the Fourth Circuit Court of Appeals expressly rejected the argument that pathological gambling could deprive a defendant of the "capacity to refrain from such criminal activity as attempted bank robbery."

(3) Diminished Capacity

In addition to insanity, in some jurisdictions, a defendant is also permitted to raise a **diminished capacity** defense. This defense is made out where permitted when defendant establishes that he lacked the mental capacity to form the specific mens rea required for the crime charged.

As the Supreme Court has recently explained, "Though the term 'diminished capacity' has been given different meanings, *see, e.g.,* Morse, Undiminished Confusion in Diminished Capacity, 75 J. Crim. L. & C. 1 (1984) ('The diminished capacity doctrine allows a criminal defendant to introduce evidence of mental abnormality at trial either to negate a mental element of the crime charged, thereby exonerating the defendant of that charge, or to reduce the degree of crime for which the defendant may be convicted, even if the defendant's conduct satisfied all the formal elements of a higher offense'), California, a jurisdiction with which the concept has traditionally been associated, understood it to be simply a '"showing that the defendant's mental capacity was reduced by mental illness, mental defect or intoxication . . . ."'"[28]

The insanity and diminished capacity defenses are different from one another. In a jurisdiction that uses both concepts, insanity is a defense to *all* criminal conduct, but diminished capacity is simply a way of establishing that the defendant did not have the capacity to possess the mens rea required for a specific criminal offense. Sometimes, diminished capacity is a complete defense; sometimes, it is used as a mitigating defense, so that a defendant who establishes that she is not guilty of first-degree murder by reason of diminished capacity might therefore automatically be guilty of commission of a lower degree of murder.

(4) Guilty but Mentally Ill

The defense of **guilty but mentally ill**, including similar variants on that language (e.g., "guilty *and* mentally ill"), sometimes shorthanded as "GBMI," has been established by statute in a number of jurisdictions. In those jurisdictions, an individual who is found by the fact finder not to be NGRI—i.e., *not* to be insane under the prevailing standard for insanity—might still be found to be GBMI on a finding that he or she was nonetheless mentally ill under the standard for that condition prevailing in that jurisdiction. Where GBMI exists as an option, defendants may also

---

[27]741 F.2d 45 (4th Cir. 1984).
[28]*Clark v. Arizona*, 126 S. Ct. 2709, 2733 n.41 (2006).

plead in that fashion where the prosecution agrees—that is, they may plead "guilty but mentally ill" to the charged crime.

However, unlike an NGRI verdict, a GBMI verdict does *not* relieve a defendant of criminal responsibility. Rather, individuals found GBMI are entitled to appropriate treatment of their mental illness, *but* when and if they regain their sanity, they are treated the same way as everyone else who has been convicted of the crime for which they were convicted, and they must usually serve the remainder of the sentence that was imposed by the trial court.

(5) Burden of Proof

A state may, if it chooses, treat insanity as an affirmative defense and impose the burden of proof on the defendant. Or it may impose on the State the burden of disproving a claim of insanity beyond a reasonable doubt. These decisions are legislative judgments made in each jurisdiction.

As the Supreme Court has recently made clear, "A State may provide, for example, that whenever the defendant raises a claim of insanity by some quantum of credible evidence, the presumption disappears and the government must prove sanity to a specified degree of certainty (whether beyond reasonable doubt or something less). Or a jurisdiction may place the burden of persuasion on a defendant to prove insanity as the applicable law defines it, whether by a preponderance of the evidence or to some more convincing degree."[29]

(6) Competency

Competency and insanity are entirely separate and distinct concepts. Unlike insanity, a defendant's mental competency to stand trial, to enter a guilty plea, to be sentenced, or to be executed is not a substantive matter—that is, it is not related to the issue of guilt or innocence. Rather, **competency** relates only to the question of the defendant's present ability or inability to understand the nature or object of the proceedings against him or to participate and assist in his defense.

> ### Sidebar
>
> **MENTALLY RETARDED ≠ INCOMPETENT**
>
> The Supreme Court has ruled that mentally retarded individuals cannot be subjected to capital punishment, as that would be unconstitutional cruel and unusual punishment. But the Court has added that that does *not* mean that mental retardation is a defense:
>
> [C]linical definitions of mental retardation require not only subaverage intellectual functioning, but also significant limitations in adaptive skills such as communication, self-care, and self-direction that became manifest before age 18. Mentally retarded persons frequently know the difference between right and wrong and are competent to stand trial. Because of their impairments, however, by definition they have diminished capacities to understand and process information, to communicate, to abstract from mistakes and learn from experience, to engage in logical reasoning, to control impulses, and to understand the reactions of others. There is no evidence that they are more likely to engage in criminal conduct than others, but there is abundant evidence that they often act on impulse rather than pursuant to a premeditated plan, and that in group settings they are followers rather than leaders. Their deficiencies do not warrant an exemption from criminal sanctions, but they do diminish their personal culpability.
>
> *Atkins v. Virginia*, 536 U.S. 304, 318 (2002).

A finding of incompetency merely postpones a criminal trial, it does not preclude it.

Similarly, a defendant who has been found competent to stand trial may still be found at trial to be insane. Insanity focuses on the defendant's mental state at the time of the criminal act charged. Competency, once again, focuses on the defendant's mental state at the time of the proceedings being initiated against him.

---

[29]*Clark v. Arizona*, 126 S. Ct. 2709, 2731 (2006) (citations omitted).

The Supreme Court's test for whether a defendant is competent or incompetent for these purposes is whether he "has sufficient present ability to consult with his lawyer with a reasonable degree of rational understanding—and whether he has a rational as well as factual understanding of the proceedings against him."[30]

C. Infancy

Questions of mental capacity also arise with respect to crimes committed by children. At the early common law, **infancy** was not a defense, although minors were often pardoned. However, the late common law rules regarding children were different and relatively straightforward. In general, children under the age of seven years old at the time of the alleged criminal act were conclusively presumed to lack the capacity to engage in criminal conduct. Between the ages of seven and fourteen years old, they were presumed to be incapable of engaging in criminal activity, but that presumption was rebuttable. And, after the age of fourteen, the reverse was true, and children were presumed to be criminally responsible for their actions. Many states continue to use this same approach of presumptive ages today, although often with statutory changes in the relevant ages.

Moreover, beginning in the early twentieth century, states began to require the adjudication of criminal complaints involving children below a certain age—most commonly, 18 years old—as delinquency proceedings to be tried in special juvenile courts, rather than criminal prosecutions tried in regular, adult criminal courts. Theoretically, in these juvenile delinquency proceedings, in contrast to adult criminal courts, the State was functioning as a paternalistic guardian of the child's "best interests."

Over time, however, for a variety of reasons, including the unhappy fact that so much serious crime in the United States is committed by juveniles, some of these juvenile proceedings began to take on a character similar to adult criminal trials, and the focus has often become simply whether the accused child has met the elements of the crime charged, just like adult proceedings. In addition, for many of the same reasons, many states have enacted statutes permitting individual juvenile defendants to be "waived" for trial into adult criminal courts when they have committed particularly serious or violent crimes.

SUMMARY

■ Excuse defenses exculpate even though an actor's conduct may have harmed society because the actor is deemed not to be blameworthy, as opposed to justification defenses, which focus on the act, not the actor.

■ The defense of duress applies when an actor commits a crime because she reasonably believes that she is being threatened with death or serious injury if she does not commit that criminal act, although this defense does not usually excuse an act of homicide.

---

[30]*Dusky v. United States*, 362 U.S. 402 (1960). *See also* more recently *Indiana v. Edwards*, 554 U.S. 164, 128 S. Ct. 2379, 171 L. Ed. 2d 345 (2008).

■ In most jurisdictions, insanity is a complete defense to criminal charges (NGRI = Not Guilty by Reason of Insanity).

■ The Supreme Court has ruled that every jurisdiction has the right to determine what if any insanity defense it chooses to use.

■ The insanity test most commonly used is *M'Naghten*: "A person is not responsible for criminal conduct if at the time of such conduct he was suffering from such a mental disease or defect as not to know the nature and quality of the act or, if he did know, that he did not know that what he was doing was wrong."

■ In some jurisdictions, a defendant may raise a diminished capacity defense, establishing that he lacked the mental capacity to form the specific mens rea required for the crime charged.

■ In some jurisdictions, a defendant may be found guilty but mentally ill where the fact finder has found him not to be insane, but nonetheless mentally ill under the standard specified for that condition.

CONNECTIONS

Relationship to Actus Reus and Mens Rea

The actus reus (see Chapter 2) and mens rea (see Chapter 3) of a crime are elements of the criminal offense. The classic defense to a criminal charge is to establish the prosecution's failure of proof of one of those or any other elements of the crime. In contrast, excuses are often affirmative defenses that need to be proven by the accused without regard to proof of the elements of the offense.

Relationship to Actus Reus (Involuntary Act)

An involuntary act might or might not be associated with an actor's mental disease or defect. See Chapter 2. In some instances, for example, an individual might possess an otherwise healthy mind, but suffer from a temporary condition such as a severe blow to the head that produces an automatistic response. If a defendant commits a criminal act under such circumstances, she may not have committed a voluntary act and, wholly aside from any possible mental illness defense she may have (e.g., insanity), she may be able to raise a complete defense to a charged crime based on involuntariness.

Relationship to Justification Defenses

Justification defenses (see Chapter 12) typically focus on the act, not the actor; they exculpate otherwise criminal conduct because such conduct is deemed beneficial to society, or because the conduct is in some other way judged to be socially useful or desirable. Excuse defenses, in contrast, traditionally focus on the actor, not the act; they exculpate even though an actor's conduct may have harmed society because the actor's conduct is deemed not to be blameworthy.

Relationship to Purposes of the Criminal Law

The commission of some criminal acts is deemed to be excused because even though an actor's conduct may have harmed society, it is not deemed to be blameworthy given the purposes of the criminal law (see Chapter 1).

Index